The
Barbra Streisand
Scrapbook

William Moore, "Moore Legends"

The Barbra Streisand Scrapbook

Allison J. Waldman

A Citadel Press Book
Published by Carol Publishing Group

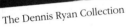

The Dennis Ryan Collection

A Citadel Press Book
Published by Carol Publishing Group
Citadel Press is a registered trademark of Carol Communications, Inc.
Editorial Offices: 600 Madison Avenue, New York, N.Y. 10022
Sales and Distribution Offices: 120 Enterprise Avenue, Secaucus, N.J. 07094
In Canada: Canadian Manda Group, P.O. Box 920, Station U, Toronto, Ontario M8Z 5P9
Queries regarding rights and permissions should be addressed to Carol Publishing Group, 600 Madison Avenue, New York, N.Y. 10022

Carol Publishing Group books are available at special discounts for bulk purchases, sales promotion, fund-raising, or educational purposes. Special editions can be created to specifications. For details, contact: Special Sales Department, Carol Publishing Group, 120 Enterprise Avenue, Secaucus, N.J. 07094

Designed by Andrew Gardner

Manufactured in the United States of America
10 9 8 7 6 5 4 3 2 1

Library of Congress Cataloging-in-Publication Data

Waldman, Allison J.
        The Barbra Streisand scrapbook / by Allison J. Waldman.
            p.   cm.
        "A Citadel Press book."
        ISBN 0-8065-1488-4
        1. Streisand, Barbra.   2. Singers—United States—Biography.   I. Title.
ML420.S915W3   1994
782.42164'092—dc20
[B]   93-45773
                                                                  CIP
                                                                  MN

*If you're lucky, some-
how, some day, some-
one in your life will
tell you that nothing's
impossible . . . that
you can do whatever
you desire as long as
you work hard, use
your talent and intel-
ligence, and never
stop believing in
yourself. Barbra
Streisand had to look
in the mirror to find
that encouragement
and validation. I
didn't. I only had to
look into my mother's
eyes. So, thanks to my
mom, Jean Corn, who
never doubted my
dreams and never
rained on my parade.
—AJW*

Contents

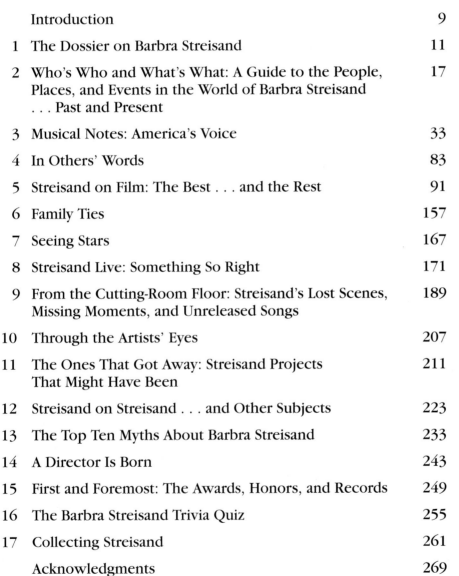

Courtesy *All About Barbra*

Introduction

Bit by bit, putting it together. Piece by piece,
Only way to make a work of art.
—STEPHEN SONDHEIM

"Much more" . . . "Gotta Move" . . . "I'm the Greatest Star" . . . "Why Did I Choose You?" . . . "All That I Want" . . . "I've Been Here" . . . "How Lucky Can You Get?" . . . "My Father's Song" . . . "Everything" . . . "Papa, Can You Hear Me?" . . . "Putting It Together" . . . "Move On" . . . Barbra Streisand has sung all these songs, and the lyrics of each one have spoken to her in a unique way. Indeed, Barbra's passionate performances of these songs (and others)—on stage, on albums, and in films—suggest that the star has tried to express herself with music, to give the listener or viewer a chance to know her, to understand her.

Or so it seems. But can we ever know a woman as "simply complex" as Barbra Streisand from her art? Are the words to songs, the images in films, the essential truth she brings to her performances, the key to who Barbra Streisand really is?

Perhaps yes, perhaps no . . . the one and only person who can and will reveal Barbra Streisand is Barbra herself. Someday she will write her memoirs, and in them, the most we'll ever know about this woman—a self-described "mass of contradictions"—will be unfurled. Until that time, the writers of books and articles will sort through reams of interviews, watch hundreds of hours of video, listen to Barbra being grilled by Mike Wallace on *P.M. East* and again on *60 Minutes*, and they still will not have more than a superficial idea of what makes Streisand tick.

And so, it comes back to the work. Maybe the only way to really know and understand and relate to Barbra Streisand is to listen to her albums, to watch her films, to behold her truth. *Bit by bit*, in each song, each scene, each performance, the kaleidoscope that is Barbra Streisand reveals new facets. *Piece by piece*, the girl from Brooklyn becomes the Hollywood director, and the award-winning actress-singer becomes America's most poignant voice. *The art of making art* is sharing all you are and all you dream you'll be . . . with all those people you'll probably never meet, but still can touch.

Putting it together, that's what this book is all about. A scrapbook of memories, achievements, projects, people, and moments. Will it tell you what Barbra Streisand is all about? Maybe . . . because it's all here. All the songs and the movies and the magic that Streisand has made in thirty something years of standing in the spotlight. Just as Barbra put it together—*bit by bit, piece by piece, reel by reel, deal by deal, doubt by doubt*—so, too, have I. You'll never know, but maybe there's more here than meets the eye. Maybe you'll find the real Barbra is here after all . . . right between the lines.

—ALLISON J. WALDMAN

No. P 1202

PERMIT NO. 544753

DATE ISSUED 5/29/62

NAME Barbra J. Streisand

ASSUMED NAME Barbra Streisand

OCCUPATION Singer

AGE 20   HEIGHT 5   5 IN.   WEIGHT 110 LBS.   SEX FEMALE

EYES Blue

Brown

NOTIFY DEPARTMENT OF LICENSES BY MAIL OF ANY CHANGE IN RESIDENCE

EXPIRES SEPTEMBER 30, 1965

1

The Dossier on Barbra Streisand

Name: Barbara Joan Streisand
Professional Name: Barbra Streisand
Occupation: Actress/Singer/Director/Producer/Writer/Composer
Height: 5'5"
Weight: 115 lbs.
Hair: Currently blond; originally brown
Eyes: Blue
Present Addresses: California—Holmby Hills; New York—Central Park West
Date of Birth: Friday, April 24, 1942, at 5:04 p.m.
Birthplace: Brooklyn, New York
Mother: Diana Rosen
Father: Emanuel Streisand
Siblings: Sheldon Streisand (born 1935) and half-sister Roslyn Kind (born 1951)
Religion: Judaism
Educational Background: Yeshiva of Brooklyn; P.S. 89; Erasmus Hall High School, Class of 1960; some college coursework in human sexuality and psychology, University of Southern California
Marital Status: Married to Elliott Gould in Carson City, Nevada, on September 13, 1963—they were divorced in Santo Domingo, Dominican Republic, in July, 1971
Children: Son, Jason Emanuel Gould, born Mount Sinai Hospital in New York City on December 29, 1966
Financial Worth (Estimated) in Mid-1994: $150 million
Salary for First Live Engagement: $108 a week (in 1961 at the Bon Soir in Greenwich Village)

Salary for Most Recent Singing Engagement: $20 million for two shows (in 1993–94 at the MGM–Grand Hotel, Las Vegas)
Political Affiliation: Liberal Democrat
Charities: Longtime supporter of liberal causes. She established the Streisand Foundation in 1985 to distribute donations to causes as diverse as Pediatric Aids, Get Out the Vote, and environmental protection. Internationally, she's anti-nuclear and pro-Israel. Currently, the Streisand Foundation has contributed over $7 million to worthy causes. In 1993, she donated her twenty-four-acre, five-home Malibu estate to the state of California to be used as a scientific and research conservancy.
Major Awards: Two Oscars (one for acting, one for songwriting); two Emmys; eight Grammys; the Grammy Legend Award; Tony Star of the Decade; ten Golden Globes; New York Drama Critics Award; American Music Award; Friar's Club Entertainer of the Year (1969); five People's Choice Awards; ShoWest Star of the Decade (1988); George Foster Peabody Award (1965); National Association of Theatre Owners (NATO) Star of the Year (1968); Scopus Laureate (American Friends of Hebrew

Jason Gould grew up on movie sets. Here he is nestled in Mommy's arms on the set of *Funny Girl*.

(Inset left) By the time Barbra got a permit to perform in nightclubs, she had dropped the extra "a" from Barbara.

Streisand made her Broadway debut as Miss Marmelstein, put-upon secretary of Maurice Pulvermacher (Jack Kruschen) in *I Can Get It for You Wholesale*.

University) (1984); National Organization of Women's Woman of Courage Award (1984); Women in Film Crystal Award (1984); Women in Film Dorothy Arzner Special Recognition (1992); ASCAP Songwriter's Award (1986); AIDS Project Los Angeles Commitment to Life Award (1992); eight National Association of Record

On the night Barbra won the Oscar as Best Actress for *Funny Girl* (in a tie with Katharine Hepburn), she was escorted to the show by estranged husband Elliott Gould.

Merchants (NARM) Awards; NARM President's Award (1988); La Croix D'Officier des Arts et Lettres (France) (1984); Directors Guild of America (nomination) (1991)

Theatre Credits: *Teahouse of the August Moon, Desk Set,* and *Picnic,* Malden Bridge Playhouse, New York, summer 1957; *Purple Dust,* Cherry Lane Theatre, New York City, fall 1957; *The Boyfriend, A Hatful of Rain, Tobacco Road,* Clinton Playhouse, New York, summer 1958; *Driftwood,* Garret Theatre, New York City, January 1959; *The Insect Comedy,* Jan Hus Theatre, New York City, May 1960; *The Boyfriend,* Cherry Lane Theatre, New York City, August 1960; *Another Evening With Harry Stoones,* Gramercy Arts Theatre, New York City, October 21, 1961; *I Can Get It for You Wholesale,* Shubert Theatre, Broadway, March 22 to December 9, 1962; *Funny Girl,* Winter Garden Theatre, Broadway, March 26, 1964 to December 26, 1965; *Funny Girl,* Prince of Wales Theatre, London, April 13 to July 16, 1966

Film Credits: *Funny Girl,* 1968; *Hello, Dolly!,* 1969; *On a Clear Day You Can See Forever,* 1970; *The Owl and the Pussycat,* 1970; *What's Up, Doc?,* 1972; *Up the Sandbox,* 1972; *The Way We Were,* 1973; *For Pete's Sake,* 1974; *Funny Lady,* 1975; *A Star Is Born,* 1976; *The Main Event,* 1979; *All Night Long,* 1981; *Yentl,* 1983; *Nuts,* 1987; *The Prince of Tides,* 1991

Most Successful Film (at box office): *A Star Is Born*

Least Successful Film (at box office): *All Night Long*

Film With Most Oscar Nominations: *Funny Girl*

Film With Most Oscar Victories: *Hello, Dolly!*

Recording Credits: *I Can Get It for You Wholesale,* 1962; *Pins and Needles,* 1962; *The Barbra Streisand Album,* 1963; *The "Second" Barbra Streisand Album,* 1963; *The Third Album,* 1964; *Funny Girl* (original cast), 1964; *People,* 1964; *My Name Is Barbra,* 1965; *My Name Is Barbra, Two,* 1965; *Color Me Barbra,* 1966; *Harold Sings Arlen (With Friend),* 1966; *Je M'Appelle Barbra,* 1966; *Simply Streisand,* 1967; *A Christmas Album,* 1967; *A Happening in Central Park,* 1968; *Funny Girl* (soundtrack),

Streisand strikes a classical pose in her television special *Barbra Streisand . . . and Other Musical Instruments.*

Volume 2, 1978; *The Main Event* (soundtrack), 1979; *Wet,* 1979; *Guilty,* 1980; *Memories,* 1981; *Yentl* (soundtrack), 1983; *Emotion,* 1984; *The Broadway Album,* 1985; *One Voice,* 1987; *Nuts* (soundtrack), 1987; *Till I Loved You,* 1988; *Barbra Streisand: A Collection, Greatest Hits . . . and More,* 1989; *Barbra Streisand Just for the Record . . . ,* 1991; *The Prince of Tides* (soundtrack), 1991; *Highlights From Just for the Record . . . ,* 1992; *Back to Broadway,* 1993; *Duets,* 1993; *Barbra the Concert,* 1994

Most Successful Album: *Guilty*

Least Successful Album: *Barbra Streisand . . . and Other Musical Instruments*

Most Successful Single: "Evergreen"

Least Successful Single: "Sam, You Made the Pants Too Long"

Album With Most Grammy Nominations: *Guilty* and *A Star Is Born* (4 each)

Album With Most Grammy Victories: *The Barbra Streisand Album* and *A Star Is Born* (2 each)

Television Credits: *My Name Is Barbra,* 1965; *Color Me Barbra,* 1966; *The Belle of 14th Street,*

1968; *What About Today?,* 1969; *Hello, Dolly!* (soundtrack), 1969; *Barbra Streisand's Greatest Hits,* 1970; *On a Clear Day You Can See Forever* (soundtrack), 1970; *The Owl and the Pussycat* (soundtrack), 1970; *Stoney End,* 1971; *Barbra Joan Streisand,* 1971; *Live Concert at the Forum,* 1972; *Barbra Streisand . . . and Other Musical Instruments,* 1973; *Barbra Streisand . . . Featuring "The Way We Were" and "All in Love Is Fair,"* 1973; *The Way We Were* (soundtrack), 1973; *ButterFly,* 1974; *Funny Lady* (soundtrack), 1975; *Lazy Afternoon,* 1975; *Classical Barbra,* 1976; *A Star Is Born* (soundtrack), 1976; *Streisand Superman,* 1977; *Songbird,* 1978; *Eyes of Laura Mars* (soundtrack), 1978; *Barbra Streisand's Greatest Hits,*

Critics despised it, but fans loved *A Star Is Born.* It remains Streisand's most successful film.

1967; *A Happening in Central Park*, 1968;
*Barbra Streisand . . . and Other Musical
Instruments*, 1973; *Funny Girl to Funny Lady*,
1975; *Barbra Streisand: With One More Look at
You*, 1977; *Getting in Shape for the Main Event*,
1979; *A Film Is Born: The Making of Yentl*,
1983; *Putting It Together: The Making of the
Broadway Album*, 1986; *One Voice*, 1986

**Most Successful TV Special (according to
Nielsen rating/share):** *My Name Is Barbra*,
21.5/31.6 share

**Least Successful TV Special (according to
Nielsen rating/share):** *The Belle of 14th
Street*, 15.4/26.7

Hobbies: Antiquing; gardening;
decorating/designing homes; shopping; eating

Astrological Sign: Taurus

Lucky Number: 24

Pet Peeves: Mispronunciation of her name;
paparazzi photographers; autograph hounds;
being misquoted

Favorite Actor: Marlon Brando

Favorite Actress: Rita Hayworth

Barbra's always ready with a good quote. Her favorite, "She
who tells the truth shall surely be caught," is from *Joan of Arc*.
Courtesy *All About Barbra*

Streisand met President John F. Kennedy when she was invited
to sing at the Washington Press Correspondents dinner in May
1962. The New York Public Library

Favorite Composers: Harold Arlen; Stephen
Sondheim

Favorite Singers: Johnny Mathis; Joni James

Favorite Directors: William Wyler; Bernardo
Bertolucci

Favorite Fashion Designer: Donna Karan

Favorite Television Shows: CNN, C-SPAN

Favorite Foods: Chinese cuisine; Breyers'
Coffee Ice Cream

Favorite Scent: Gardenia

Favorite Political Figure (Past): John F.
Kennedy

Favorite Political Figure (Present): Bill
Clinton

Favorite Quote: "She who tells the truth shall
surely be caught."—*Joan of Arc*

Professional Motto: "The audience is the
greatest barometer of the truth."

THE DOSSIER ON BARBRA STREISAND

Favorite Things: Craftsmanship; shoes; sea smells and country sounds; Oriental philosophy; being in the middle of reading ten books at a time; soft drinks; all kinds of hats; antiques; French silks; big, sloppy, fluffy beds in early morning; working hard and being lazy, too; muted, subtle colors; people who really care about what they do

Dislikes: New Year's Eve; eggs; hospitals; bright, red colors; liquor; the smell of ammonia; flat notes; vulgarity; people who assume too much familiarity too soon

Little Known Talent: Expert speller

Little Known Medical Ailment: Tinnitus, a lifelong ringing in the ears—she never hears silence

Childhood Dreams, Other Than Acting: To be a doctor or a biologist or a landscape architect

While in Rome, Barbra laid down the rules for this photographer. "I'll pose for one picture, then you leave me alone to shop. Okay?"

A page out of the Erasmus High School yearbook.

Pierluigi/Columbia Records

2

Who's Who and What's What: A Guide to the People, Places, and Events in the World of Barbra Streisand ... Past and Present

Agassi, Andre Flamboyant tennis champion who won Wimbledon in 1992. In September 1992 at the U.S. Open in Forest Hills, Barbra attended the matches and cheered for Agassi. When interviewed, she explained they were good friends. She was widely quoted as saying, "He plays like a Zen master." A year later, Streisand showed up at Wimbledon to watch him in the semifinals. Speculation again rose that the fifty-one-year-old Streisand was having a fling with the twenty-seven-year-old athlete.

All About Barbra British fan publication devoted to the career of Streisand which has been in print since 1983.

Another Evening With Harry Stoones An Off-Broadway musical revue which featured Streisand, Dom DeLuise, and Diana Sands, among others. It opened on October 21, 1961, at the Gramercy Arts Theatre and closed the same night.

Arlen, Harold Streisand's favorite songwriter; among the songs he's written are "Over the Rainbow," "When the Sun Comes Out," and "Come Rain or Come Shine," all of which Barbra has recorded. He penned the liner notes for her debut album *The Barbra Streisand Album*. Barbra sang two songs for his album *Harold Sings Arlen (With Friend)*.

Barbra A shortened version of Barbara, which Streisand devised to set herself apart from the rest of the world of Barbaras. It was also Streisand's way of changing her name—which she was encouraged to do early in her career—without changing it substantively. Advisers wanted her to change her name to Barbara Sands or Barbara Streis, but she refused. She explained later that she wanted the people she had grown up with to know who she was when she became famous. To spite those who insisted on a change, she altered Barbara by dropping an "a." She became the first Barbra. Since then, many have followed her lead by spelling the name as she does.

Barbra Quarterly The first serious fan publication devoted to Streisand's career. It spawned imitators, like *Barbra Now & Then*, but also inspired *All About Barbra* (which is still publishing). *Barbra Quarterly* set the tone for the others with its high-quality content, glossy production, and heavy emphasis on photos.

Barwood The name of Barbra Streisand's production company. The name was formed by combining **Bar**bra and Holly**wood**.

Beaton, Cecil Oscar-winning costume designer who created the clothes Barbra wore in the regression sequences for *On a Clear Day You Can See Forever*. He had also worked with Streisand early in her career when he photographed her for *Vogue* magazine and witnessed her transformation from star to superstar. "Barbra is one of two kinds of superstars. The two types are the coolly detached and the fanatically involved. Barbra was the latter during our collaboration in *On a Clear Day*. . . . Barbra and

(Inset left) Barbra Quarterly was the first Streisand fan magazine, setting the tone for *All About Barbra*, a British publication which is still thriving.

In *The Belle Street of 14th Street*, Barbra sort of previewed her *Yentl* look. She played a young boy and sang "Mother Machree."

I talked our way into everything and I trusted her judgment, something I seldom do with any actor, especially a relative neophyte. She obviously thought everything out; I've never to this day, met anyone so young who had such an awareness and knowledge of herself. Pleasing her was very difficult, but it pleased me, inwardly, because I myself am extremely hard to please. I think each of us is ever aware of the name we've been given and, more importantly, what we've each done with it."

Belle of 14th Street, The
Streisand's third television special. It was an homage to the vaudeville era and featured Barbra with costars Jason Robards Jr., Lee Allen, and John Bubbles. It was a major flop.

Bergman, Marilyn and Alan
Two of Barbra's dearest friends, Marilyn and Alan have also collaborated with her and have been her professional sounding board. They wrote the lyrics for many of her biggest hit songs, including "The Way We Were" and "You Don't Bring Me Flowers." Their greatest Streisand collaboration (with composer Michel Legrand) came on *Yentl*. Marilyn recounted her impres-

Barbra's *Wholesale* bio in *Playbill* caused a major controversy when she claimed she was "born in Madagascar and reared in Rangoon." The Michel Parenteau Collection

sion of Barbra, when they first met her in 1962 at the Bon Soir, to James Spada in *Billboard*: "I was totally unprepared. She started to sing and I remember that my eyes filled up with tears and I couldn't stop crying. I was so overwhelmed. Then we went backstage, which was a joke, because her dressing room was as big as a closet. I just said to her, 'You must know how wonderful you are.' "

Bon Soir, The Greenwich Village nightclub where Barbra appeared in engagements in 1961 and 1962.

"Born in Madagascar, raised in Rangoon"
For her *I Can Get It for You Wholesale* biography in *Playbill*, Barbra decided to invent a more exotic background for herself. She wrote that she was "born in Madagascar and raised in Rangoon," among other flights of fancy. *Playbill* threatened to drop her biography entirely if she didn't write it truthfully. According to Streisand, she wanted audience members to be amused by the notes, and she considered her own biography to that point much too commonplace.

Brice, Fanny Singer-comedienne whose life was depicted on stage and screen in the musical *Funny Girl*. Streisand played Brice in the Broadway show, the film version, and the film's sequel, *Funny Lady*.

"Brooklyn is boredom, baseball, and bad breath!" Infamous quote that was attributed to Streisand even though she never said it. When it turned up in the introduction to an October 1977 *Playboy* interview, she wrote to the magazine to say she never said that about Brooklyn, explaining: "That statement has been following me like a bad scent, and in trying to set the record straight, you missed that one."

Caan, James Barbra's leading man in *Funny Lady*, playing Broadway producer and songwriter Billy Rose. Caan also appeared with Barbra on stage at the Kennedy Center in Washington for the television spe-

A pair of Oscar winners — Richard Dreyfuss was Barbra's leading man in *Nuts*.

cial *Funny Girl to Funny Lady*, where they sang the duet "Paper Moon"/"I Like Him" from the film. In 1975, he commented on working with Streisand: "The most important thing to me is that I have a good time when I work, that I can laugh. If I'm not going to get along with someone, it's really not worth being miserable three or four months of my life. You hear all kinds of funny stories about Barbra and it's all garbage. . . . It's not hard to get bad words out of me because I'm very opinionated, and if I don't like somebody I'd sure say so. There's nobody like Barbra. She's talented and fun and we had a terrific time."

Cammermeyer, Margarethe Lieutenant colonel in the Washington National Guard who was forced to resign when the military learned she was a lesbian. Barbra has optioned her story for Barwood Films and plans to produce it as a television movie for NBC with Glenn Close in the starring role.

Chaplin, Sydney Broadway's original Nick Arnstein in *Funny Girl*, he clashed with Streisand and left the show before his contract was up. He was replaced by Johnny Desmond in June 1965.

Choy, Muriel and Jimmy Brooklyn neighbors

to the Streisands when they lived at 3102 Newkirk Avenue. The Choys befriended teenage Barbra when she baby-sat for their children. Later, Barbra went to work as a cashier at their local Chinese restaurant, Choy's Orient. She credits Muriel Choy with teaching her many things, including the facts of life.

Clinton, Bill Arkansas governor who became the president of the United States in 1992. Streisand's fund-raising concert and campaigning helped Clinton win. After the election, she sang at his inaugural ball and later was an overnight guest at the White House on a visit to Washington.

Columbia Records Streisand's recording label for her entire career (except for the cast album to *Funny Girl* and the soundtrack album to *Funny Lady*).

"Coffee Talk" Title of the *Saturday Night Live* sketch with Mike Myers in drag as Long Island Jewish American Princess Linda Richman, who loves Barbra Streisand. On February 22, 1992, Myers appeared with Madonna and Roseanne Barr, and as the skit came to an end, Streisand surprised the actors and the television audience by walking onto the set.

Corman, Cis The president of Barwood,

Barbra's association with personal manager Marty Erlichman has endured over thirty years — including about ten apart.

Barbra's marriage to Elliott Gould produced one child, their son Jason Gould.

Streisand's production company. Formerly a casting director, Corman is Barbra's best friend. Their friendship began in 1957.

Crawford, Michael British actor-singer who appeared with Streisand in *Hello, Dolly!* Years later, Crawford received international acclaim as the Phantom in Andrew Lloyd Webber's *Phantom of the Opera*. Streisand and Crawford performed the Phantom's most memorable song, "The Music of the Night," as a duet on Streisand's *Back to Broadway* album in 1993. Their recording was nominated for a Grammy Award as Best Pop Vocal Duet.

Davis, Clive Former CBS Records president (now the head of Arista Records) who was responsible for encouraging Streisand to sing in a more contemporary vein to take advantage of the changing musical tastes of the country. He put Barbra together with record producer Richard Perry, resulting in the *Stoney End* album and the hit song of the same title.

Dennen, Barry Actor-singer whom Streisand met in 1960 when they did an Off-Broadway show called *The Insect Comedy*. The two became intimately involved. He encouraged her theatrical aspirations, emphasizing her singing voice. He helped her pick material to compete in the talent show at The Lion. Dennen has had an undistinguished acting career. His claim to fame is costarring in the film version of *Jesus Christ Superstar*.

Diamond, Neil Brooklyn-born pop singer–songwriter who met Barbra when they were both in the Chorale Club at Erasmus Hall High School. Years later, as hugely successful recording artists for Columbia Records, they recorded the duet "You Don't Bring Me Flowers." It was a number-one hit on the *Billboard* singles chart. He also presented Streisand with the Oscar when she and Paul Williams won for "Love Theme From *A Star Is Born* (Evergreen)."

Dreyfuss, Richard Oscar-winning actor (for *The Goodbye Girl*) who won the role of Aaron Levinsky in *Nuts* when Dustin Hoffman and Streisand could not come to terms over money. On *The Today Show* in 1987, to promote *Nuts*, Dreyfuss spoke about Streisand's particular film persona: "You can see a clear line around Katharine Hepburn's personality and Bette Davis's personality and Joan Crawford's personality. And Jean Arthur and Barbra Streisand. That is what sets them apart. And this is what makes it compelling for us to watch them."

"Dust Mop of the Year" Tag line on the controversial movie poster for *Up the Sandbox* (1972). The Richard Amsel artwork showed Streisand tied to an oversized baby bottle on the cover of *Time* magazine, whose headline was "Dust Mop of the Year." Time Inc. objected to the use of their publication in the artwork. The posters and print ads were pulled and a new campaign launched.

Eastwood, Clint Macho Hollywood star and director whose career has run parallel to Streisand's. They are friends and colleagues and have discussed working together. In 1970, they shared the honor of World Film Favorites at the Golden Globes, and in 1992, Streisand presented Eastwood with the Oscar as Best Director for *Unforgiven*.

Ellbar Name of the television production company (formed from the names Barbra and Elliott [as in Mr. and Mrs. Gould]) which produced *My Name Is Barbra, Color Me Barbra,* and *The Belle of 14th Street.* They also had another company called Barbel. In both instances, they were no doubt inspired by Desilu, created by Desi Arnaz and Lucille Ball when they started *I Love Lucy.*

Erlichman, Martin Barbra's personal manager. "I always treated Barbra like a star, not by giving her limousines, but by making decisions for her as if she were a star, not settling, but demanding the best treatment for her by everyone," Marty said in 1983, reflecting on the early days before Barbra became so successful. Erlichman and Streisand teamed up in 1961 and stayed together until 1977. They resumed their professional relationship in 1986, and it continues to this day. According to Barbra: "The others love money. Marty loves me. You know why I liked him right away? Because he was real. He was wearing glasses."

F.O.B. According to the Washington press, F.O.B. stands for Friends of Bill, i.e., President Bill Clinton's closest associates. Streisand is an F.O.B.—and conversely, Clinton is also an F.O.B.—Friend of Barbra.

First Artists The film production company created in 1969 by Streisand, Paul Newman, and Sydney Poitier to create and distribute their films. Steve McQueen and Dustin Hoffman would join First Artists in subsequent years. Streisand's First Artists motion pictures were *Up the Sandbox, A Star Is Born,* and *The Main Event.* The company disbanded in the early eighties.

4 for McGovern Fund-raising concert held at the Los Angeles Forum in 1972 for Democratic presidential candidate George McGovern. Streisand closed the show, following performances by Quincy Jones, James Taylor, and Carole King. Streisand's portion of the show was recorded and released as the album *Live Concert at the Forum.*

Friars Club Famous previously all-male entertainment club which traditionally honors accomplished performers with roasts. At the roast, stars kid, insult, and tease the honoree in an affectionate, often bawdy, way. In 1969, Streisand became only the second woman ever to be honored by the Friars as Entertainer of the Year. The first was Dinah Shore.

Gould, Elliott Barbra Streisand's ex-husband. As a young actor, Gould was the star of the Broadway musical *I Can Get It for You Wholesale.* He met Streisand when she auditioned for the role of Miss Marmelstein. They fell in love during rehearsals, and when the show opened, they were living together. The reviews for the musical were tepid, except for Barbra, who garnered all the raves. Gould and Streisand were married on September 13, 1963, in Carson City, Nevada. They had one child, a son named Jason Emanuel. Barbra and Elliott's marriage suffered considerable strain because of her skyrocketing success in the sixties while Elliott was struggling to get work. Ironically, his greatest success would come a decade later when he was hailed as the new antihero by Hollywood in films like *M*A*S*H* and *Bob and Carol and Ted and Alice.* The Goulds divorced

Funny Girl's classic first words: "Hello, Gorgeous!" When she won the Academy Award, Barbra greeted her Oscar with the same line.

amicably in 1971 in the Dominican Republic. In the years since, they have remained friendly and supportive of one another. He has two other children, Sam and Molly, from his marriage to Jennifer Bogart. In 1984, he was asked about his relationship with Barbra: "Barbra is a very special case for me—and I may be for her. We love one another. At the age we began together, there were certain predestined situa-

High Society magazine tried to publish pictures of a nude scene which was supposedly cut out of *The Owl and the Pussycat.* The Michel Parenteau Collection

tions neither of us could deal with without destroying one another. So at some point, we conceded our relationship, which right now is beautiful. I don't care what anybody else thinks."

Gould, Jason The son of Barbra Streisand and Elliott Gould, born on December 29, 1966. He studied filmmaking at the University of California at Berkeley before pursuing an acting career in 1988. After working as a production assistant for Steven Spielberg and making brief appearances in the films *Listen to Me, The Big Picture,* and *Say Anything,* Jason was cast in his moth-

er's film, *The Prince of Tides,* playing her son. He received excellent notices.

Guthrie, Gary Enterprising Louisville, Kentucky, disk jockey who spliced together Streisand and Neil Diamond's solo versions of "You Don't Bring Me Flowers" to create a duet. After finding out about his unauthorized effort and the duet's popularity in the region, Columbia Records contacted Streisand and Diamond about recutting the song in a studio together. Their official duet came out five months after Guthrie's "version," and it immediately became a number-one single. Guthrie later sued Columbia for $5 million, trying to get more than a finder's fee from the label. The suit was eventually dropped, and the case was settled out of court.

Hamlisch, Marvin Composer of "The Way We Were," Hamlisch had previously worked with Streisand when he was the rehearsal pianist for *Funny Girl* on Broadway. For *The Way We Were,* he won two Oscars (for the song and for original score) and a Grammy. In 1993, Hamlisch conducted the orchestra for Streisand's two New Year's concerts at the MGM-Grand in Las Vegas, and in 1994 he conducted the orchestra for her world tour.

A Happening in Central Park Name given for Streisand's live 1967 concert which was recorded as an album and television special. Over 135,000 people showed up for the event, a record at that time for the largest audience to see a single performer.

"Happy Days Are Here Again" Barbra's first recording success. Her version of the traditional Democratic Party theme song was a radical departure. She took the normally uptempo 1929 ditty and sang it as a ballad. It remains one of her seminal songs.

Holmes, Rupert Singer-songwriter-record producer who produced *Lazy Afternoon.* Before that, he was relatively unknown. Streisand had heard his solo album and wanted to work with him, and the album put him on the map professionally. He worked on material for *A Star Is Born* (the songs "Everything" and "Queen Bee") and arranged and produced sessions.

The Insect Comedy Streisand's first Off-

Broadway play. It lasted three performances at the Jan Hus Theatre in New York in May 1960.

I Remember Barbra Documentary about Barbra Streisand told from the perspective of the people in Brooklyn who remembered her. For it, filmmaker Kevin Burns won the Best Documentary award at the Eighth Annual Student Film Awards sponsored by the Academy of Motion Picture Arts and Sciences.

It's Up to You Student film made by seventeen-year-old Jason Gould in 1983. It starred Jason's dad, Elliott Gould; his grandmother, Barbra's mother, Diana Kind; his aunt, Roslyn Kind; and assorted extended family members. Barbra assisted her son during production and in the editing room.

Johnson, Don Handsome, virile American actor who achieved his greatest success on television as Detective Sonny Crockett in *Miami Vice*. In 1988, Streisand and Johnson met in Aspen, Colorado, and began an affair. She did a cameo walk-on in the *Miami Vice* episode "Badge of Dishonor"; later, Johnson recorded a duet with Streisand called "Till I Loved You." Their relationship lasted nine months, ending when Johnson reunited with and remarried ex-wife Melanie Griffith. Streisand and Johnson have remained friendly.

Karan, Donna Successful fashion designer who came to the fore in the eighties and by the nineties was a household name. Streisand became close friends with Karan and Karan's husband, Stephan Weiss. Since then, Barbra has worn many personally designed Donna Karan outfits—like the pin-striped skirt suit for the Clinton inauguration concert. For the MGM-Grand concerts in 1993, Karan codesigned Streisand's gowns with Barbra.

Kelly, Gene Legendary movie song-and-dance man, choreographer, and director. He directed Barbra in *Hello, Dolly!* Although the film was marred by difficulties, Streisand and Kelly had a good relationship. During rehearsals, Kelly got in the habit of giving Streisand the thumbs-up sign when things were going well. When the movie wrapped, Streisand gave Kelly the classic James Montgomery Flagg three-sheet poster of Uncle Sam, pointing his finger and saying, "I

Want You!" "[It's] a real collector's item. On it she wrote, 'To Gene, thumbs up, and thanks for everything. Love, Barbra,' " Kelly told biographer Clive Hirschhorn in *Gene Kelly*.

Kelley, Virginia The mother of President Bill Clinton, Mrs. Kelley died two days after attending Barbra's concerts at the MGM-Grand Hotel in Las Vegas on December 31, 1993, and January 1, 1994. Barbra introduced Mrs. Kelley to the audience each evening, and after the

Barbra's romance with television star Don Johnson came to an end soon after this appearance at the premiere of his movie *Sweethearts Dance*. Randy Emerian

shows, Virginia was a guest at the post-concert parties. Streisand attended the funeral for her and then, a week later, established the Virginia Kelley Breast Cancer Research Center at the Arkansas Cancer Research Center in Little Rock. In announcing the creation of the center,

Thumbs-up was special signal between Streisand and director Gene Kelly. Barbra gave Gene a gift when the picture wrapped to remind him of their working relationship.

Streisand said, "She leaves her optimism, tenacity, and compassion as a legacy to her son, to the nation, and to all of us privileged to have known her."

Kind, Diana Barbra's mother. She was born in 1907, the child of a garment worker-cantor and a housewife. Diana was blessed with a beautiful soprano voice and claims that Barbra's musical gifts come from her. She married Emanuel Streisand, and together they had two children, Sheldon and Barbara (later changed to Barbra by the actress).

Kind, Louis Diana Kind's second husband, Barbra's stepfather. As a young girl, Barbra disliked the new man in her mother's life. They married in 1949, and Barbra claimed years later that Kind never like her, never showed her any affection, and mentally abused her. Diana and Louis separated in 1953 and divorced many years later.

Kind, Roslyn Barbra's half-sister, seven years younger, the daughter of Diana and Louis Kind. She was named Rosalind but later shortened it to Roslyn—much as Barbara was shortened to Barbra. At eighteen, she decided to follow in her sister's footsteps and become a singer, with mixed results. She had two minor RCA albums, *Give Me You* and *This Is Roslyn Kind*. She is still pursuing her career and recently appeared on Broadway in *Three From Brooklyn*.

Kristofferson, Kris After discussions with Elvis Presley, and rumors about Mick Jagger, it was Kristofferson who was selected to play the fading rock star John Norman Howard in *A Star Is Born*. He was in the middle of all the controversy the film attracted, but in the end, he and Streisand were close friends. "I thought she'd be pretty forbidding to work with. I found it a real good experience. I think in the back of my mind I knew it'd be something real good or we'd end up killing each other," he said in 1977. In 1984, he appeared in Barbra's first music video, "Left in the Dark," playing her leading man.

Laurents, Arthur Broadway director of *I Can Get It for You Wholesale*, he is best known as a writer. He wrote *The Way We Were* for Barbra, basing the character of Katie Morosky on a woman he'd known.

Legrand, Michel Oscar-winning French-born composer and arranger who produced Streisand's French album, *Je M'Appelle Barbra*. Legrand teamed with Marilyn and Alan Bergman to compose the score for Barbra's first film as a director, *Yentl*.

Lieberson, Goddard Former head of Columbia Records who gave Barbra her first contract with the label in 1962. Although he doubted her popular appeal, Lieberson was persuaded to sign her when it appeared Capitol Records was going to get her.

"Like Butter" What Barbra is, according to *Saturday Night Live* character Linda Richman. The idea is that nothing is richer and better and sweeter than butter. The term "like butter" has now become associated with Barbra. When Streisand sang at the Clinton inaugural in January 1993, audience members were heard telling her, "You're like butter!" There are also T-shirts which advertise the phrase.

Lion, The Greenwich Village gay nightclub where Streisand first achieved notoriety as a singer. She won a talent contest on June 6, 1960, by singing "A Sleepin' Bee" and "When Sunny Gets Blue." The victory, worth $50 and an engagement at the club, was the start of her singing career.

MGM-Grand Hotel Huge Las Vegas hotel complex which opened on December 18, 1993, with Streisand as the first act booked into the Grand Garden arena. Her fee for two shows, New Year's Eve and New Year's Day, was reportedly $20 million.

"Ma Première Chanson" Streisand's first attempt at song-writing. She wrote the music; Eddy Marnay penned the lyrics. It was recorded on *Je M'Appelle Barbra*, Streisand's French album.

Mastroianni, Marcello Italian movie icon who was featured in a 1965 *Esquire* magazine article, telling about the tour of Italy he would give to Streisand. This prompted Barbra to reply in a column called "Aftermath," wherein she offered her wry tour of New York and Brooklyn for Marcello.

Matthau, Walter Streisand's costar in *Hello, Dolly!* While they were shooting on location in Garrison, New York, a fight erupted, and Streisand and Matthau exchanged angry words. Their feud was blown up by the press, and Matthau did little to dispel the notion that he did not care for

Barbra. However, years later, Matthau was one of the many stars who attended Streisand's *One Voice* concert at her home, and his wife, Carole Saroyan, wrote a letter to the *New York Times* in 1983 in response to Isaac Singer's criticism of Streisand's film version of his short story, "Yentl, the Yeshiva Boy." In 1969, Matthau told *Esquire* magazine: "Barbra operates like a Japanese Kabuki dancer. I don't dislike her. I have a kind of fondness for her that is very real. She's a very unique actress. She has a great sense of over-lap—and underlap."

Mengers, Sue One of the most powerful agents in Hollywood during the seventies. Streisand was Mengers's top client, and Mengers negotiated deals which capital-ized on Streisand's box-office clout and made her one of the highest-paid movie stars in the world. Mengers persuad-ed Streisand to take over Lisa Eichhorn's role in *All Night Long*, which was directed by Jean-Claude Tramont, Mengers's hus-band. Streisand and Mengers's professional rela-tionship ended in 1981, in part because of the agent's negative attitude about *Yentl*. In 1987, she talked about what happened in a *Los Angeles Times* Calendar piece: "She always wanted to do the picture, and I was always negative about it. . . . But mostly, I think [our professional relationship] had run its course by then, with Barbra. Barbra was like my little sister and how in the world was she going to direct this difficult picture and play a boy? To my chagrin, I was wrong. I never had enough belief. I remember going to see it—at the time

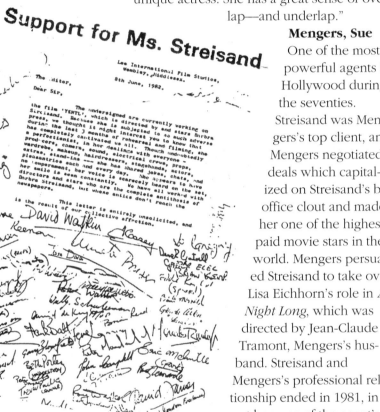

(Above) The cast and crew of *Yentl* felt it was neces-sary to set the record straight with "The Letter." Courtesy of the Lincoln Center Library for the Performing Arts.

we weren't speaking—and crying and saying, 'Thank god she didn't listen to me!' Right after that I called her, and we are friends again."

Merrick, David Legendary theatrical producer who hired Streisand for her first Broadway show, *I Can Get It for You Wholesale*, and then nearly fired her because of her tardiness during rehearsals. Later, he and Ray Stark teamed up to produce *Funny Girl*, but Merrick was eventually bought out. Finally, he was the producer of Broadway's *Hello, Dolly!*, and because he would not close the show, Twentieth Century-Fox was forced to shelve the Streisand film version for a year.

Miller, Allan A teacher and actor, introduced to Streisand by his wife, Anita, who met her at the Cherry Lane Theatre in New York City in 1957. She arranged for a scholarship for Barbra to study acting with her husband. Streisand baby-sat for Anita and Allan's son to earn extra money.

Nixon's Enemy List Infamous litany of well-known Americans who campaigned against the reelection of President Richard Nixon. During the Watergate hearings, John Dean testified about the existence of the list. Barbra Streisand was one of the liberal celebrities deemed an enemy.

October 31, 1964 The week when five Streisand albums were listed on the *Billboard* Top 100 Albums chart: *The Barbra Streisand Album*, *The "Second" Barbra Streisand Album*, *The Third Album*, *Funny Girl*, and *People*.

Oscar 1. Nickname for the Academy Award. Streisand has won two Oscars, one as Best Actress in *Funny Girl* in 1968, another for writing the music to "Love Theme From *A Star Is Born* (Evergreen)." 2. Name for the rat which invaded the Third Avenue railroad flat Streisand shared with Elliott Gould before they were married.

O'Neal, Ryan Streisand's costar in two comedies, *What's Up, Doc?* and *The Main Event*. They were also romantically involved before and during filming of *Doc* and have remained close friends. In 1979, while filming *The Main Event*, O'Neal said of his leading lady: "She's a lot of human being, Barbra Streisand."

Walter Matthau found little appealing about Barbra when they costarred in *Hello, Dolly!*

Pacific Jewish Center Small synagogue in Venice, California, which was chosen by Streisand for her son Jason's bar mitzvah. The Orthodox Jewish shul was a highly unlikely choice, but after meeting with the rabbi and attending sabbath services there, Barbra, Jason, and Elliott Gould all decided it was the right temple for the bar mitzvah. Later, Streisand presented the synagogue with a six-figure donation. In April 1981, Barbra, brother Sheldon, and their mother, Diana Kind, attended the dedication of the Pacific Jewish Center School in honor of the late Emanuel Streisand.

"Papa, Watch Me Fly" 1. Streisand's finale in *Yentl*. 2. Title of a special edition of the ABC-TV newsmagazine *20/20* devoted to Streisand and the making of her first film as a director, *Yentl*. Geraldo Rivera conducted the interview, and the special episode featured behind-the-scenes footage of the filming, as well as the recording of the music.

Patinkin, Mandy Barbra's costar in *Yentl*, he is one of the leading Broadway musical stars of the eighties and nineties. About *Yentl*, he says, "I was touched by how much she cared about the project. She was obsessed with the idea of making the movie and that impressed me. And the fact that it would be her first time as a director was a turn-on as far as I was concerned. I wanted to be part of that venture. And it was a

great experience working with her. She never hesitated to show how nervous she was and I found that endearing. Of course, it made everyone anxious to help." Nevertheless, after *Yentl* was long over, Patinkin was still upset that he didn't get a chance to sing in the film.

"People" Poignant ballad written by Jule Styne and Bob Merrill for *Funny Girl*. Streisand's version of the song, recorded for the cast album as well as her own album of the same name, became a classic. It's since become her signature song. Ironically, she originally felt the lyrics to the song were all wrong. She claimed people who don't need people are much luckier than people who need people. But the notion that she didn't want to sing the song is nonsense; she knew immediately it was a terrific ballad.

Perry, Richard Record producer who worked with Barbra on a trio of albums—*Stoney End*, *Barbra Joan Streisand*, and *Live Concert at the Forum*—in the early seventies. With his help, Streisand adapted a more contemporary musical image by beginning to sing pop/soft rock music.

Peters, Jon The man who became Streisand's partner, lover, and constant companion for nearly ten years beginning in 1974. Peters was a millionaire when Streisand met him, owner of a string of successful beauty salons in Southern California. Still, he was accused of riding on

Streisand's coattails when he expressed his ambition to become a movie producer. He designed the wig Barbra wore in *For Pete's Sake*, which led to their meeting. They became romantically involved soon after that first encounter. Peters produced Streisand's *ButterFly* album in 1974, then moved into moviemaking. His first film was *A Star Is Born*, with Barbra as executive producer. It has made more money than any other Streisand film to date. Peters subsequently became enormously successful as an independent producer in tandem with Peter Guber. They produced *Flashdance*, *Missing*, and *Batman*, among other films. Sony Entertainment hired Guber and Peters (for astronomical salaries) to run Columbia Pictures when buying the studio in 1990. Peters left Columbia in 1991 and returned to independent producing. Streisand and Peters severed their romantic relationship in 1982, but their lives are still intertwined. Jon married in

Sue Mengers *(center)* was Streisand and O'Neal's agent in 1978 when she visited them on the set of *The Main Event*. The Michel Parenteau Collection

Jon Peters's first producer credit was on *A Star Is Born*, a multi-million-dollar success that starred Barbra and Kris Kristofferson.

1985, and when he and his wife adopted a daughter, Callie, Barbra became the child's godmother, and she and Callie are extremely close. Peters continues to be very involved in Streisand's life. In 1992, Peters hosted a massive fiftieth birthday party for Streisand.

Pierson, Frank Writer who agreed to work on the screenplay of *A Star Is Born* if Streisand and Peters would allow him to direct it. Admiring Pierson's screenwriting, Peters and Streisand said yes on the condition that he would be their collaborator. During filming, however, Pierson became increasingly uninterested in incorporating Streisand's ideas into the film. After principal photography ended, Pierson delivered his cut of the picture, but Streisand recut the movie, and it was her version which was released. Before the film's premiere, Pierson vented his anger at Streisand and Peters in a scathing article about the picture called "My Battles With Barbra and Jon," which was published in *New York* and *New West* magazines.

Pollack, Sydney Producer-director-actor and close friend of Streisand and her director on *The Way We Were*. In 1985, Barbra presented him the Best Director Oscar for his work on *Out of Africa*. Pollack also appeared on *The Broadway Album* as part of the executive chorus on the cut "Putting It Together." In a 1983 interview

with reporter Joseph Morgenstern, Pollack commented on working with Barbra: "My recollection is that it was an absolutely perfect collaboration [on *The Way We Were*]. I could not have wanted in any of my dreams or fantasies anyone more talented or cooperative. As a matter of fact, when I used to read stories about her being difficult, I'd think, 'That must be somebody else they're talking about; it's not the person I worked with.' "

Presley, Elvis Streisand considered casting "The King" as the washed-up rock star in the version of *A Star Is Born* she and Jon Peters were producing. The two visited Presley in Las Vegas to discuss the project but realized after seeing the bloated, dissipated entertainer that he was in no condition to do a film. If anything, he seemed to be living the sad existence of the John Norman Howard character in the script. Reportedly, Presley's manager, Colonel Tom Parker, wouldn't even consider the project because he didn't want Elvis "playing second fiddle to Streisand."

Rainbow Road Joan Didion and John Gregory Dunne's screenplay for a remake of *A Star Is Born* set in the world of rock music. When Streisand and Jon Peters decided to produce their screenplay, one of the first things they did was change the title back to *A Star Is Born*.

Redford, Robert Streisand's costar in *The Way We Were*. Like Barbra, he has branched out into directing. He and Streisand have long talked about reuniting for a sequel to *The Way We Were*, and for a while both were developing *The Prince of Tides*. Redford backed out of *Tides* at a certain point and let Streisand have the project. She has said of him, "He's a person and I'm a person. He's a pretty perfect person and making the film [*The Way We Were*] was really fun. He's one of my best friends." As for Redford, he, too, has only good things to say about Streisand. In 1986, he reminisced about *The Way We Were* in *USA Today*: "I think it was the subtle stuff the audiences responded to. I think it had to do more with Barbra Streisand and myself than what we were doing. I like Barbra a lot. I really enjoyed working with her. In fact, every minute was a pleasure."

Richman, Linda Character created by *Saturday Night Live* comic Mike Myers, who hosts a fictional public-access talk show on Long Island called "Coffee Talk." Among the favorite chats on the show is Barbra Streisand, whom Linda describes as "like butter." When Streisand performed live at the MGM-Grand Hotel in Las Vegas on December 31, 1993, and January 1, 1994, Myers was a surprise guest—in drag as Linda—and appeared on stage with Barbra in a seemingly impromptu comedy sketch.

Rill, Eli One of Streisand's acting coaches when she began studying in New York City at age sixteen.

Sadie Barbra's dog, a white miniature French poodle given to Barbra by the cast of *Funny Girl* on Broadway at her birthday party on April 24, 1965. Barbra introduced Sadie to the world on the *Color Me Barbra* television special; she sang "Look at That Face" to Sadie. The dog died in the mid-seventies. Jon Peters gave Barbra another white poodle, one who looked very much like the first Sadie. She was named Sadie II, and it was she who appeared on the cover of the *Songbird* album with Barbra.

Scarangella, Angelina Streisand's pseudonym when she attended more than one acting school in New York in 1958–60. She claims that she found the name by going through dozens of phone books. To make others believe she really was Angelina, Barbra had matchbooks made up with that name on it. Years later, Barbra used the alias when she was admitted to Mount Sinai Hospital to give birth to her son, Jason Gould, on December 29, 1966.

Seaman's Savings Special passbook savings account Barbra started in the early sixties and still maintains in the name Barbara Joan Streisand. She told *Life* magazine in 1983, "I started it just before I took the third 'a' out of my name, and I've still got it. I put money in it only when I feel it's really mine, like $750 my mother gave me when I married Elliott. I think I have about $17,000 there now. I feel really rich. If I ever have to escape, if I ever want to leave this life, I'd take the money out of that account."

Sharif, Omar Streisand's matinee-idol leading man in the film version of *Funny Girl.* Although Egyptian, Sharif pulled off the role of Jewish gambler Nick Arnstein and even sang his own songs. Years later, he wrote in his memoirs about a brief affair with Streisand while making the film. He briefly reprised the role of Nick in *Funny Lady.*

Simmons, Richard Well-known diet and fitness expert who is a devout, very public Barbra Streisand fan. He was a special correspondent for *The Tonight Show* at the MGM-Grand in Las Vegas on January 31, 1993, covering Barbra's return to the concert stage. He credits Barbra

Sydney Pollack and Barbra began their longtime friendship when he directed her and Robert Redford in *The Way We Were.*

A meeting of the minds: Streisand and Redford filming *The Way We Were* in Malibu.

with being his role model and the motivation for his personal success.

Singer, The An album Streisand was preparing when she was persuaded to do a more contemporary record instead. Subsequently, the material was on the retrospective boxed set *Just for the Record. . . .*

Singer, Isaac Bashevis Award-winning author who wrote the short story, "Yentl, the Yeshiva Boy," which was filmed in 1983 as Barbra's directorial debut, *Yentl.* Singer condemned Streisand's interpretation of the story, particularly making it a film with music. Singer's criticism ran in the Arts and Leisure Section of the Sunday *New York Times.* In response, Streisand issued a statement expressing her disappointment in his opinion but adding pointedly, "If a writer doesn't want his work changed, he shouldn't sell it."

Sondheim, Stephen The most influential Broadway composer of the seventies, eighties, and nineties, Sondheim collaborated with Streisand on *The Broadway Album,* reworking many of his songs for her. Their successful teaming led to another album, *Back to Broadway.* In 1992, Sondheim presented Streisand with the Grammy Legend Award.

Soundtracks Possible title of an album of music from the movies Barbra has been planning since 1986. According to columnist Liz Smith, Barbra would like to dedicate the album to Harold Arlen, and it would include this quo-

tation from Einstein: "Great spirits have always encountered opposition from mediocre minds."

Stars Salute Israel at 30 All-star musical television special in honor of the State of Israel's thirtieth anniversary. It aired on May 8, 1978, with Streisand's segment comprising the last twenty-five minutes of the show. Aside from singing, Streisand also conducted an interview with former Israeli prime minister Golda Meir via satellite.

Streisand Foundation, The Created by Barbra in 1985 to support qualified charitable organizations committed to antinuclear activities, preservation of the environment, civil liberties, and human rights. Profits from the *One Voice* concert album and video release, as well as other endowments from Barbra, are funneled through The Streisand Foundation. As of 1993, over $7 million has been distributed by the foundation.

Streisand, Sheldon Barbra's brother. Sheldon is seven years older, and when she was just starting in show business, he was an advertising executive. He eventually went into real estate and has been very successful. He lives in Long Island and has a grown daughter named Erica, four years older than Jason. According to Barbra: "My brother is not a dreamer, he's structured right in the world." She stated this as an ironic preface to the explanation that it was Sheldon who introduced her to the psychic who helped her to receive a message from their father, Emanuel.

Styne, Jule Broadway composer of *Funny Girl* as well as dozens of other musicals, he was instrumental in Barbra being cast as Fanny Brice. He was one of her earliest and most influential supporters.

Summer, Donna A popular singer who had her greatest recording success in the seventies with the advent of disco dance music. Streisand and Summer teamed up for a disco opus called "(No More Tears) Enough Is Enough," which made it to the top of the charts. In 1983, Summer sang "Papa, Can You Hear Me?" from *Yentl* at the Oscars.

Trudeau, Pierre Former prime minister of Canada, he and Streisand dated in 1969 and 1970. Her appearance at a session of the Canadian Parliament in 1970 caused a sensation.

Walters, Barbara Television newswoman and interviewer who has featured Streisand as a guest on two of her specials. On the debut of *The Barbara Walters Specials* in 1976, Walters interviewed her and Jon Peters about their relationship and their film, *A Star Is Born* (the other couple featured in the hour show was newly

One of Barbra's most glamorous beaux was Canadian prime minister Pierre Trudeau.

elected President Jimmy Carter and his wife Rosalyn). In 1985, Walters visited Streisand's home for another special, and they talked about *The Broadway Album*. Prior to these specials, Walters first interviewed Streisand on *The Today Show* in 1975. Most recently, Streisand was interviewed by Walters on a segment of *20/20* (November 19, 1993).

"With One More Look at You" 1. In *A Star Is Born*, the climactic song performed by Esther at the end of the film. 2. A syndicated television special about the making of the film.

What Becomes a Legend Most? Distinctive print advertising campaign for Blackgama Furs. Streisand did the ad in 1968, and the photo, which was shot by Richard Avedon, became the company's most requested reprint.

Work in Progress, A The title Streisand had considered for the album *Classical Barbra*, her first attempt at classical music. She finally decided against the title because she didn't want to be seen as apologizing for the album.

Streisand's love-hate relationship with producer Ray Stark resulted in some very successful films: *Funny Girl, The Owl and the Pussycat, The Way We Were, For Pete's Sake,* and *Funny Lady.*

3

Musical Notes: America's Voice

According to Quincy Jones, one of the most accomplished men in the music business, Barbra Streisand's singing voice "is a Stradivarius." To many admirers, it's something more magical than that. The esteemed musician Glenn Gould wrote in *High Fidelity* in 1976 that "the Streisand voice is one of the natural wonders of the age, an instrument of infinite diversity and timbral resource." But what she does with this instrument, the way she uses the inherent quality of the sounds she creates, how she has set her mark on the world of music—becoming one of the best of America's voices—is Streisand's greater gift.

To rise above the rest, to set oneself apart, a singer needs much more than a nice voice. In fact, there have been singers who have accomplished individuality without benefit of a good sound. They rely on style, attitude, phrasing, and interpretation. The fundamentals of vocalizing—the attention to the details of pitch, tempo, dynamics, lyrics—are the singer's cornerstones. These basics are the foundation of vocal musicianship, the very building blocks of singing, and no performer can achieve greatness without mastering

these principles. Learning the craft of singing, how to breathe and how to sustain a note, how to match a pitch and how to change keys, how to carry a melody or how to sing in harmony— these are skills both learned and instinctive. They involve not only the voice but the ear, the brain, the lungs—and the soul.

In the realm of American pop music, there are but a handful of singers who have it all—a beautiful sound, great style, distinctive phrasing, superb musicianship, and the unique ability to create a mood and a moment within the confines of thirty-two bars of music. And within that elite handful are two names which have come to define the term "best ever" . . . Frank Sinatra and Barbra Streisand.

It is perhaps ironic that Barbra Streisand should have reached such a rarefied position in popular music considering the fact she's always bristled at being labeled just a singer. While Sinatra has happily boasted of being first and foremost a saloon singer, Streisand always chafed at being pigeonholed. From the very first, she made it clear she was "an actress who sings." Approaching her songs like three-act plays, Barbra created entire scenes and characters with her music. Then with a seemingly instinctive gift both to interpret material and to communicate with people, she performed her musical plays—three minutes at a time—and drew audiences into the spell she wove. In those first nightclub dates in 1960, Barbra Streisand discovered the way to create her very special, very individual, very personal musical artistry.

(Above) Even in her earliest recording sessions, Streisand had ideas about how things should be done. The Michel Parenteau Collection

(Left) Nineteen-year-old Barbra at one of her first recording sessions for Columbia Records. The Michael Parenteau Collection

(Inset left) Barbra's top-notch performance on the *Pins and Needles* album encouraged Goddard Lieberson to sign her to a Columbia Records contract. The Dennis Ryan Collection

The actress in song had found a way to express herself, to receive audience approbation, and to explore new creative challenges. At that time in music, no one else had ever done what she was doing in quite the way she did it. Yes, Ella Fitzgerald captivated listeners with a voice both pure and soulful, but Ella's magic was to ride on the wave of music and improvise . . . to become an extension of the song. And no one could deny that Judy Garland's voice was a clarion of emotion, the embodiment of feelings. But Fitzgerald played with the lyrics, using them to launch deeper into the melody, and Garland's emotional take on a song did not approach the lyric as does Streisand, with her commitment to dramatic analysis. Garland's response was a catharsis, a reaction to the lyric. Streisand takes a song apart, breaking down the lyric to its essence. It was this kind of synthesis which led her to ask Stephen Sondheim to rework his most famous ballad, "Send in the Clowns." "Every time it's been recorded, people have had to sing [the stage] version because there was no second release. [Barbra's] instincts were absolutely right because on stage the scene needed something else," agreed Sondheim.

Whether a listener actually imagined the character Streisand created with her interpretation, or merely perceived it on a subconscious level, the desired effect was achieved. It would only be in later years, particularly when singing pop-rock music, which was unable to withstand the weight of her dramatics, that Streisand's interpretive skills would fail her. But ever the adaptive talent, Streisand would discover how to sing even that material and make it work, most notably on the lyrically light hit album *Guilty*, produced by Barry Gibb.

The sound of a voice is perhaps the most abstract element in a singer's suc-

cess. Whether an alto or soprano, a woman is born with a particular vocal range and a sound which is uniquely her own—good or bad. Streisand always knew she could sing. "I liked singing. I mean, my identity was the kid on the block who had a good voice," she recalled in a 1992 interview. That good voice has been one of the most distinguishing characteristics of Barbra Streisand. It is pure and smooth, feminine and lyrical, unimpinged by a heavy vibrato. Streisand's voice could best be described as a rather wide-ranging alto. If you were to compare it to a man-made musical instrument, her voice is more like a viola than a flute. This range gives her singing voice a quality similar to her speaking voice, and the result is pleasant and very easy on the ears (especially when Streisand refined the sound, getting away from the tendency toward stridency early in her career). It's a voice that's also comfortable to sing along with, a factor which should not be discounted when talking about pop singers.

There is a uniqueness about Barbra Streisand's vocal style. It is more than being an actress in song, because, after all, there are many wonderful Broadway actresses with magnificent voices. Jule Styne, who wrote the lyrics for *Funny Girl*, has his idea about what Streisand does, which he explained in the liner notes for *Michael Feinstein Sings the Jule Styne Songbook*: "Girls phrase their music instead of phrasing their lyrics. Barbra Streisand is one of the few women who is an exception—her concept of singing, because she sings the words all the time—a great word singer. A lot of people think by phrasing that way, they can get it. But no, you have to have the sound that goes with the phrasing, and you have to have your own identification, your own sound. She is a one-of-a-kinder."

The inherent quality of Streisand's voice; her

(Above) Barbra live at the Bon Soir. Columbia recorded two shows and considered releasing the tapes as her first album. Hank Parker/Columbia Records

innate ability to sell a song; her rock-solid musical foundation; and, finally, the intelligence to adapt and develop as an artist . . . all these factors have contributed to Streisand's musical success. But as with the enduring musical giants of the recording era—Sinatra, Elvis Presley, the Beatles—Streisand's achievement lies in all that coupled with a sustained appeal that is both artistic and commercial. Her contemporaries are ever-changing. In the sixties, they were Garland, Eydie Gorme, Dionne Warwick, and Vikki Carr; in the seventies, Olivia Newton-John, Bette Midler, Donna Summer, and Karen Carpenter; in the eighties, Madonna, Whitney Houston, Sheena Easton, and Cyndi Lauper; in the nineties, Mariah Carey, Bonnie Raitt, and Natalie Cole, among others. The one constant among female vocalists in the past thirty years is Streisand, and few would argue that she has set a standard of excellence which is unparalleled. As the millennium approaches, Streisand stands alone as the preeminent female vocalist of the century, having earned the respect and admiration of musicians, composers, critics, and, perhaps most important, the masses. And in the future, there's no reason to believe she will not continue to add luster to her musical legacy. For an actress who sings, it is an application she can wear with pride.

Barbra Streisand's album catalog reveals all the elements of her enduring musical success story. The albums also graphically demonstrate a star's metamorphosis from young, developing songstress to accomplished musical legend . . . and along the way, the transformations that shaped her as an artist.

Neophyte in Song

1962   I Can Get It for You Wholesale
1962   Pins and Needles
1963   The Barbra Streisand Album

With a voice like hers, you would imagine Barbra Streisand had little trouble early in her career convincing theatrical producers and record executives to give her a chance to show her stuff. However, with her "exotic" looks—

As Fanny Brice in *Funny Girl*, Barbra became a star. Capitol Records got the original cast album recorded and into the stores three days later!

My Name Is Barbra produced two albums, an Emmy, and a Grammy for Barbra. Barwood Films

which were labeled offbeat by the kind, and homely by many others—Streisand was considered a major risk. But Streisand persevered, getting work as a singer in small Greenwich Village clubs like The Lion and the Bon Soir. In Barbra's mind, singing was an extension of acting: "Each song to me is a different play, a different character. In one song, I'm six years old, in the next I'm thirty-five."

She began to get noticed for her unique song stylings, as well as her idiosyncratic personality. At the Bon Soir, she opened for comedienne Phyllis Diller, who remembers, "It was extremely exciting to me because on her opening night—when she was only eighteen years old—I knew that this was a star. It was all there. On her third note, every hair stood up all over my body. I am, basically, a musician and [to hear] that voice and that heart, that thing that came out! It was a great thrill to work with her, to watch that happen and know where it was going. She was a disciplined, devoted worker, a brilliant genius . . . and she was a child!"

Ultimately, it was her work on Broadway in *I Can Get It for You Wholesale*, as the hero's mousey, put-upon secretary Miss Marmelstein (a role which was written for an older woman, so that Streisand's looks didn't matter) which helped pave the way for her recording career. According to *Wholesale* author Jerome Weidman: "The character of Miss Marmelstein, as she appears in the novel, was changed considerably when I did the play. The reason for this is simple. A totally unknown, young actress named Barbra Streisand came into the theater one day and read and sang for the part. Harold Rome, the composer, and I were entranced with her and went right home to enlarge the part and tailor it more to her quite remarkable talents. I'm delighted that we did. She was the hit of the show."

Because of Streisand's emergence as the show's only scene-stealer, she was given lead vocals on chorus numbers and inclusion in the scenes where her character could legitimately be placed as the musical wended its way to New York. On the album, her voice is heard on the first number, "I'm Not a Well Man," in her solo "Miss Marmelstein," and leading the chorus in "The Ballad of the Garment Trade" and "What Are They Doing to Us Now?" Listening to the album now, it is clear that the best voice of the bunch is Streisand's, and it's a voice the microphone loves. Her precise diction and original phrasing and the ease with which she navigates the scale were prime assets to the generally uninspired cast album. Streisand's strong vocals impressed composer Harold Rome, and Barbra became one of the principal singers in the anniversary edition of *Pins and Needles*, a thirties musical revue about the garment industry, which was being produced as an album by

Erlichman, was campaigning to get his client a recording contract, and Columbia Records was the one label he truly wanted for her. But Columbia president Goddard Lieberson was doubtful about Streisand's appeal: he thought she'd have a cult appeal, popular only with urban record buyers. But if Lieberson was judging Streisand by the *Wholesale* and *Pins and Needles* albums, he should have taken into account the quality of the material itself. As Streisand would prove in just a short time, she had excellent musical taste and canny intelligence in picking songs. In those first two albums, she had had little choice. "Everybody

The front cover of *My Name Is Barbra* showed the star as a five-year-old. The back cover revealed a shapely, sexy Streisand.

Columbia Records. Like *Wholesale*, Streisand was the best thing on the record, spicing up the gentle satire of a number like "It's Not Cricket to Picket" with a healthy dose of indignation, playing up the broad humor of "Four Little Angels of Peace," and bringing unexpected poignancy to the ballad "What Good Is Love." Both albums were evidence of not only her raw musical talent but her developing dramatic technique as well.

Streisand's personal manager, Martin

said, 'She has a beautiful voice, but it's more Broadway than records, and certainly the voice and the material are not what is being bought at the moment. We don't think she'll sell records,' " Marty Erlichman remembered in a 1983 special supplement to *Billboard* magazine, *The Legend of Barbra Streisand*.

"The first label that wanted her was Atlantic," said Marty. "But that label was basically jazz, and I told them that I thought she had great potential as an album seller. And since

Columbia was the best album-producing company, I had my heart set on them." The next label to come up with an offer was Capitol Records. When it became apparent to Columbia that Capitol was in the game—and that Marty and Barbra might say yes—Lieberson relented and signed her. The terms of Streisand's first Columbia contract were financially modest: Streisand chose to accept less money in exchange for creative control. What it meant for the singer was that the label could not dictate either the material she sang or anything else. Streisand's albums would reflect her musical taste and style; she would not be packaged or "re-created" by any "experts" at Columbia Records. Whether she was to succeed or fail, she would do so on her own terms.

When *The Barbra Streisand Album*, her solo debut, hit the stores in February 1963, it was soon evident that Streisand would succeed. *The Barbra Streisand Album* featured her in a variety of song stylings and dramatic scenes and was proof positive that she was a singer with both a beautiful voice and a great ability to interpret a lyric. There were many appealing elements to this album, starting with the choice of material. Many of the songs were those she was singing in clubs at the time: "Happy Days Are Here Again," "Cry Me a River," "Who's Afraid of the Big, Bad Wolf," "A Sleepin' Bee," and two numbers from the musical *The Fantasticks*, "Much More" and "Soon It's Gonna Rain." Most critics were enchanted with the new singer; a few were not, but their criticism had little effect on listeners. Goddard Lieberson would discover that Streisand's appeal went far beyond the urban record buyers. As if fulfilling some musical destiny, Streisand's premiere solo album would climb the charts, landing in the top ten (the highest point it reached was number eight).

(Above) My Name Is Barbra, Two was originally advertised as "My Name Is Barbra, Act Two."

Her commercial success was then topped by artistic recognition. *The Barbra Streisand Album* was nominated for three Grammys, winning two important accolades: Album of the Year and Best Female Vocalist.

Streisand's huge, immediate success was undoubtedly a shock, albeit a happy one, for Columbia Records. But for Barbra, the results were expected. With an air of confidence bordering on arrogance, she said at the time: "Everyone is surprised, but I always knew it would happen this way. People were ready for me."

The Barbra Streisand Album marked the first collaboration between Streisand and arranger-conductor Peter Matz. Composer Harold Arlen had worked in the theatre with Matz and suggested to Marty Erlichman that he would work well with Barbra. Arlen was on target as a matchmaker: Streisand and Matz proved to be a winning combination. "I was immediately attracted to her when we met, and I realized this was a very special person," Matz told author James Spada in his book *Streisand: The Woman and the Legend*. Matz brought energy and vibrance to the arrangements, adding the colors and tones Barbra felt in the material but was unable to articulate because she was not a trained musician. "She had a strong instinct about what was going to work for her," he said, "both in material and down to specific things in the music. Many of the ideas in the arrangements . . . were really hers." As she had with accompanist Peter Daniels, who worked with her until she jumped from nightclubs to stadiums, Barbra could communicate her musical desires to Matz, and he could add nuances and shadings which complemented her vocalizing. She could say, "I think it should sound like this," then hum a few notes, and Matz understood.

To appreciate the quality of Peter Matz's contributions to Streisand's first album (and many subsequent ones), you need only listen to her initial Columbia singles. In those first sessions, released prior to *The Barbra Streisand Album*, versions of "Happy Days Are Here Again" and "Right as the Rain" (as well as "When the Sun Comes Out" and "Lover Come Back to Me") were recorded with arrangements by George Williams. His arrangements are labored and stagnant, and despite Barbra's superb singing, the singles went virtually unnoticed. The same songs were redone on her first and second albums with new arrangements by Peter Matz. The difference is tremendous. "When a singer is very passionate or dramatic, it wouldn't do to have blandness in an accompaniment. When there's a lot of heat in the voice, you have to back it up with equal heat. But you have to draw the line at where it gets intrusive." Undoubtedly, Matz knew exactly what he was doing with Barbra, and he is one of the main reasons *The Barbra Streisand Album* made the impression it did.

Broadway Baby

1963   *The "Second" Barbra Streisand Album*
1964   *The Third Album*
1964   *Funny Girl*
1964   *People*

In 1963, Barbra Streisand had the Midas touch. She was winning awards by the armful; she had proven herself to Columbia Records and was elevated to major star status; she was earning money hand over fist on the nightclub-concert circuit; and on television, Barbra was Ed Sullivan's guest, did comedy shtick with Bob Hope, and sang with Judy Garland. Her follow-ups to *The Barbra Streisand Album*—*The "Second" Barbra Streisand Album* and *The Third Album*—were very much in that debut album's spirit, although with a greater sense of assurance and an accent on elegance. *The "Second" Barbra Streisand Album* included more of her club material, like the spirited song

For her television special *Color Me Barbra,* the opening sequence was filmed on location at the Philadelphia Museum of Art. Barwood Films

written for her by Peter Matz, "Gotta Move," and a cynical John Kander–Fred Ebb number called "I Don't Care Much." The album had a heavy dose of Harold Arlen material: "Any Place I Hang My Hat Is Home," "Down With Love," "When the Sun Comes Out," and "Like a Straw in the Wind." Streisand was adept at traversing the musical terrain of Arlen's sprawling melodies, and with an intensity that bordered on melodrama, she made a classic Greek tragedy out of the lyrics of "When the Sun Comes Out" and a biting Shavian comedy with the bitter medley "Down With Love."

"A great actress rides on emotion, she makes people feel the emotion behind the lines. A great singer does the same," Barbra revealed, explaining her musical philosophy. "You have to act to be a good singer. There's no trick in getting up in front of an audience and closing your eyes and singing. That's easy. But to get up there and keep your eyes open and look at your audience and make them feel what you want

Barbra's French album was enhanced greatly by her collaboration with Michel Legrand.

them to . . . that's hard. Standing up there without doing anything at all, that's the hardest. I can do that, too." She could also bring that same excitement to her records. *The Third Album* had dramatic turns similar to her first two albums, such as "Never Will I Marry" and "I Had Myself a True Love," but it differed in tone. There was an air of sophistication and grace, and the album

benefited from a beautiful, definitive version of "Bewitched, Bothered, and Bewildered" and distinctive renditions of the standards "It Had to Be You" and "As Time Goes By." Streisand's second and third albums climbed even higher on the *Billboard* chart than had her debut. *The "Second" Barbra Streisand Album* nearly became Streisand's first number-one record: it peaked at number two. *The Third Album* went to number five.

Still, Streisand was looking for more . . . much more. Her dreams of stardom were nurtured in the theatre. As a fifteen-year-old kid, she had sweated and slaved in summer stock, imagining the moment when she would someday step out onto a Broadway stage. With *Wholesale*, Streisand got that moment . . . but as part of an ensemble she could only fly so high. On March 26, 1964, at the Winter Garden Theatre, Barbra Streisand opened in *Funny Girl*. The show was a hit, but Streisand was a sensation. It would be hard to imagine a better set of reviews than she received. She was hailed as Broadway's newest, perhaps greatest hope for the future. And in a mythical moment in the spotlight, Streisand sang, with soaring emotion, a plaintive ballad of love and yearning called "People." Music, drama, desire, and destiny came together in that moment. If it were written into a script, it would have seemed like cliché, but it happened to Streisand. Her stardom was ensured following *Funny Girl*, and the lyrics to "I'm the Greatest Star," her first song in the show, seemed truly prophetic.

Less than two weeks after it opened, the *Funny Girl* company gathered in the recording studio to recreate the musical for the Capitol original cast album. In an amazing turnaround, the album was released three days later. The speed was impressive, but compared to Streisand's solo albums, the *Funny Girl* cast album was subpar in quality. It had a tinny, unpolished sound . . . one which might have been avoided if Columbia had recorded the album instead of Capitol. Ironically, Lieberson had chosen to record *Anyone Can Whistle* instead of *Funny Girl*, in anticipation of the former's success. Therefore, Capitol won the contract for the *Funny Girl* LP and got Streisand. And as fate would have it, Stephen Sondheim's *Anyone Can Whistle* was a major flop, closing a week after it opened. The cast album is the only record of its run. *Funny Girl*, on the other hand, was a major success and ran over a thousand performances. Before the show opened, Streisand had recorded a single of "People" (for Columbia), and with the publicity generated by the opening, the record received heavy radio play. It made it onto the *Billboard* pop chart a week after the show opened and reached number five. With all the excitement Streisand was creating—appearing within weeks on the covers of *Life* and *Time*—and having a top-ten single, the original cast album sold 400,000 units in a month. And as it flew out of record shops, it soared up the *Billboard* Top 200 chart. Ultimately, it reached number two, and anxious to take advantage of *Funny Girl*'s success, Columbia urged Streisand to record an album and put "People" on it. Still, it would take a few months before the busy star would get back to the recording studio. In May, just six weeks after her Broadway bonanza, Streisand attended her first Grammy Award presentation and came home a winner as *The Barbra Streisand Album* was chosen Album of the Year and she won as Best Female Vocalist. Columbia could push her for a new album, but Streisand was now in the driver's seat. After a very short two years, the young artist was at the point where she decided when and what to record. Her star was in the ascent, and she was making the most of her new status.

People was Streisand's first post–*Funny Girl* album, and it would be her first to reach the coveted number-one spot on the

(Above) Barbra recorded "Free Again" in English and French; "Non C'est Rien" was on *Color Me Barbra* and "Free Again" was on *Je M'Appelle Barbra*.

Billboard chart. *The "Second" Barbra Streisand Album* in the fall of 1963 and the *Funny Girl* cast album in winter 1964 both made it to number two, but neither were able to climb to the number-one perch. But with the high recognition of the title cut (which made it to the top ten in *Billboard* as a single), the *People* album attained the top spot and stayed on the *Billboard* chart for eighty-four weeks. In addition to a pre-sold hit song, *People* had everything going for it as an album. Streisand's choice of material ranged from the pathos of Irving Berlin's "Suppertime" to the comedy of "When in Rome," the Broadway ballads "Will He Like Me?," "Don't Like Goodbyes," and "My Lord and Master," along with other gems like "How Does the Wine Taste?," "Love Is a Bore," and "I'm All Smiles." She also recorded with a new arranger, Ray Ellis, who, like Matz, developed a strong working relationship with Streisand, one which would last throughout the decade.

The *People* album was a Grammy winner for Streisand— 1964 was her second year in a row as Best Female Vocalist. The dramatic, iconoclastic cover design— showing Barbra standing alone on a beach, her back to the camera—set *People* apart from the typical 1964 record album. It was Streisand's own audacious and bold concept (especially for an album called *People*), and it won the Grammy for Best Album Cover.

Remarkably, on October 21, 1964, Barbra Streisand had five albums—*The Barbra Streisand Album*, *The "Second" Barbra Streisand Album*, *The Third Album*, *Funny Girl*, and *People*—listed on the *Billboard* album chart. The twenty-two-year-old American singer had only one rival in

Barbra recorded the music from *The Belle of 14th Street* as a possible album but when the show did so poorly, the plans were scrapped.

record popularity—those four Liverpool lads, the Beatles.

Chanteuse

1965　*My Name Is Barbra*
1965　*My Name Is Barbra, Two*
1966　*Color Me Barbra*
1966　*Harold Sings Arlen (With Friend)*
1966　*Je M'Appelle Barbra*

For Streisand, the real thrill of making her Broadway dream come true was not, ultimately, in the glory of the spotlight. She loved the pursuit, the hours and days and weeks of rehearsal and revisions that went into the creation of the show. Once it was frozen, however, Streisand was faced with the burden of having to deliver the same show, the same songs, night after night. On one hand, the challenge of Broadway was tremendous, especially for a performer obsessed with perfection. Could she make *Funny Girl* magical eight times a week, thrilling suburban theatregoers and matinee ladies the way she did first-nighters and the critics? But there was the other hand, and Streisand found

the ritual of doing the same role over and over again creatively stifling. Fortunately, she was able to turn to her music for new roles to play. Streisand's records in this era feature some of the best vocalizing of her catalog. Although it was just a couple of years since *The Barbra Streisand Album*, Barbra had refined her singing, and her voice took on a smoother, fuller, more mature sound. "I was desperate before, like on my first album . . . I think you can tell that. I was giving my all, and it's too much. Your all is too much. You must give only three-quarters, five-eighths. Maybe you won't understand what I'm saying because they say all the great people give their all. They don't really though. All kinds of great people, like Frank Sinatra . . . hold back. It makes the audience want more and come to them."

That was certainly the case with *People*. The number-one, Grammy-winning high of the album was sort of an unofficial close to Streisand's initial entree into records: her next three albums would be the result of her exploration into another branch of popular entertainment. On June 22, 1964, Streisand signed a $5 million deal with CBS Television for a group of specials. As she did with her music, Streisand negotiated for artistic control of the shows and didn't ink the deal until she got it. *My Name Is Barbra* was her nationwide introduction to people who were still unfamiliar with her Broadway and recording successes. The special—a song-filled, one-woman show—was both a critical and ratings hit. Soon after it aired, a new album incorporating and expanding upon material from the special was released, and, like *People*, it climbed up the charts.

My Name Is Barbra was in many ways Streisand's first theme album, as she took listeners on a musical progression from childhood to adulthood. Symbolizing the album's thematic journey was the front (and back) cover artwork. The front cover was a photograph of Streisand at age five (taken by her brother Sheldon when he was twelve), while the back revealed a grown Streisand seductively reclining in an evening gown. Most of side one—"My Name Is Barbra," "A Kid Again"/"I'm Five," "Sweet Zoo," and "Where Is the Wonder"—was graphically re-created for the television special as Streisand romped in an oversized playground set. However, for the album, Streisand added two more numbers to the childhood sequence—"My Pa," a love song from a little girl to her perfect father, and "Jenny Rebecca," which is a mother's lullaby to her newborn daughter. Side two plunges the listener into romance, beginning with "I Can See It," which provocatively flirts with reckless adventure. Innocent love and all its fantasy follow, with "Someone to Watch Over Me," "I've Got No Strings," and "If You Were the Only Boy in the World." Finally, there is the reality of being part of a relationship: "Why Did I Choose You?" and "My Man." (These are the only side-two songs on the television special, both sung in Streisand's concert finale.) Like the special, the *My Name Is Barbra* album was as ambitious as it was entertaining. It succeeded in taking the magic of the special to another level.

My Name Is Barbra, Two was only a sequel in that it included the medley from the television special which was not on *My Name Is Barbra*. Streisand's romp through Bergdorf-Goodman's department store to a medley of poverty songs was a visual feast on television. On *My Name Is Barbra, Two*, the medley seems oddly piggy backed onto the album. But it was important to commit the medley to vinyl, and it certainly didn't mar the overall quality of the LP. It was an album filled with luscious standards and theatre-oriented music, including the Fanny Brice comic classic "Second Hand Rose," Rodgers and Hart's "Where's That Rainbow" and "Quiet Night," the Gershwins' "I Got Plenty of Nothin'," and some splendid, new numbers: "He Touched Me," "The Kind of Man a Woman Needs," and "The Shadow of Your Smile." In all, it was a program perfectly

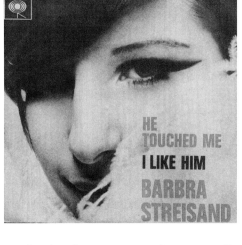

suited to Streisand's actress-in-song. She won a third straight Grammy as Best Female Vocalist for *My Name Is Barbra*, and both albums charted very well (each peaked at number two).

Streisand's second television extravaganza, *Color Me Barbra* was very similar to the first. In fact, Barbra called the two shows "bookends." But with the addition of color, and dramatic location shooting in the Philadelphia Museum of Art, *Color Me Barbra* was a sumptuous treat all its own. Once again, she was surrounded with top-notch people: Joe Layton, who conceived the production numbers; director Dwight Hemion; and producer Gary Smith. This collaboration would become a constant in most of Streisand's TV projects. But as Smith and Hemion pointed out in a 1987 *TV Guide* interview, there is but one driving force when doing a Streisand special: "When you do a show with Barbra, it's her vision. She's such a perfectionist that she pushes you to limits you don't think you can go. It's like a test. Every shot, every song, every idea, you need an answer and you damned well better find it."

The album version of *Color Me Barbra* followed the TV special much more closely than had the two *My Name Is Barbra* LPs, although the record did not include all the songs from the TV show. Still, there was an overall flow to *Color Me Barbra*, as Streisand rendered new takes on oldies like "Yesterdays," "Where or When," and "One Kiss"; bit into the jumpy rhythms of "Gotta Move"; and excelled on new material: "Where Am I Going?" and "Starting Here, Starting Now." Amid these songs lay Barbra's first foray into the international market: "Non C'est Rien" was the French version of Streisand's latest single, "Free Again," and it was a preview of her next project, *Je M'Appelle Barbra. Color Me Barbra*

(Above) Streisand recorded two songs from the Broadway show *Drat, the Cat*, a failed Elliott Gould/Lesley Ann Warren musical. The Michel Parenteau Collection

reached number three on the *Billboard* chart, and the National Academy of Recording Arts and Sciences nominated it as Album of the Year, and Streisand as Best Female Vocalist.

Streisand's French album, *Je M'Appelle*

With 135,000 adoring New Yorkers at her feet, Barbra's free concert in the park became quite a "happening."

Barbra, represented an artistic challenge, to be sure, and it also succeeded in altering people's image of Brooklyn/Broadway Barbra. Streisand started the project on the right foot by choosing Michel Legrand, a French composer, to arrange and conduct most of the album (along with Ray Ellis). Legrand could bring an authenticity to the French album which a Peter Matz or Robert Mersey probably could not. For *Je M'Appelle*, Streisand recorded classic French songs like "Once Upon a Summertime," "Autumn Leaves," "Speak to Me of Love," and "Clopin Clopant" so well that she was compared favorably with the great French torch singer Edith Piaf. Streisand wrote her first song for the album . . . a slight, sweet melody to which Eddy Marnay added lyrics. Appropriately called "Ma Premiere Chanson (My First Song)," it hinted at the undeveloped talent Streisand has as a composer, which was later realized with "Evergreen."

Legrand and Streisand's collaboration was the beginning of a beautiful friendship. *Je M'Appelle Barbra* laid the groundwork for their future teamings, most notably on *Yentl*, for which Michel wrote the entire score. "I love working with Barbra," Legrand has said. "She's very demanding, very disciplined, and serious as a person, but also, like myself, she is a child and loves what is really good and beautiful." Despite the exotic nature of *Je M'Appelle Barbra*, the album reached number five on the *Billboard* chart, although it never achieved the status of a gold album.

In between the French album and *Color Me Barbra*, Streisand was a guest on *Harold Sings Arlen (With Friend)*, lending her voice to composer Harold Arlen's solo album. Together, they did a jazzed-up duet of "Ding-Dong, the Witch Is Dead!" from *The Wizard of Oz*, but the real gem of the album was Streisand's solo rendition of the Arlen–Truman Capote song "House of Flowers."

In the four years since her first album, Streisand had made an indelible mark on the music world, as a recording artist and a record-seller. She had gone from a rebellious kook with a great voice to an established singing star with an elegant, sophisticated air. Where would she go from here? For a time, the answer was clear. Streisand became pregnant while in London during *Funny Girl*'s limited run there. Her planned American concert tour, which was to commence as soon as she returned to the States, had to be cut back from twenty-six cities to four. From July 30 to August 9, 1966, Streisand was on stage in Newport, Philadelphia, Chicago, and Atlanta. In September, she recorded *Je M'Appelle Barbra* in New York, then went into semi-retirement to await the birth of her baby. On December 29, 1966, Jason Emanuel Gould was born. But there was little time to enjoy a maternity leave. Three months later Streisand was back in the recording studio ready to start a new album. However, it was a new year, and the times had quite suddenly and radically changed.

Coasting

1967   *Simply Streisand*
1967   *A Christmas Album*
1968   *A Happening in Central Park*

In 1967, the world, musically and otherwise, was undergoing incredible change. The Beatles revolutionized music with *Sgt. Pepper's Lonely Hearts Club Band.* People were reexamining society, challenging the status quo, questioning authority . . . and the music reflected the moody unrest of an America being changed forever by the fight for civil rights, the pros and cons of the Vietnam War, and the antiestablishment sentiment of the under-thirties. Barbra Streisand was only twenty-five at the time, yet her work and her image firmly represented the establishment. Rather than being a part of her generation, Streisand seemed older and entrenched in traditional show business. She was suddenly out of step with the times. Where she had been the antiestablishment rebel in the early sixties, singing songs that nobody else was doing and looking like her own version of a beatnik, in 1967 she reeked of wealth, privilege, and mainstream society. She had the right to enjoy the fruits of her labor, and her nouveau-riche period was part of her maturation. For a lower-mid-

Rehearsing for the concert in Central Park.

dle-class kid from Brooklyn, Streisand had come a long, long way. Why shouldn't she go to swank parties where she could mingle with royalty, or sit with the likes of Marlene Dietrich at couture fashion salons? Perhaps she was living the dreams which had nurtured her all through her childhood.

Streisand and musical director Walter Scharf recording the
Funny Girl soundtrack.

For Marty Erlichman, there were miles to go before he and Barbra could rest on their laurels. Barbra's next challenge was the movies, and their attention was turned in that direction. "For nine months I tried to get her a job. Every record company in the business had turned her down. 'Change the clothes, change the nose, stop singing the cockamamie songs,' " Marty recalled at the time. "Now it'll start all over when she hits Hollywood to make *Funny Girl.* They'll want to make her into a Doris Day. But she sells the public Barbra, nothing else. She's never been bastardized or exploited. The main thing she's going to learn is not to trust too much. The public is very fickle. Ten million people love you when you're an underdog on the way up, but nine and a half million hate you when you hit the top."

Streisand taped her third television special in April 1967, and it was conceived as something very different, something dramatically opposed to her other specials. *The Belle of 14th Street* was a nostalgic pastiche about the world of vaudeville, giving Streisand the chance to do a handful of different characters and a variety of songs from the era. And it would not be a one-

woman show; Streisand would share the television screen with guest stars Jason Robards Jr., Lee Allen, and John Bubbles. Everything about the show would be a re-creation of a bygone era. Unfortunately, the nostalgia craze was still five years off, and *Belle* was an unruly, rambling, occasionally entertaining mishmash. CBS decided to shelve the special and did not air it for six months. When it was broadcast, Streisand experienced her first out-and-out failure. The critics were merciless in their condemnation. For Streisand, the woman with the Midas touch, it was a rude awakening, but she owned up to the show's shortcomings. The proposed album of music from the special was scrapped.

Two days before *Belle* aired, Columbia released two new Streisand albums: *Simply Streisand* and *A Christmas Album.* The material on *Simply Streisand* was very much in keeping with the songs on her previous sets, but while her renditions of "My Funny Valentine," "The Nearness of You," and "When Sunny Gets Blue" were lovely, they seemed from another era when compared to the Beatles' "Lucy in the Sky With Diamonds" and "A Day in the Life." Quite simply, *Simply Streisand* was more of the same from Barbra, and to some it seemed like retro-Streisand. Musically, she seemed to be idling in neutral, even though the album reached number twelve on the *Billboard* chart.

But Streisand was on surer ground with *A Christmas Album,* a 1967 release which would become one of the most enduring albums in her catalog. Exactly why Streisand felt compelled to do a Christmas album, which included beautiful renditions of religious material like the Gounod "Ave Maria," "I Wonder as I Wander," and "The Lord's Prayer," is unclear. It may have been that she was veering from the predetermined image people had of her, as she did with *Je M'Appelle Barbra.* Perhaps it was simply good business. As it turned out, creating *A Christmas Album* was a savvy move for the singer. The album reached number one on the *Billboard* Christmas chart. To this day, *A Christmas Album* does brisk business every holiday season, perennially a top-seller. It is divided between religious and popular music, offering Streisandesque versions of "The Christmas Song," "White Christmas," "Have Yourself a Merry Little Christmas," and "Jingle Bells." Still, while the album was entertaining and commercial, it was not a step forward in her development.

What was holding Streisand back at this time was one massive distraction. In May 1967, Barbra left New York for Hollywood to begin filming *Funny Girl*, and she was immediately thrust into rehearsals, costume fittings, and other aspects of preproduction. In June, she got a few days off from the film in order to return to New York for a special, one-night-only concert in Central Park. All of Manhattan was invited to come to the park and hear one of their own, singing under the stars—for free! Over 135,000 people showed up, and the two-hour-plus concert was filmed as Streisand's fourth television special and recorded for an album. *A Happening in Central Park* was Streisand's first live album and contained old favorites— "Second Hand Rose," "People," "Happy Days Are Here Again"—as well as two lovely new songs: "A New Love Is Like a Newborn Child" and "Natural Sounds." The spectacle of Streisand on stage before a record-breaking crowd made for a drama that could not have been scripted, and Barbra had not lost her natural ability to create an aura of intimacy and rapport, even in such a setting as this.

Fifteen years later, Streisand revealed that she had received death threats before this concert from the Palestinian Liberation Organization. Ignoring the threats, Streisand did the show, but at one point she forgot the lyrics to a song. The sequence was edited out of the special as well as the album, but the memory of that moment, coupled with her fear of the audience's expectations ("How great do I have to be?"), became so intense that Streisand developed chronic stage fright. "When she's off, her singing is about twenty-five percent better than anyone else's, but that's not good enough for her," explained husband Elliott Gould. "She isn't satisfied unless she's operating at her own full capacity. Why? I suppose you could call it a searching for love, respect, affection. She's always been a fantastic

perfectionist, but now, you see, she's expected to be perfect. When you have to be a queen every time you perform and you're only twenty-five and you're a very thoughtful, vulnerable lady, well, it's hard."

Ultimately, both the *Happening* album and its television special were transitional for Streisand. The special did well in the Nielsen ratings, but the album version of *Happening* only reached thirty on the *Billboard* Top 200 chart; high marks for most, but for an artist whose first ten solo albums were almost always in the top five, it was a disappointment.

The times were changing, and it was clear that Streisand needed to adapt. But Barbra was

The soundtrack for *Funny Girl* was a vast improvement on the Broadway cast album and interpolated standards like "I'd Rather Be Blue."

The cover for *What About Today?* was very dramatic and artistic, but it gave the wrong idea about the music on the album. Richard Avedon/Columbia Records

going through a metamorphosis. She wasn't going counterculture, nor was she donning a peasant dress and painting flowers on her face. Streisand was becoming a movie star, and her music for the next few years would take a backseat to her moviemaking.

Like the Movie? Try the Soundtrack

1968   *Funny Girl*
1969   *What About Today?*
1969   *Hello, Dolly!*
1970   *Barbra Streisand's Greatest Hits*
1970   *On a Clear Day You Can See Forever*
1970   *The Owl and the Pussycat*

On Broadway, *Funny Girl* was a star-making role for Barbra Streisand. The film version made

her a superstar. According to respected critics, her luminous performance on screen was even more brilliant than her stage version (no doubt it derived a benefit from her seven hundred performances in the theatre). But Streisand took to film like a duck to water, thriving under the hot lights and acquiring filmmaking know-how like an eager student. Molding her performance for the screen was a Hollywood legend, director William Wyler. Contrary to the popular rumor of the day, Streisand and Wyler had an excellent rapport on *Funny Girl*. It was not too surprising that she was nominated for an Oscar for her performance. It was a surprise when, for her very first film, she received it, tying with Katharine Hepburn; but then this was Barbra Streisand—she already had won Grammys and Emmys and been nominated for two Tonys. Clutching the Oscar in her hand, Streisand was catapulted to the top shelf in Hollywood. And with *Hello, Dolly!* in the can and *On a Clear Day You Can See Forever* filming, Streisand was not only the new kid on the block but a force with which to be reckoned.

The soundtrack from *Funny Girl* was the perfect companion piece to the film. It was far superior to the original cast album, with improved arrangements provided by music supervisor Walter Scharf. After working with Barbra, Scharf was a confirmed fan. In 1968, he declared, "Barbra Streisand is the greatest talent of my lifetime. Barbra is endowed with something that's hard to explain. Something more than the next person. She has a remarkable intuition about the sound of music." The soundtrack includes quintessential versions of "My Man," "I'm the Greatest Star," "You Are Woman/I Am Man," "Sadie, Sadie," and "Don't Rain on My Parade," plus songs which were added to the movie like "Funny Girl" (a lovely ballad that was quite different than the 1964 comic single of the same name which was dropped from the Broadway show) and "I'd Rather Be Blue Over You." "My Man," perhaps Fanny Brice's best-known song, was interpolated into the film, although it wasn't part of the stage show. At that time, composer Jule Styne and lyricist Bob Merrill were dead-set against it because they wanted the score to be totally original. However, for the movie, producer Ray Stark and director William Wyler overruled the songwriters and had Barbra do the classic torch song as the movie's dramatic climax. She gave a tour-de-force performance, and it became a highlight of the film. "My Man" took the place of "The Music That Makes Me Dance." Other songs lost in the transition from stage to screen were "Cornet Man," "Who Are You Now?" and "Rat-Tat-Tat-Tat." The soundtrack, like the movie, was an immediate sensation. *Funny Girl* reached number twelve on the *Billboard* Top 200 chart, and Streisand was once again nominated for a Grammy as Best Female Vocalist.

In the next two years, record buyers would find three more Streisand soundtracks in stores—even one from *The Owl and the Pussycat*, which wasn't a musical. For the latter, dialogue from the sexy comedy as performed by Streisand and costar George Segal was interspersed with the film's incidental music, provided by Blood, Sweat and Tears. While Streisand's vocals on the soundtracks for *Hello, Dolly!* and *On A Clear Day . . .* were excellent, the albums were doing little for her recording career. *Dolly!* reached only forty-nine on the *Billboard* chart, and *Clear Day* didn't even crack the Top 100, stalling at 108. But *The Owl and the Pussycat* was the real loser, ranking 186, which makes one wonder why Columbia even released it as an album.

There was only one solo Streisand album produced in this era, a paean to modern, young songwriters called *What About Today?* It was Barbra's first attempt to get in touch with the changing musical times and included material by singer-songwriters Buffy Saint Marie, Paul Simon, and Lennon-McCartney; also represented were contemporaries Burt Bacharach and David Shire. But Barbra's first out-and-out pop album was a timid effort, cloaking many of the songs in inappropriate arrangements which rarely captured the spirit of the original versions, like "Honey Pie," "Punky's Dilemma," and "With a Little Help From My Friends." Streisand fared better on versions of "Alfie," "Goodnight," and "Until It's Time for You to Go," and she was

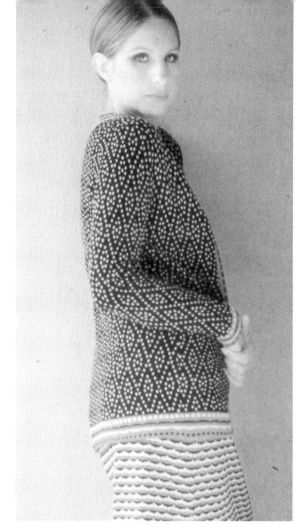

One of the looks Barbra tried for *The Way We Were* album cover.

able to really belt out the title cut and "The Morning After" (both energetically arranged by Don Costa).

Still, the album was a mixed bag, and it wasn't helped by the cover photo—a hand-tinted, anachronistic shot of Streisand which made her look like a shady lady from the 1890s rather than a with-it, up-to-the-minute star of 1969, the image the album was clearly trying to evoke. Not surprisingly, *What About Today?* was a relative flop with record buyers, and it only made it to thirty-one on the *Billboard* chart.

Six months after *What About Today?*, Columbia put out *Barbra Streisand's Greatest Hits*, which comprised her most popular songs from 1963 to 1969. But some of the choices were questionable hits: "Sam, You Made the Pants Too Long," "Why Did I Choose You?" and "My Coloring Book" were nice songs, but hardly hits. Also, unlike other musical acts, Streisand was uniquely an album seller—her singles, with the exception of "People," were not her best sellers. Streisand fans were more inclined to buy her albums than her singles. Therefore, *Barbra Streisand's Greatest Hits* didn't engender the kind of mass appeal that most "greatest hits" albums do; it peaked at number thirty-two on the Top 200 chart and wasn't classified as a gold album (signifying sales of 500,000 copies) until 1971, a year and a half after its release. So, as the decade came to a close, Streisand found herself in something of a predicament, career-wise: her films were thriving, but her music was in a rut.

Changing

1971   Stoney End
1971   Barbra Joan Streisand
1972   Live Concert at the Forum
1973   Barbra Streisand . . . and Other
          Musical Instruments

In early 1970, Columbia Records president Clive Davis (he had succeeded Lieberson) met with Streisand about the state of her recording career. He tactfully urged her to scrap the album of ballads she was working on (called *The Singer*) in favor of a more contemporary release. He suggested she work with a new young producer named Richard Perry, and after hearing his work and meeting with him, Streisand agreed to do so.

Change was happening all around Streisand, and she was very cognizant that her musical image was in need of repair. And she was undergoing a personal transformation as well. After finishing her 1969 engagement at the International in Las Vegas, she viewed a videotape of the performance and knew it was time to freshen her act and update her music. Either adapt or become a dinosaur. Streisand adapted. When she came back to Vegas a year later, she had replaced the designer gowns with simple, elegant pantsuits; instead of bejeweled wigs, a more down-to-earth Barbra wore her hair long and straight. Gone were the affectations of a sophisti-

cated diva with occasional injections of Borscht Belt humor. The revised Streisand looked younger simply by looking her own age—twenty-eight. Achieving great success when she was still in her early twenties, Streisand was perceived by many as much older than she was. Changing her look was important, but a hip exterior would have meant little if she had not updated her music. Thanks to the input of Richard Perry, and with her recording of the songs of Carole King, Laura Nyro, Randy Newman, and others, Streisand had finally caught up to the music of her generation.

Stoney End was the first Streisand-Perry collaboration, and it is an album culled from the music of singer-songwriters Joni Mitchell and Harry Nilsson, as well as Nyro and King. In the

The soundtrack for *On a Clear Day* marked the only time Barbra worked with arranger Nelson Riddle.

1983 *Billboard* magazine special, *The Legend of Barbra Streisand*, Perry told James Spada about Streisand's fears at the time. "The night before our first recording session, she called me up, freaking out. She said, 'I can't do it. This isn't me. I don't feel it.' So I tried my best to calm her down. I said, 'Trust me, you're gonna love it . . . it's gonna blow your mind as soon as we get into it a little bit.' The next day, the first song we did was 'Maybe.' All of Barbra's first takes are sheer excitement, listening to her sing the song . . . with the whole orchestra. So, after we did the first take of 'Stoney End,' we came in and listened to a playback. . . . She leaned over and whispered, 'You were right and I was wrong, but it's nice to be wrong.' "

Columbia was so excited about the prospects for that album that the title cut was released as an advance single—a full six months before the album. "Stoney End" was the first Streisand single since "People" to land in the top ten and become a major radio hit. In fact, "Stoney End" proved to have crossover appeal. Rock-'n'-roll stations which had never deigned to play her singles before were playing "Stoney End," and listeners liked it. When "Time and Love" was released, they played that song, too, although it didn't do nearly as well as "Stoney End." Even those critics who lamented that Streisand seemed to be covering the material rather than interpreting it were nonetheless eager for her to continue delving into this kind of music.

Streisand had broken through musically with a younger audience, and the success of *Stoney End*—the album reached number ten in *Billboard*—was a welcomed return to the top of the charts. Its success was repeated with *Barbra Joan Streisand*, which came out later that same year. More adventurous than its predecessor, *Barbra Joan Streisand* attempted to combine a hipper Streisand on songs like "Mother" and "Where You Lead" with her more classic chanteuse stylings of "The Summer Knows" and "One Less Bell to Answer"/"A House Is Not a Home" (which she introduced on *The Burt Bacharach Show* television special). The schizophrenic nature of *Barbra Joan Streisand* was present not only in Streisand's choice of music

Barbra Streisand . . . and Other Musical Instruments looked good on television, but the album was Barbra's least successful.

but in the album packaging as well. The picture on the front cover portrayed Streisand looking pensive and perplexed, and the title over the picture read Barbra Joan Streisand. But on the back cover, a smiling, almost goofy picture of the star (from the same sitting) was topped with Barbara Joan Streisand, her name for the first eighteen years of her life. Whatever the meaning behind the mixed message, record buyers were unaffected. On the *Billboard* Top 200 chart, *Barbra Joan Streisand* reached number eleven. Streisand had rebounded from her recording slump in a big way; she was successfully managing to stay on top of both her film and music careers.

Between the sessions spent in the recording booth, Streisand took a long break after filming *The Owl and the Pussycat*. She had been working nearly nonstop throughout the sixties (except for her pregnancy), and she had earned the time off. In a return to Las Vegas in late 1970, Streisand incorporated her *Stoney End* and *Barbra Joan Streisand* material, and even spoofed her new, hip image on stage with an

Funny Lady was one of the first albums recorded for Clive Davis's new company Arista.

allusion to smoking pot. Taking a toke of a faux joint, Barbra pretended to get high as she explained why people shouldn't rely on drugs or booze for relaxation. Streisand immortalized this routine forever when she performed it on her next album, *Live Concert at the Forum*. The concert was meant to raise money for George McGovern's 1972 presidential campaign. Streisand was one of the "4 for McGovern"; the other three performers in concert that night were Carole King, James Taylor, and Quincy Jones. Although King was riding a huge wave of success thanks to her monster album *Tapestry*, and Taylor was at his peak thanks to the hit song "You've Got a Friend," it was Streisand's performance that blew the roof off the Los Angeles Forum on April 15, 1972. Columbia recorded it all and released *Live Concert at the Forum* as Streisand's second live album. As with *Barbra Joan . . .*, Columbia included a poster with the initial release of the concert album—a marketing ploy to attract a younger crowd—and

while not as popular as the previous two studio albums, *Forum* reached number nineteen in *Billboard* and stayed on the chart for twenty-seven weeks. By July, Streisand was back to work on the film *What's Up, Doc?* where she was able to show off her updated, young, natural image while she sang a seductive "As Time Goes By" to costar Ryan O'Neal, and belted a rousing version of Cole Porter's "You're the Top" over the opening credits. Looking youthful, singing oldies, Barbra seemed to have found a perfect balance.

Or so it seemed. . . . Streisand's efforts to update her image and her music took a step backward with her next project, her final television special for CBS, *Barbra Streisand . . . and Other Musical Instruments*. Like her other studio specials, this one was glitzy, glossy, and extravagant. But where *My Name Is Barbra* and *Color Me Barbra* were driven by set pieces which were both visually stimulating and musically superb, *Musical Instruments* seemed more concerned with costumes, props, exotic musical instruments, and overstuffed arrangements. Streisand was dwarfed by the overproduction. The songs were primarily standards and show music—"I've Got Rhythm," "Glad to Be Unhappy," "By Myself"—harking back to Streisand's albums from the sixties. There was a brief nod to her more recent albums when she belted "Sweet Inspiration"/"Where You Lead" with Ray Charles's backup group, the Raettes. The high points of the show were, in the end, the most simple, unpretentious sections: Ray and Barbra singing "Cryin' Time" together; Barbra by herself on a stool, singing a lovely, soulful rendition of the Harold Arlen–Truman Capote tune "I Never Has Seen Snow"; and finally, the star performing "The Sweetest Sounds" with an angelic choral backup. The album version of *Barbra Streisand . . . and Other Musical Instruments* was basically just a soundtrack; there were no new songs added, and unfortunately, the duet with Ray Charles was cut. The album did not succeed the way Streisand's previous television soundtracks did, and it only made it to number sixty-four on the *Billboard* chart. The message was clear for Streisand . . . keep moving forward.

The Best of Both Worlds?

1974   Barbra Streisand . . . Featuring "The
        Way We Were" and "All in Love Is
        Fair"
1974   The Way We Were
1974   ButterFly
1975   Funny Lady
1975   Lazy Afternoon
1976   Classical Barbra

Just before leaving for London to shoot *Musical Instruments*, Streisand wrapped production on her latest film, a dramatic love story set against the turbulent World War II years and postwar Hollywood called *The Way We Were*. Playwright-novelist Arthur Laurents, who had directed Streisand in *I Can Get It for You Wholesale*, wrote the piece with Barbra in mind, and after reading a fifty-page treatment outlining the poignant romance between a left-wing, radical Jewish woman and an all-American WASP hero with feet of clay, Streisand was hooked. She called producer Ray Stark, to whom she owed two more pictures, and told him this would be her next film. Streisand costarred with Robert Redford, and their onscreen chemistry was electrifying. Critics would quibble and grouse about the way in which the Hollywood blacklisting storyline (which was so crucial in Laurents's novel) was subordinated to the emotional fireworks of Katie and Hubbell's failing marriage, but audiences were unanimous in their approval of the love story. Director Sydney Pollack seemed to understand that, and he put his faith in his stars' ability to wring every drop of longing out of Hubbell and Katie's ill-fated relationship. The final scene, shot in front of the Plaza Hotel in New York, would become a cinematic classic: Hubbell and Katie meet years after their divorce and share a few moments together catching up and remembering the love they shared . . . and still feel for each other. As they part and the end credits roll, Streisand's aching, heartfelt version of the title song fills the theatre. In the same way that "As Time Goes By" is integrally tied to the greatness of *Casablanca*, so, too, is

On *Lazy Afternoon*, Barbra was relaxed, comfortable, and happy mixing musical styles, from Broadway to disco to synthesized pop music.

Streisand's rendition of "The Way We Were" linked to this 1973 release. This was the first and perhaps the most significant time that Streisand's musical gifts were perfectly wed to one of her straight dramatic films.

It is interesting to note there were two different title songs written for the film, and Streisand recorded both. "The Way We Were," which is now so familiar, was used in part because it complemented the images on the screen better than the alternate tune. The second song, dubbed "The Way We Weren't" by Streisand, was a slightly more complex tune and had a darker tone. According to Marvin Hamlisch, he had considered writing "The Way We Were" in a minor mode. "[But] it might have told you too much in advance, that Streisand and Redford were never going to get together. So I wrote a melody that was sad, but also had a great deal of hope in it." The Bergmans' lyrics echoed that sentiment, creating a sense of loss but also the possibility of reuniting:

*If we had the chance to do it all again,
Tell me, would we? Could we?*

For Hamlisch, who had been the rehearsal pianist for *Funny Girl* on Broadway, having Streisand sing his composition was a defining moment. "The most exciting thing that ever happened to me was getting in front of an orchestra, putting on the headset, beginning to conduct, and hearing Barbra sing that song. That was a thrill."

"The Way We Were" was released as a single, the centerpiece of a Streisand pop album, and in a Columbia soundtrack of the Hamlisch score. The single benefited from the success of the movie, eventually moving up the *Billboard* chart until it reached the vaunted number-one spot, but it didn't stop there. It was the top single for all of 1974.

Streisand had finally achieved the kind of twenty-four-karat success with a single that she had so often achieved with her albums. Streisand's pop album featuring the hit single was initially called *The Way We Were*, but it was later changed to *Barbra Streisand . . . Featuring "The Way We Were" and "All in Love Is Fair"* when Ray Stark threatened to sue because the title duplicated the soundtrack. Nevertheless, it was Streisand's album which climbed the *Billboard* chart and made it to number one, just like the single. The album blended Streisand versions of contemporary composers' songs—Paul Simon's "Something So Right," Carole King's "Being at War With Each Other," and Stevie Wonder's "All in Love Is Fair"—with three songs from the team of Marilyn and Alan Bergman and Michel Legrand: "What Are You Doing the Rest of Your Life," "Summer Me, Winter Me,"

(Above) "The Way We Were" was a monster hit for Barbra, the most popular song of 1974.

and "Pieces of Dreams." *The Way We Were* ultimately veered closer to Streisand's more traditional albums from the sixties, but thanks to experiences with *Stoney End* and *Barbra Joan Streisand*, she was broadening her musical horizons. To be sure, *The Way We Were* went number one in part because of the hit single and the movie, but the album's balanced program would entice record buyers to keep on buying Barbra Streisand albums.

After all the commotion about the title of the album, Ray Stark's soundtrack—the official *The Way We Were*—made it to the twentieth spot on the *Billboard* chart. At Academy Award time, Streisand was nominated as Best Actress for *The Way We Were*, losing to Glenda Jackson (for *A Touch of Class*). The Bergmans and Marvin Hamlisch were honored for the title song, and Hamlisch won another Oscar for his original score for the film. The songwriters also won two Grammys for *The Way We Were*: Song of the Year and Best Original Score for a Motion Picture. Amazingly, Streisand was not nominated either for her single rendition of the song or her soundtrack vocal. It was one of the few times that the National Academy of Recording Arts and Sciences had overlooked a certified Streisand classic, but it would not be the last. In 1982, Streisand's version of "Memory" would be similarly passed over.

Riding high on the success of *The Way We Were*—onscreen as well as on vinyl—Streisand returned to work on a musical project which was even riskier then her French album and musically her greatest challenge. *Classical Barbra* was her stab at singing art songs—*lieder* by Schumann and Schubert, a *vocalise* by Fauré, and more.

Without attempting to sing operatically (which almost exclusively involves use of the head voice), Streisand molded the music to her own unique sound; she sang some of the material in lower keys and utilized her chest voice for the most part (where she was most comfortable in any case). Barbra's reasoning was simple: "What's the point of me singing classical music if it comes out sounding like a weak Beverly Sills?" Her instincts were correct, even if her execution occasionally faltered. On songs like "Vershwiegene Liebe" and "Brezairola," Barbra's interpretive skills reveal a loving sensitivity to art songs as a genre. Streisand selected some off-the-beaten-path compositions, just as on her pop-ballad albums, and she approached each one individually and with intelligence. True to her dramatic sense, Barbra found the emotional center of each song and brought it to the surface, completely honest in her interpretations.

In the *Carmina Burana* solo "In Trutina," she sang in a voice devoid of vibrato, creating a youthful, pure, and incredibly beautiful moment in time. Her French songs were, without exception, lovely. But on more grandiose work, such as Handel's "Dank sei Dir, Herr," Streisand seemed overwhelmed by the material, unversed in how to carry the song over all those strings.

Still, Streisand could be proud of her work: it was an ambitious project and, by and large, a good one. But when Columbia executives heard the tracks as Streisand was preparing them, they worried about the commercial viability of the project . . . or perhaps they were concerned that their premier vocalist would embarrass herself. Hearing their doubts, and probably experiencing a few of her own, Streisand temporarily shelved the album. It would take three more years for her to finally feel confident enough to release *Classical Barbra*. She need not have been so concerned. The criticism was mixed, but some noted experts like Glenn Gould went into lengthy dissertations in praise of Streisand's classical album. And in some rehearsal rooms of college music departments, her record was a big hit with the students majoring in applied voice. The album reached an amazing forty-six on the *Billboard* Top 200 pop chart, and on the classical chart, the album climbed all the way to number six. For the first time in her career,

The soundtrack album of *The Way We Were* was recorded with all of Marvin Hamlisch's score and two renditions of the title song by Barbra.

Barbra Streisand was nominated for a Grammy in the category Best Classical Vocalist–Solo Performance. Her competition included Beverly Sills, Jan de Gaetani, Janet Baker and James King, Margaret Price, Marni Nixon, Carlo Bergonzi, and Dietrich Fischer-Dieskau. Streisand lost to Sills, who ironically won for *The Music of Victor Herbert*, a more popular music album than a classical one!

In 1985, Streisand recalled the experience doing the album in a Stephen Holden piece for the *New York Times*: "The most difficult singing project was my classical album, because classical singing is such a disciplined art form. As in rock, the rhythms are very specific. I wanted to write 'This is a work in progress' on the back cover, but my record company asked me not to. But even though I'm not satisfied with it, I'm still happy I made it."

In the midst of one of the most successful and fertile professional periods in her career, Streisand's personal life was in a lull. It turned out to be the calm before the storm. In 1973, as she was preparing to film a new comedy called *For Pete's Sake*, Barbra met beauty salon entrepreneur Jon Peters. Their romance was explosive and was played out in tabloid headlines and full-color photos. The movie magazines made Peters out to be Streisand's Svengali, a manipulative, ambitious hustler who was using his relationship with Barbra to get ahead. Peters was up front about his ambition to get into the movie business as a producer, but both he and Barbra resented the notion that she was under his hypnotic control. She opened doors for Peters, but it was up to him to walk through them and make his own opportunities.

BurterFly was Jon Peters's first step into the world of producing, albeit music production. As a followup to the top-of-the-pop success of *The Way We Were*, it was experimental and unwieldy. Barbra valiantly sang in a variety of music styles—trying gospel ("Grandma's Hands"), reggae ("Guava Jelly"), and hard rock ("Life on Mars"). However, the diversity of material didn't add up to a successful album. It was savaged by the critics—as much for Streisand's allowing Peters to produce the album as for her vocals and for Peters's conceptual cover—the shot of a fly perched on a stick of butter. What was beyond criticism, however, were the cuts which worked, in particular the

(Above) Streisand considered calling *Classical Barbra* "A Work in Progress."

quiet beauty of "Simple Man," a solo version of the country song "Cryin' Time," and the album's seductive opening number "Love in the Afternoon." Despite all this, *ButterFly* climbed the *Billboard* Top 200, stopping at number thirteen.

Streisand's other pop album in this era was a successful collaboration with singer-songwriter Rupert Holmes called *Lazy Afternoon*. Streisand had heard Holmes's solo album *Widescreen* and decided she would like to sing some of his material. Holmes was asked to produce the entire album, and to this day, he credits Streisand with being the catalyst to his subsequent success, which includes composing the score for the Tony–winning Broadway musical *The Mystery of Edwin Drood* and enjoying a top-ten pop hit with the single, "The Piña Colada Song (Escape)." "As I've gotten a tiny bit of success myself and had a sampling of what that can do for you, to you, and against you, my respect for Barbra grows," Holmes said in 1983. "I [can] better realize what she's accomplished artistically, what she's been able to preserve in terms of her own integrity and identity. I'm probably even more of a Streisand fan now than I was when I was working with her, and I was a fan then."

Holmes's work with Streisand resulted in an album far less eclectic than *ButterFly*. In fact, it was more like *The Way We Were*. The Holmes material included "Letters That Cross in the Mail," "Widescreen," and two special cuts: "My Father's Song," which the composer wrote especially for Streisand after talking with her about her childhood, and "By the Way," with music by Streisand and lyrics by Holmes.

One of the album's pluses

was the variety of musical backdrops Holmes created to frame Streisand's vocals: for example, a bluesy, nightclub arrangement for "Moanin' Low"; synthesized electronics for "Widescreen"; and a simple, single piano accompaniment for "A Child Is Born." As Columbia executive Bruce Lundvall said at the time, "You could put Barbra in front of a rock band or a symphony orchestra, she would still be Barbra Streisand, not compromising, not uncomfortable; the audience would not think she was out of her territory. And that's the basis of a great talent, a great singing voice and interpretive skill."

For the fans, *Lazy Afternoon* also included liner notes written by Barbra: her personal observations about the songs on the album and why she chose to sing each one. It was a wonderful touch by the star and offered valuable insight into the way she approaches music. *Lazy Afternoon* made it to the twelfth spot on the *Billboard* Top 200 and paved the way for Holmes's work on *A Star Is Born*.

As her recording career progressed, so, too, did Streisand's film career. She completed her contractual obligation to Ray Stark with a sequel to *Funny Girl* called *Funny Lady*. The music for the picture was recorded for Arista Records, a new company headed by Clive Davis, and one of the label's first coups was landing the Streisand soundtrack. The score for *Funny Lady* included new songs by *Cabaret* composers Fred Ebb and John Kander, plus a smattering of oldies written primarily by Billy Rose, Fanny Brice's second husband (who was played by James Caan in the film). Although essentially a hodgepodge of a soundtrack—not nearly as well-produced as *Funny Girl*—*Funny Lady* did very well. Streisand belted "How Lucky Can You Get," "Great Day," and "Let's Hear It for Me" with gusto, and the presold audience who had loved *Funny Girl* welcomed *Funny Lady*, pushing the soundtrack to number six on the *Billboard* chart.

As America approached the Bicentennial, Barbra Streisand was the top female star in records and onscreen. It would have been very easy to stay the course and continue doing more of the same. Instead, she chose this

moment in her career to veer from the tried and true and strike out on her own. Encouraged by Peters, Streisand announced her intention to produce and star in a second musical remake of *A Star Is Born* (Judy Garland headlined the first in 1954).

Streisand and Peters inadvertently started a firestorm of controversy. Fat was then thrown on the fire when Frank Pierson, who had adapted the screenplay and directed the film, wrote an article (which was published in two national magazines) which painted a portrait of the *Star Is Born* moviemaking process as a chaotic, dangerous three-ring circus, with Barbra and Jon as temperamental children calling the shots. Based on his story, as well as the negative industry buzz, it was predicted that *A Star Is Born* would go down in history as Barbra's *Titanic*.

Interestingly, Pierson seemed to miscalculate a key factor regarding this film: its setting in the pop music world and boasting a soundtrack filled with Barbra Streisand in song. Barbra had rarely erred when it came to her musical

Streisand and Kristofferson blended their very different musical styles for *A Star Is Born*. Like the movie, the album was number one in the country.

A copy of the French sheet music for "Love Theme From *A Star Is Born* (Evergreen)": Barbra recorded the song not only in English, but also in French, Spanish, and Italian.

Pop Diva

1976   A Star Is Born
1977   Streisand Superman
1978   Songbird
1978   Barbra Streisand's Greatest Hits, Volume 2

A Star Is Born was a turning point in Barbra Streisand's career. For the first time, she had put her reputation and power on the line—it would be her name on the picture as executive producer. With the mounting anticipation of disaster surrounding the film, Streisand was understandably apprehensive about what would happen. She believed in the work and fed on Jon Peters's indefatigable enthusiasm and marketing savvy. He worked closely with Columbia Records on the promotion for the film's soundtrack and made sure the word was delivered to radio station managers that the advance single, "(Love Theme From *A Star Is Born*) Evergreen," was a sure-fire hit.

"Evergreen" was a romantic, gentle love song and featured the most lovely, evocative melody Barbra had ever written. The rest of the score was soft rock 'n' roll (even though it was supposedly set in the hard-rock milieu of 1976); songs like "Woman in the Moon," "Everything," and "With One More Look at You' were all geared for Streisand's pop-music audience. Kris Kristofferson also had a couple of songs on the soundtrack—growling and groaning to approximate the sound of a washed-up rock star—but the strength of the album, as well as the film, rested firmly on Streisand's shoulders. Before *A Star Is Born* opened in theatres around the country, many fans were already familiar with "Evergreen."

But would the popularity of the music score pave the way for filmgoers to embrace the picture? The answer would be a loud and definitive yes! While the great majority of film critics were unmercifully negative (many used the forum to launch personal attacks on Streisand and Peters), ticket buyers stood in line to get into the theatre to see Streisand and costar Kris Kristofferson. And it was more than mere

instincts. What were the chances that she would let a project as important as *A Star Is Born* be saddled with anything less than her best effort? Pierson commented recently about Streisand's music: "She's like Brando about her voice. The world's greatest actor who has nothing but contempt for his skill." Perhaps that is true of Brando, not Streisand. She has never had contempt for either her voice or her audience. And *A Star Is Born* was proof of that. While music critics complained the music in *A Star Is Born* was not rock-'n'-roll, most buyers didn't seem to care.

Unperturbed by critics and naysayers, Streisand and Peters persevered with their $6 million baby. "Let the public decide" was her philosophy. She put her faith in her talent, her instincts, and the people who had nearly always responded to her most personal projects—her fans. The fate of *A Star Is Born* rested with the audience; and to many prognosticators, the fate of Barbra Streisand rested with *A Star Is Born.*

curiosity; fans went to see the film more than once, and non-fans went to see it based on the positive word of mouth. In the media, however, it was open season on America's number-one movie star, and Streisand was the target. Both *A Star Is Born* and Streisand were left unscathed by the onslaught. The movie was a huge hit in America and around the world. Streisand's gamble had paid off handsomely, both financially and in industry esteem. The icing on the cake came for the star when "Evergreen," only the third song she'd ever composed, won both the Grammy (as Song of the Year) and the Oscar (for Best Song).

Columbia Records was anxious for Barbra to capitalize on the momentum *A Star Is Born* had generated. Six months after the film's opening, *Streisand Superman* was in record stores. The ads boasted it was "faster than a speeding bullet . . ." and the single from the album, "My Heart Belongs to Me," zoomed to number one on the adult contemporary charts (and to number four on the *Billboard* pop chart). The album lived up to the hype. In a little over a month, *Superman* reached number three on the *Billboard* album chart. *Superman* included two songs originally written for *A Star Is Born*—another Streisand composition called "Answer Me" and the clever, feminist-oriented ballad by Rupert Holmes, "Lullaby for Myself." It also contained an easy mix of contemporary pop tunes including Billy Joel's "New York State of Mind" and Kim Carnes's "Love Comes From Unexpected Places." Another song on the album, "Don't Believe What You Read," featured Streisand's first attempt at writing lyrics and was prompted by the star's displeasure with the kind of nonsensical gossip of which she and Peters had been the victims as a result of *A Star Is Born*. As she did with *Lazy Afternoon*, Streisand wrote the liner notes for *Superman* and used the opportunity to thank the fans who had supported *A Star Is Born*. It was a revealing indication of the star's growing admiration and gratitude for her fandom.

There was one other *Superman/A Star Is Born* connection: the cover photo was inspired by a scene from the film. The album cover

Barbra visited the set of *Eyes of Laura Mars*, Jon's first movie without her. She did record the film's theme song.

showed Streisand in skimpy white shorts and a tight, white T-shirt, with the Superman comic book logo on the front. The look was so provocative that *Playboy* magazine, which was planning an in-depth interview with Barbra, asked Streisand to pose for their cover in the same getup. In a playful move, Barbra took off her socks and sneakers and quipped to the editors, "Now you can say I took it off for *Playboy*!"

Streisand assembled the same creative team for her next album, another pop melange called *Songbird*. The mix was unusual, including the haunting title song, the Broadway hit "Tomorrow" from *Annie*, and a wonderfully sensual, ethereal tune called "Honey, Can I Put on Your Clothes." It was the title cut which was released as the single, and although it managed to reach only twenty-five on *Billboard*'s pop chart, it went to the top spot on the adult contemporary chart. Overall, the album performed strongly. It climbed to number eleven on the *Billboard* Top 200 and remained on the chart for twenty-seven weeks.

Ironically, the number which attracted the most attention from *Songbird* was the Neil Diamond–Alan and Marilyn Bergman song, "You Don't Bring Me Flowers." Streisand's rendition was a solo, and it had never occurred to either Barbra or Neil to do the song as a duet. Diamond and Streisand were both under contract to Columbia Records, and they were acquaintances. Both had attended Brooklyn's Erasmus Hall High School. "Barbra and I went to school together. We sang in the same chorus for two years, [but] we never knew each other then. She was in the alto section and I was in the baritone section."

Gary Guthrie, a disc jockey for WAKY-AM in Louisville, Kentucky, heard Neil's version of "You Don't Bring Me Flowers" while visiting a friend's house. Guthrie and his wife were breaking up at the time, and he noticed her reaction. "She started crying. I couldn't help feeling there was something missing, but I couldn't figure it out." He came up with the missing element when he heard that Streisand had the same song on her upcoming album. "It set off this image in my mind. It needed two people singing it to each other." Guthrie took the solo

Scavullo's provocative photograph of Donna Summer and Barbra Streisand no doubt helped sell the disco hit "Enough Is Enough." Francesco Scavullo/Columbia Records

recordings by Streisand and Diamond (from his LP *I'm Glad You're Here With Me Tonight*) and "created" a duet with the aid of the radio station's recording equipment. The results were magical, far more effective than either star's single take. He played the song on the radio, and a furor erupted. It became the most requested song in the area. When Columbia Records executives learned about the success of Guthrie's creation, Streisand and Diamond were asked to go back into the studio and make the duet a reality. Both stars were thrilled by the serendipity of the situation and readily agreed to team up. Four months later, the duet was recorded and immediately released as a single; it was number one on the *Billboard* chart within five weeks! Streisand benefited greatly by the timing: the duet was featured on *Barbra Streisand's Greatest Hits, Volume 2* (which was released earlier than planned) and helped the album go to number one.

In December 1977, Barbra Streisand celebrated her fifteenth anniversary with Columbia Records. The company threw her a party in New York and announced that Streisand had re-signed for five more albums. In the seven years since *Stoney End*, she had righted her recording career and reemerged as one of the world's most enduring voices.

High Notes and Lows

1978   Eyes of Laura Mars
1979   The Main Event
1979   Wet
1980   Guilty

Jon Peters's first solo film production was *Eyes of Laura Mars*, a thriller starring Faye Dunaway. Peters enlisted Streisand's help with the movie, asking her to sing over the credits and on the soundtrack album. "Prisoner (The Theme From *Eyes of Laura Mars*)" was the hardest rock that Streisand had ever done, and to her credit, she threw her heart and soul into the recording. It was released as a single but only went to number twenty-two on the *Billboard* pop chart. The film was not a hit, and

Barbra's concept for *Wet* was songs all about water. For the cover, she did a photo session in a Jacuzzi.
Mario Caselli/Columbia Records

the soundtrack was not boosted by the addition of Barbra Streisand. It made a poor showing on the *Billboard* chart, stalling at 124.

On the other hand, the soundtrack for Barbra's latest film, *The Main Event*, was far more successful. The centerpiece of the album was her first disco hit, the title tune "The Main Event"/"Fight." The soundtrack wound up at number twenty on *Billboard*'s Top 200, and the single made it all the way to number three on the pop chart. The disco craze was in full swing in 1979, and the success of "The Main Event"/"Fight" prompted songwriter Paul Jabara to concoct a disco duet which would bring together his favorite singer—Streisand—with the reigning disco queen—Donna Summer. Streisand was planning a new album and decided to sing only songs which related to water. The theme would lead to a final product, appropriately called *Wet*. To convince Streisand to sing his disco opus "Enough Is Enough," Jabara wrote an introduction which alluded to rain and tears. Streisand was further influenced when her son Jason let her know he'd like to meet Summer. In August 1979, Streisand and Summer met in the recording studio and put Jabara's work on vinyl. The single was released in October, and within three weeks "(No More

Tears) Enough Is Enough" was the number-one song in the country.

There was speculation that Donna and Barbra had clashed during the recording session, rumors which were denied by both women. "[The duet with Donna Summer] was a good idea. It worked. I am always open to new ideas, creatively speaking. And I enjoyed working with Donna. Discount any of the stories that said otherwise," said Streisand about the experience. Photographer Francesco Scavullo shot a provocative black and white picture of Streisand and Summer for a possible album cover. He put both women in low-cut, Merry Widow corsets, revealing lots of skin. The image was used on the long-form (twelve-inch) 45, and photo stickers of that record were slapped on Streisand's *Wet* album to remind record buyers that the song was on it as well.

Professionally, as the decade came to an end, Barbra Streisand seemed to have the world on a string. Onscreen, she followed the monumental success of *A Star Is Born* with *The Main Event*, a strained romantic comedy which nevertheless did big box office. Musically, Streisand closed out the era in far better standing than she had the previous decade. The seventies were truly a time of transformation for Streisand. She began

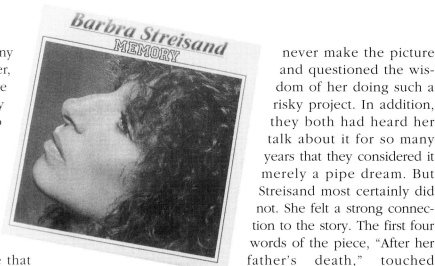

as everybody's favorite funny girl, a plucky overachiever, an ugly duckling with the voice of a nightingale. By 1979, Streisand was no longer anybody's notion of an ugly duckling: she was a full-fledged swan. In the next decade, she would spread her wings and fly to heights beyond her childhood imaginings.

It's interesting to note that prior to her collaborations with Neil Diamond and Donna Summer, Barbra Streisand had been, for the most part, a musical loner. But the success of these duets, as well as fruitful experiences working with songwriter-producers Rupert Holmes and Michel Legrand, could not be denied. Columbia encouraged Streisand to pursue teaming up with other talent, hoping for continued financial re-wards. But for Streisand in 1980, there was only one artistic endeavor occupying her mind. In fact, it had become an obsession for the star, and the next three years of her life would be devoted to the realization of her most ambitious, artistic dream: producing and directing the film *Yentl*. Streisand had first read the Isaac Bashevis Singer short story in 1968, and she was so captivated by it that she purchased the rights immediately. She fully intended it to be her next film.

Ultimately, it would take Streisand—the most powerful female movie star throughout the seventies—fifteen years to get a studio to give her the go-ahead to do the film. Many of her closest associates, including Jon Peters and her agent, Sue Mengers, believed she would

(Top) Streisand's rendition of Lloyd Webber's "Memory" was one of her finest recordings ever.

(Bottom) Guilty was a golden project for Streisand, her most successful album to date.

never make the picture and questioned the wisdom of her doing such a risky project. In addition, they both had heard her talk about it for so many years that they considered it merely a pipe dream. But Streisand most certainly did not. She felt a strong connection to the story. The first four words of the piece, "After her father's death," touched Streisand (whose father died when she was just a toddler) very deeply. But was the tale of a young, Jewish woman who disguises herself as a boy to attend the yeshiva (university), only to find herself in love with a male student and coerced into marrying his ex-fiancée, a commercial film property? Streisand believed she could make it one, and the lack of encouragement from her associates and film executives only made her more determined to bring *Yentl* to the screen.

Then, in 1979, Streisand visited her father's grave in New York with her brother Sheldon and was photographed standing beside the tombstone. When she looked at the developed photo, Streisand noticed the name Anshel on a nearby stone. In Singer's short story, Anshel is the name Yentl uses when she pretends to be a yeshiva boy. For Barbra, it was an omen ("Anshel is not a normal name . . ." she told *20/20* reporter Geraldo Rivera). Finally, Streisand was convinced by her brother to participate in a séance to try and contact their father. Although skeptical and somewhat frightened, Streisand agreed to give it a try. The communication she received during the session—her father's message was tapped onto a table and spelled out—Sorry-Sing-Proud—was powerful and influential. Whether it was real or not, Streisand chose to believe it and to use it as fuel to get *Yentl* made. On the plane back to California, Streisand began writing the screenplay for the movie.

It was while working on the script that Streisand began a musical collaboration with Barry Gibb of the rock group the Bee Gees. Unlike her pairings with Diamond or Summer, Gibb would not only sing with Streisand; he would produce the album, and all the material would be written for Barbra by Barry and his cowriters. While industry insiders wondered exactly how Gibb would adapt his musical stylings for Streisand, the two worked with remarkable ease in creating *Guilty*. In September 1980, the first single, "A Woman in Love," was released and went to the top of the charts. The album came out soon after, and it, too, rose to the top spot on the *Billboard* Top 200. *Guilty* would become a multi-platinum phenomenon, an international success. At the 1981 Grammys, *Guilty* would be nominated for Album of the Year, Song of the Year (i.e., for "Woman in Love"), Outstanding Performance Duo or Group (for "Guilty") as well as individual Grammys for Streisand's vocal performance and Gibb's production. Although an odds-on favorite, *Guilty* won only a single Grammy: Streisand and Gibb shared it for their duet of the title song.

Guilty was a unique album for Streisand in that all the music on it was written and arranged for her and her alone. Gibb was trying to make

Barbra did everything on *Yentl,* including all the singing.

the best Streisand album ever, and in the opinion of many critics, he did. More important, *Guilty* became Barbra's most successful album (thus far), selling over five million copies worldwide. For Streisand, *Guilty* was the pinnacle of pop success. Her efforts to reach out to a younger audience, which began in 1970, were more fully realized with *Guilty* than with any other album, including the soundtrack to *A Star Is Born*, which was also a worldwide hit. Additionally, *Guilty* did not have the hook of a feature film to boost its popularity; its appeal lay solely in Streisand and Gibb's music. In retrospect, Barry Gibb commented on *Guilty* in 1983: "I wanted to produce her best-selling album. But to me, none of the songs on that album match the greatness of some of the songs she's done with the Berg-mans, or 'People' or 'Evergreen.' I would love to work with her again. I have a lot of ideas for her, a lot of directions she could go in."

All or Nothing at All

1981   Memories
1983   Yentl

For another artist, *Guilty* would have immediately been followed by a sequel or an album which could (hopefully) capitalize on its monu~mental success. But for Streisand, another *Guilty* was not on the agenda. After fifteen years of planning and contemplating, Barbra was at last ready to bring *Yentl* to the screen. And to ensure that it was exactly the film she intended it to be, Streisand took total responsibility for the film: she would star in the title role, cowrite the screenplay, coproduce, and direct the entire production. It was a monumental task, the kind only undertaken in the past by filmmakers Charles Chaplin, Orson Welles, and Warren Beatty.

Understandably, the size of the film project would relegate Streisand's recording efforts to a back burner. Still, Columbia was anxious, if not desperate, for a 1981 Christmas release from Streisand. While she was in London recording musical tracks for *Yentl*, Columbia prevailed upon Barbra to produce something . . . anything. After discussions, it was decided that Streisand would record two new songs (and include a solo rendition of "Lost Inside of You" that had been recorded for *A Star Is Born*) which would anchor an album of previously recorded love songs. It would be a pseudo-greatest-hits package, and it mattered little to anyone that *Barbra Streisand's Greatest Hits, Volume 2* had been released a mere three years before. The new numbers were "Coming In and Out of Your Life," a pop ballad which would presumably appeal to the *Guilty* fans, and, for longtime Streisand devotees, "Memory," a soaring, haunting anthem from Andrew Lloyd Webber's recently open-ed stage musical, *Cats*. Lloyd Webber himself produced and arranged the song for Streisand, and her recording was masterful. It is generally regarded as the finest rendition of the song ever produced. Surprisingly, Columbia chose to release "Coming In and Out of Your Life" as the album's single, even though "Memory" was the far superior cut. Additionally, "Memory" was gaining familiarity because of the worldwide success of *Cats*.

The album was called *Memories* (*Love Songs* in the United Kingdom), and Columbia put it in record stores in November 1981, just in time for Christmas. Despite the fact that there was relatively little new material, the album was a strong seller. It climbed to the top ten, stop-

ping at number six on the *Billboard* chart. It was also an enduring album, staying in the Top 200 for 106 weeks. "Coming In and Out of Your Life" benefited from Streisand's re-newed radio popularity thanks to *Guilty* (which had had four single releases reach the Top 50 on *Billboard's* pop chart); it was widely played around the country and made it to number eleven in *Billboard*. On *Billboard's* adult contemporary chart, it made it to the number-two spot. Three months later, "Memory" was released as a followup single. It charted well on the adult contemporary chart (number nine) but only reached fifty-two on *Billboard's* pop chart.

In the fall of 1983, Barbra's most personal film and musical project was at last completed. *Yentl*, more than *Funny Girl* or *A Star Is Born*, more than *The Barbra Streisand Album* or *My Name Is Barbra*, was Barbra Streisand's total creation. She said it was like giving birth, and she desperately wanted both critical and commercial approbation for her "kid." The first indications that the film was a knockout came when Columbia released the soundtrack album in November 1983, just a week before the movie's premiere. As Streisand had revealed with her soulful, passionate, and dynamic version of "Memory" on the previous album, she was in magnificent voice for these sessions. On *Yentl*, she would be called upon to display her complete range of musical expression and vocal dexterity . . . and do it without the aid of other characters singing along. Yentl's songs would be the thoughts inside her head; her internal monologue was to be the audience's key to the character as she evolved during this incredible journey.

"The style of the music needed to be romantic and timeless, rather than reflective of a period," said Michel Legrand about his approach to the film. Having a past working

Columbia put out a single of "Papa, Can You Hear Me?" from *Yentl*, hoping for some radio play.

relationship with Barbra was a plus for him as well. "I soon learned that the music had to reflect Yentl's inner life—her secret longings and emotions. What Barbra was looking for was a feeling of magic, a fairy-tale-like quality. . . . She has an extraordinary voice, a unique voice, which I know very well. There is a special emotion in her voice which is very personal and makes it even more beautiful. It is different from writing for anyone else, because you are writing for her whole personality."

With each cut on the album, Streisand was at her best. She employed expert comic timing for "No Wonder," bared her soul in "Papa, Can You Hear Me?" explored sexual awakening for "The Way He Makes Me Feel," and seemingly took flight for the finale, "A Piece of Sky." *Yentl* was custom-made for Barbra Streisand; each note and lyric was shaped for her talents. It is no wonder, then, that *Yentl* is a musical gem and one of Streisand's greatest albums. The recording sessions were intense and emotional for Barbra. She broke down in tears during one take of "Papa, Can You Hear Me?" She had rehearsed the song countless times in anticipation of the recording, but she revealed later: "No matter how much thinking and planning you do, no matter how much intellectual thought goes into something, the moment of truth is being. . . . It's the aliveness of the moment."

Yentl charted well for Streisand, reaching the *Billboard* top ten and stopping at number nine. A pop version of "The Way He Makes Me Feel" was specially recorded as a single; it made it as high as number forty on the *Billboard* pop chart, but on the adult contemporary chart, it was number one. The primarily positive critical response for the album and the film was a great reward for Streisand. She had risked a lot to prove to the many doubters she had encountered that her commitment to *Yentl* was worthwhile. The only negative came when the Academy Awards failed to recognize her remarkable accomplishment. The musical score from *Yentl*, however, did not go unnoticed at Oscar time. Two songs were nominated—"Papa, Can You Hear Me?" and "The Way He Makes Me Feel"—as well as the entire score.

Barbra turned on the sex appeal as a lounge singer in the music video for "Left in the Dark."

Marilyn and Alan Bergman and Michel Legrand received *Yentl's* only Oscar, for the original song score. It was only fitting that when they went onstage to accept their awards, they recognized the inspiration and creative force responsible for their work—the director and star, Barbra Streisand.

Am I Standing Still in Time?

1984   Emotion

In 1984, there was a return to pop music for Streisand with the album *Emotion*. However, in the four years since *Guilty*, popular music had been inexorably changed with the advent of music video. The MTV revolution had altered the way hit music was measured—now a song, in order to succeed, had to have a good video in addition to a good beat! And more than that, MTV was geared to the youth market . . . ignoring the adult contemporary artists like Streisand

in favor of heavy metal, dance music, and traditional rock. *Emotion* was Streisand's first
attempt to reach the MTV crowd, and as material and musicians were enlisted, it soon became
clear that *Emotion* was an ill-conceived corporate fantasy at best. With Columbia now pushing for an album as contemporary and hit-ori-
ented as *Guilty*, Streisand was hampered by the
simple fact that she did not have a Barry Gibb at
the controls to write and produce the album.
Emotion was instead an amalgam of talents,
some of which complemented Streisand, some
of which did not. In essence, *Emotion* was an
album more like *Songbird* or *Wet* than *Guilty*.

Perhaps what was most interesting about
Emotion was how ill-timed it was. Streisand is
an artist who has always had the gift of timing—
the knack of being in the right place with the
right project at the right time. She knew when
to make the jump from nightclubs to Broadway,
from Broadway to Hollywood, from musicals to
comedies, from acting and singing to directing,
and on and on. *Emotion* was never in synch,
and that was especially evident with the choice
of its single release. "Left in the Dark" was a big,
dramatic, overblown opus by Jim Steinman,
whose greatest successes had been Meat Loaf's

Streisand's *film noir* look for her first official music video, "Left
in the Dark," was one of the only highlights of *Emotion*.
Columbia Records

"Bat Out of Hell," Bonnie Tyler's "Total Eclipse
of the Heart," and Air Supply's "Making Love
Out of Nothing at All." But Steinman's mini-
operas were on the decline, and Barry
Manilow's version of "Read 'Em and Weep"
failed to make a ripple on the charts. Still,
Columbia pushed "Left in the Dark" as the best
choice for the album's prerelease . . . and
Streisand's first official video. (Streisand had
done some simple, single-camera video pro-
mos, including one for "Memory," which aired
in England and was used as part of a commerical in America.)

Streisand enlisted feature director Jonathan
Kaplan to helm the video and asked *A Star Is
Born* costar Kris Kristofferson to be her leading
man for the mini-drama. But as adept as
Streisand is at filmmaking, the scorned woman
storyline conceived for "Left in the Dark" did
nothing to energize the dour ballad. Both the
song and the video were long and joyless, with
only Streisand's popularity to explain its margin-
al success. The single made it to number four
on the adult contemporary chart, but on the
Billboard pop chart, it only hit number fifty.
The album stopped at nineteen on the Top 200.
Although respectable for many other acts, it was
Streisand's poorest, non-pop music outing since
Live Concert at the Forum.

A second single—the title track—was
released in hopes of pushing the album back up
the charts. It was a better cut, and it reteamed
Streisand with Richard Perry. The "Emotion"
single also boasted a superior video, one codi-
rected by Streisand and Richard Baskin. Baskin,
a songwriter who had done music for the
Robert Altman film *Nashville*, contributed to
Emotion (writing lyrics for "Here We Are at
Last," the tune of which was composed by
Streisand as a possible theme song for *The Main
Event*) and would continue collaborating with
the star on other projects. (He had also become
the most constant companion in Streisand's personal life since Jon Peters.) The "Emotion"
video was the antithesis of "Left in the Dark"—it
sparkled with wit and charm, and burst off the
screen with color and energy. It also emphasized many of the same attributes Streisand had

Streisand and producer David Foster both won Grammy Awards for their work on *The Broadway Album.*
Mark Sennet/Columbia Records

used in her most successful films . . . glamour, self-deprecating humor, and romance. Unfortunately, most people never saw the "Emotion" video. It didn't help the single, and the album did not reverse course and sail up the charts. If "Emotion" had been the first single and video release, perhaps the results would have been different, but this was an instance where Streisand was done in by timing. If *Guilty* was Streisand's pop album zenith, *Emotion* was her nadir.

Full Circle

1985   The Broadway Album
1987   One Voice

Streisand was not defeated by the poor showing of *Emotion.* If anything, she was enlightened by the failure. Since the *ButterFly* recording sessions, she had longed to do an entire album of the music of her youth, the Broadway songs she had sung in nightclubs and on her early albums. While Columbia executives advised her to ignore the *Emotion* experience and go right back to creating another pop album, Streisand had made up her mind to go

back to her roots. It was time to come full circle.

In the months following *Emotion,* Streisand and Baskin pored through Broadway song-books and original cast albums looking for material. She made long lists of both classic and obscure songs by some of the finest composers ever to work on Broadway—George and Ira Gershwin, Frank Loesser, Jerome Kern, Rodgers and Hammerstein. And she called upon former colleagues, most important being arranger-conductor Peter Matz, to come on board to help her create the album. But the greatest contribution to *The Broadway Album,* aside from Streisand, was Stephen Sondheim. As Streisand perused her song list, she found Sondheim songs at every turn . . . from "Somewhere" to "Send in the Clowns" to "Not While I'm Around," and more.

Once Barbra had narrowed her song list to a workable number, she turned to Matz, who hadn't worked with Streisand since *Funny Lady,* to create the arrangements. Barbra wanted the music to have a unique and distinct sound, something beyond the original arrangements from the Broadway shows. Matz was well aware that Barbra was encountering plenty of label resistance to her doing this kind of album:

"A lot of people were hesitant about the whole concept, how it would fare commercially, and some were unsure about my involvement. Barbra, though, was straight-ahead about the project, as she is with everything she does. She made all the decisions about the material, and always has total control of everything, from the songs to the liner notes."

The Broadway Album was a return to Barbra's theatre roots, and to the top of the charts. Richard Corman/Columbia Records

The most difficult songs to adapt were Sondheim's. Because Sondheim writes his songs for specific scenes and characters, they are often seamlessly woven into the fabric of a show. Streisand and Sondheim were acquainted and had almost worked together; he was Jule Styne's first choice for lyricist on *Funny Girl* after their brilliant collaboration on *Gypsy*, but Sondheim bowed out in order to complete the score (words and music) for *A Funny Thing Happened on the Way to the Forum*. Still, Barbra wondered if the composer would agree

to "customizing" some of his songs for her new album. Considering the fact that Sondheim is the preeminent Broadway composer of our day, and a multiple Tony winner, who also has Grammys, an Oscar, and a Pulitzer Prize to his credit, Streisand approached him with apprehension and a healthy dose of awe. To her pleasant surprise, Sondheim was very open to discussion and to change. "Sondheim told us, 'The music as it was done then made that particular statement, and now that's over,' " Peter Matz explained in *Cash Box* magazine.

While Streisand was humbled to work with Sondheim, the composer possessed equal respect and admiration for her accomplishments. It was in many ways a professional marriage made in heaven. According to Sondheim: "Barbra has one of the two or three best voices in the world of singing songs. She has the meticulous attention to detail that makes a good artist. Frank Sinatra and Barbara Cook are the same way." Sondheim was curious about how Streisand worked in the recording studio and asked if he could attend some of her sessions. She readily agreed and invited him to take an active role in the recording.

Sondheim was in attendance for "Putting It Together," perhaps the most personal of Streisand's numbers on *The Broadway Album*. As written for *Sunday in the Park With George*, "Putting It Together" is a modern artist's take on the difficulties of balancing art with business. Streisand wrote an introduction for the song depicting a dialogue between a singer and record executives who try to tell her what kind of music she should be recording. She asked three friends—director Sydney Pollack (*The Way We Were*), actor Ken Sylk, and David Geffen, the head of Geffen Records—to play the Executive Chorus. Sondheim then reworked the song's main lyrics to fit the "music business" opening. "I did a good deal of changes which were the results of long and intensive talks at her house on two separate visits, as well as further talks over the phone," Sondheim reflected after the album was completed. "She worries over every given detail and, like all true artists, she'll make the final decision on her own work.

But she listens to the input of people she respects and with whom she works, and pays attention, a rare gift indeed." The reworked "Putting It Together" was a direct assault by Streisand on Columbia, albeit a defense of her artistic choices and a venting of her anger at the label's overinvolvement with *Emotion*. With little regard for Columbia, Streisand audaciously placed "Putting It Together" as the first cut on the album.

Barbra also had Sondheim's input on the medley of "Pretty Women"/"The Ladies Who Lunch," but it was his flexibility in agreeing to rework "Send in the Clowns"—his best-known popular song—which floored Streisand. "He didn't close his mind to the experience of having something changed. He was fabulous to work with and fabulous to argue with," Barbra told Craig Zadan in his biography *Sondheim*. "This was one of the most exciting collaborations I've ever had, because we both talk fast, we think fast; so it was like shorthand half the time . . . we practically didn't have to finish sentences. It was so exhilarating; there were moments I was screaming with joy over the phone!" From Sondheim's perspective: "I could tolerate any discussions we had [about changes]. It was all for the sake of the song and the album, not for self-glorification. She's a consummate artist worrying over every detail the way I do. Nothing escapes her attention, nothing is sloppy, nothing is left to chance, and she has opinions on everything."

The rest of *The Broadway Album* was equal in quality with its opening cut. Streisand was passionate and powerful in her renditions of "Being Alive," "Somewhere," "If I Loved You," a medley from *The King and I*, and a challenging "I Loves You, Porgy"/"Porgy, I's Your Woman Now" from *Porgy and Bess*. Singing the classic torch song "Can't Help Lovin' Dat Man" from *Show Boat*, Barbra has a gentle vulnerability and softness to her vocal, and the arrangement includes a soulful harmonica obbligato by none other than Stevie Wonder. The initial arrangement was bluesy, with a muted trumpet solo, but it felt wrong to Streisand. Barbra preferred the one used in the 1951 MGM film version. It

was Richard Baskin who suggested using that arrangement, with the addition of a harmonica. Although they'd never worked together, Streisand called on Stevie Wonder to provide the harmonica solo . . . and anything else which felt right when they did the song. The resulting collaboration was charming and beautifully done. Playfully, Wonder concludes the song with a slight musical reference to "People."

The compact disc release included a bonus cut: "Adelaide's Lament" from *Guys and Dolls*, which showcased Barbra's comic talents. The time Barbra had spent working on pop albums, singing music which was not strictly from Broadway or Tin Pan Alley, had a profound influence on the way she sang the songs on *The Broadway Album*. In many ways, the pop music informed her singing of Broadway music in 1985; she could not have sung these songs in 1965 as she did twenty years later. Needless to say, twenty years of living had its influence too.

In all, *The Broadway Album* was filled with aces. David Foster was brought in to create the arrangement for "Somewhere." Barbra told him her idea for the song: she wanted it to sound "like it wasn't made on this planet." Foster claimed that he and Barbra spent three whole days alone just working on the vocals, "looking for that extra five percent in the arrangement." Their hard work paid off at Grammy time.

Still, there were critics (perhaps more in tune to rock music than to songs from the Great White Way) who didn't like *The Broadway Album*, preferring the pop diva Streisand to Broadway Barbra. Whatever the critics' qualms, the record buyers of America weren't in agreement. *The Broadway Album* sold out fast and galloped up the charts, landing Barbra her sixth number-one album on the *Billboard* Top 200.

"Somewhere," the album's single, stalled at number forty-three on the *Billboard* pop chart but reached number five on the adult contemporary chart. "Somewhere" was also filmed as a video by director William Friedkin, and when filled out with an interview and behind-the-scenes footage of Streisand in the recording studio, a long-form video documentary called *Putting It Together: The Making of "The*

Broadway Album" was created and shown on the cable channel HBO as a television special and later released for the home video market. Proceeds from the sale of the "Somewhere" single were donated to two worthy causes—AmFar (for AIDS research) and Pro-Peace.

The appeal and number-one status of *The Broadway Album* was, perhaps, a surprise to some. Stephen Sondheim, though, was not one of them. "It's all about Barbra. If anyone else had recorded the exact same set of songs and sung them very well, it might not have sold. But she's got one of the best voices on the planet. And it's not just her voice, it's her intensity, her passion, her control. Although every moment has been thought out, you don't see all the sweat and decisions that went into the work. It is as though she just stepped out of the shower and began singing at you." The album's success was especially gratifying for Streisand. According to her contract with Columbia at the time, the label was only required to give her the agreed-upon advance financing for the album if they approved it. Since the label preferred another pop album from Barbra, *The Broadway Album* was not approved. Columbia gave Streisand half her usual financing. The only way she could make up the difference was for the album to sell 2.5 million copies (at that point, it would automatically be deemed an "approved" album). When *The Broadway Album* was certified triple platinum—three million units sold—Streisand collected her advance and a sweet victory. Barbra and *The Broadway Album* were nominated for three Grammys—Album of the Year, Best Pop Female Vocal Performance, and Best Arrangement Accompanying a Vocal—winning two: David Foster's otherworldly arrangement for "Somewhere" took the award, as did Streisand. It was her eighth Grammy, and when she accepted, she noted that it had been exactly twenty-four years since she had won her first Grammy. Considering the difficulties she had had in convincing Columbia to back the project and her connection to the material, Streisand's Grammy was truly gratifying to the star.

Throughout the seventies and up to that point in 1986, Streisand had withdrawn from the concert stage in favor of recording and film work. She had developed terrible stage fright in part because she had received death threats when she did the concert in Central Park in 1967. Even when she did Las Vegas in 1969, 1970, and 1971, she was gripped with fear. The idea of singing before live audiences became anathema to her. Altogether, there were only a few instances when she was persuaded to face the crowd and sing, and the reason had to be a good one. Money was not a consideration: she turned down offers of millions from promoters around the world. But in April 1986, an incident occurred at the Chernobyl nuclear plant in Russia which would have a profound effect on Streisand. The magnitude of the disaster in the Soviet Union was tremendous, and the worldwide ripple effect touched nearly everyone in some way. In order to reach people and deliver an antinuclear message, as well as speaking out about other issues of concern to her, Barbra decided to use her voice.

With Marilyn and Alan Bergman, Streisand prepared a live concert—dubbed *One Voice*—to be held in her Malibu backyard. With the support and cosponsorship of the Hollywood Women's Political Committee (of which she was a member), Streisand's concert would raise money for Democratic senatorial candidates. The invitations were sent out in the form of a personal message on an audiocassette from Barbra. The intimate concert would take place on the grounds of Streisand's Malibu estate, in an outdoor amphitheater built just for the night. Hollywood's A-list celebrities were asked to pay $2,500 each for the privilege of hearing Barbra in concert . . . one night only. The evening was a complete sellout as soon as the invitations were received.

On September 6, 1986, with the stars shining above, Streisand stepped out of a misty manmade fog into the spotlight singing the opening words to "Somewhere," and the star-filled audience gave her a welcoming standing ovation. Dressed in white, Streisand sang a program of her tried-and-true favorites—"Evergreen," "People," and "Happy Days Are Here Again"— as well as recent hits from *The Broadway*

Album. She also gave a poignant rendition of "Papa, Can You Hear Me?," a set of *Guilty* duets with special guest Barry Gibb, and some inspired new songs prepared especially for the evening ("Over the Rainbow," "It's a New World," and "America, the Beautiful"). The concert was recorded as both an album and an HBO television special, and in December—three months after the concert—it was broadcast for home viewers. It immediately became HBO's most requested program. In April 1987, Columbia released the soundtrack to *One Voice*. Buoyed by the success of the television special, the album charted well, reaching number nine on the *Billboard* Top 200. Streisand received two Grammy nominations for *One Voice*: Best Female Vocal and Best Performance–Music Video.

Taking Chances or Taking Stock

1987   *Nuts*
1988   *Till I Loved You*
1989   *Barbra Streisand: A Collection:*
**   *Greatest Hits . . . and More***

Following *Yentl*, it was four years before Streisand was ready to make another film. *Nuts* was a gripping courtroom drama in which she was cast in a role unlike anything she'd ever played. Claudia Draper, an intelligent, high-priced call girl who kills a client in self-defense, is fighting for her right to stand trial for her crime. Her parents try to have her declared mentally impaired and committed; and Claudia must prove to the court that she is not "nuts." Complicating matters is Claudia's belligerent, sardonic attitude and the dark past she is reluctant to reveal even though it will help her case. *Nuts* was a plum role for an actress, and many Hollywood stars had been in pursuit of it, including Debra Winger, Bette Midler, and Susan Sarandon. It was Streisand, though, who acquired the film rights and produced the picture through her company, Barwood Films. Acting as producer and star, Streisand had the choice of music for the film, and although another writer was commissioned to do the

score, Barbra rejected it. With little time left before the picture's November release, Streisand decided to compose the score herself. Although her score was subtle and slight, it was also her first attempt at film-music composition. To her credit, it was an effective complement to the movie. Columbia collected the five main musical themes—all thirteen minutes and eleven seconds—and released the material as a mini-CD soundtrack.

Barbra on the streets of New York for the big finish of *Nuts*. Streisand's minimalist score — all thirteen minutes and eleven seconds — was released as a mini-album by Columbia.

When critics reviewed *Nuts*, Streisand was given mostly excellent notices for her performance. However, she was also criticized by some for taking on too many roles in the production, like composing the score. Barbra mused on that kind of criticism in an interview following the film's release: "I don't get angry. I get hurt. It's a strange phenomenon that our society is not ready for a Renaissance woman. It is only ready for a Renaissance man. Society still wants to keep women in their place. It's too threatening somehow to most people, women as well as men. We women are not very generous about one another's success. I think women are still uneasy with feminism. Having gotten our freedom, we're not sure how to use it, and

The dramatic pose for *Till I Loved You* didn't help make the album a hit. Columbia Records

some women take on some of the worst aspects of men."

Streisand was planning an album of music from the movies, similar to *The Broadway Album*, and had even mentioned it during *One Voice* when she introduced "Over the Rainbow." However, in 1988, she released *Till I Loved You*, a thematic album detailing the beginning, middle, and end of a romantic relationship. The production of the album became entwined with Streisand's personal life when

she began dating Don Johnson. Barbra had met the *Miami Vice* television star the previous December in Aspen, and as she began to record cuts for *Till I Loved You*, Johnson was included in the sessions. Streisand and Johnson sang the album's title cut, "Till I Loved You (The Love Theme From *Goya*)," a ballad from a Broadway-bound musical. (*Goya*, which was being heavily promoted by Columbia Records, never did make it to Broadway.) Streisand called on a multitude of talents to lend their expertise to the album, including Quincy Jones and Phil Ramone. Songwriters were also asked to contribute material geared just for the album, much as they did for the *Wet* album. Still, *Till I Loved You* was a pop album which lacked focus. It also lacked promotion. On the eve of the November 1988 release, Streisand and Johnson's affair ended, and the prospect of a romantic video of the title song or their joint appearances to boost record sales never materialized.

"Till I Loved You" was the album's single release, but it suffered in comparison to Streisand's other superstar duets. In fact, disc jockeys were more inclined to make Streisand and Johnson's duet the butt of jokes than to play the song. The other songs on *Till I Loved You* wavered in quality, from the soulful, gospel-oriented "The Places You Find Love" (which included an all-star background chorus of Dionne Warwick, Jennifer Holliday, James Ingram, and Luther Vandross, among others) to the saccharine "Love Light" and the awkward version of "All I Ask of You" (a duet from Andrew Lloyd Webber's *Phantom of the Opera*, which Streisand sang as a solo). In between, there were some especially fine cuts, including "On My Way to You," "What Were We Thinking Of?," and "Two People," the latter Streisand's original composition (the theme from *Nuts*) to which the Bergmans added lyrics. As an album, *Till I Loved You* made it as high as number ten on the *Billboard* chart, and the single was number one on the adult contemporary chart (it reached twenty-five on the *Billboard* pop chart).

For most of 1989, Streisand was hard at work on preproduction for her next film project—an adaptation of Pat Conroy's sprawling novel *The Prince of Tides*. As with *Yentl*, she would direct, produce, and star in the picture, and although she did not get a screen credit for *Tides*, she also worked on the screenplay extensively. As an artist who is often prone to tunnel vision when working on a project, Barbra had nothing substantive to offer Columbia Records when it was planning its holiday releases for 1989. With the same inspiration Streisand and Columbia

had had while putting *Memories* together, *Barbra Streisand: A Collection, Greatest Hits . . . and More* was conceived.

A Collection was yet another compilation album to which two new songs had been added: "We're Not Making Love Anymore" and "Someone That I Used to Love." "We're Not Making Love Anymore" was a big, dramatic ballad written by Michael Bolton and Diane Warren, and the arrangement was produced by Grammy-winner Narada Michael Walden, who had shaped Whitney Houston's smash album *Whitney*. Walden was enthusiastic about getting a chance to work with Streisand. "Barbra is a great soul. She's not much in tune with what's going on [in music]—she knows that Whitney sang 'The Greatest Love of All' and that's about it. But her voice is amazing. Barbra has what I call psychic sorrow. She sings sad songs with such passion and such a tender cry, that tears come to her eyes. Nobody else does that. I want to give her a

"Till I Loved You" was Barbra and Don Johnson's one and only duet. Disk jockeys liked making jokes about it more than they did playing it.

Barbra's classic duets with Judy Garland from *The Judy Garland Show* were included in *Just for the Record*, and will be on the video set when it's released someday.

real heartwrencher and have her sing it."

"We're Not Making Love Anymore" was an attempt at a big ballad, like "Comin' In and Out of Your Life," another contemporary love song presented to Barbra (in 1980) as a ready-made hit. It was emotional and strenuous but hardly memorable. Streisand filmed a video for the song, but unlike "Emotion," it was an uninspired one which only showed her lip-synching the words. *A Collection*, overall, was uninspired and made it only as high as number twenty-six on the *Billboard* chart. "We're Not Making Love Anymore" and "Someone That I Used to Love" were both released as singles, appearing only on the *Billboard* adult contemporary chart. The former made it to number ten, the latter to twenty-five.

Looking Back for Inspiration

1991   *Just for the Record . . .*
1991   *The Prince of Tides*
1992   *Highlights From Just for the Record . . .*

The earliest recording of Barbra Streisand singing was made in 1955 when Streisand and her mother, Diana Kind, went to the Nola Recording Studio with an accompanist they'd met while vacationing in the Catskill Mountains the previous summer. An acetate copy of thirteen-year-old Barbra doing "You'll Never Know" was saved, and for twenty years it sat on a shelf waiting to be rediscovered or to disintegrate. When Streisand found the scratchy old record, it became the catalyst for an album. She would use the acetate as the opening for a musical retrospective of her career, and for a finish, the forty-nine-year-old Barbra would sing along with thirteen-year-old Barbra. She first mentioned this project in 1983 when critic Gene Shalit interviewed her about *Yentl* on *The Today Show*. At that time, Barbra explained that the record would include many unreleased recordings—such as her duet with Judy Garland on *The Judy Garland Show*—and she would call it *Just for the Record . . .*

Just for the Record . . . was an ongoing project which came closer to becoming a reality when Streisand rekindled a professional relationship with personal manager Martin Erlichman. The two had been together from the time of Barbra's first nightclub gigs at the Bon Soir until the completion of *A Star Is Born*. With Jon Peters taking over many of the duties Erlichman had handled for Streisand, Marty moved on to other non-Streisand projects, and he became an independent producer. But even if they were not working together professionally, Streisand and Erlichman were always connected, and in 1986, they teamed up once more. *Just for the Record . . .* was one of the projects Erlichman threw his efforts into, pushing Columbia to commit to a multi-album format and the full, red-carpet treatment for Streisand.

In 1991, *Just for the Record . . .* was at last ready for release. It encompassed four CDs, covering Streisand's music (and a tad too much talk) from 1955 to 1988 and included ninety-five cuts, sixty-seven of which were never before released on record. Packaged in a pink, cloth-covered box, *Just for the Record . . .* also offered Streisand's personal reminiscence for each sequence and a plethora of

unpublished photos and mementos, although many were reproduced postage-stamp size to accommodate the tall, narrow shape of the box. But whatever the qualms about the packaging, the quality inside the wrapper made *Just for the Record . . .* a valuable [chcollectible for Streisand admirers and anyone curious about the superstar and her three-decades-long preeminence in popular music. Early cuts were highlighted by a live set recorded in 1962 at the Bon Soir in New York, which Columbia had considered releasing as a debut album for Streisand. Also included were the audio portions of television shows: *The Tonight Show, The Judy Garland Show*, and later Barbra's appearances on *The Burt Bacharach Special, The Stars Salute Israel at 30*, and others. Material from Streisand's television specials, like *The Belle of 14th Street*, and songs cut from some of her films ("If I Close My Eyes" from *Up the Sandbox* and the alternate version of "The Way We Were," called "The Way We Weren't") were also welcome additions. But the true treasures on *Just for the Record . . .* were the cuts

(Bottom) The soundtrack album for *The Prince of Tides* had two vocal tracks by Barbra, neither of which was included in the movie.

(Top) *Just for the Record . . .*, once called *Legacy*, Streisand's first boxed set.

from albums which never came to pass: songs from *The Singer* and *Between Yesterday and Tomorrow*; material which never made it onto released albums, like "A Quiet Thing"/"There Won't Be Trumpets" from the *ButterFly* sessions, "I Know Him So Well" from *The Broadway Album* sessions, "Warm All Over" from the *Back to Broadway* sessions (an album still two years into the future), and other songs which had long been buried in Columbia's vault.

The boxed set was a holiday re-lease, and considering its high ticket price (four CDs and all that packaging brought the retail price to nearly $80, although on sale it was closer to $65), *Just for the Record* made an immediate impact. It was certified platinum (one million units sold), and after its release, it reached thirty-eight on the *Billboard* Top 200 chart, which at that time did not have a format for measuring boxed sets separately. At Grammy time, Streisand's performance of "Warm All Over" was nominated for Best Traditional Pop Performance, as was the art director for the album's packaging design. A proposed video retrospective to accompany *Just for the Record . . .* was originally to be released along with the CD set, but delays in production made that impossible. The video version of *Just for the Record . . .* (in two parts) is expected to be released some time in 1995. Nine months after

Back to Broadway not only hit number one but it made Barbra the only performer to have number-one albums in four decades — the sixties, seventies, eighties, and nineties. Firooz Zahedi/Columbia Records

the boxed set came out, Streisand compiled an assortment of cuts from the retrospective into a single CD and repackaged the booklet. The abbreviated version was simply called *Highlights From Just for the Record . . .*, and for the cost-conscious, it was significantly less expensive than the boxed set.

On the heels of the release of *Just for the Record . . .*, Streisand's second film directorial effort, *The Prince of Tides*, premiered in New York and Los Angeles. It garnered even better notices for her direction and production than had *Yentl*. The music for *The Prince Of Tides* was originally to have been written by Oscar-winning composer John Barry. However, long before the film was set for release, Barry left the project with little explanation. Streisand replaced Barry with James Newton Howard, a successful young composer who was dating her at the time. Newton Howard came up with an evocative, wistfully romantic score . . . very

much in the tradition of *The Way We Were*. Streisand coproduced the soundtrack, working hand in hand with Newton Howard on the score. It was an area in which she felt more than qualified to take an active role, and as a very hands-on director, she left nothing to chance.

The Prince of Tides soundtrack album, released in December 1991, featured two vocals by Streisand . . . vocals which were not in the film. The classic standard "For All We Know" was heard as an instrumental in the film, and the soundtrack repeated that version as well as a jazzy, sensual rendition of the same number by Streisand. For the other vocal, Barbra recorded "The Places That Belong to You," the film's love theme with lyrics by the Bergmans. The original intent was for her vocal to play over the end credits, but as Streisand explained in the soundtrack's liner notes, she felt her singing would have been a distraction . . . it would have called attention to Streisand the singer. Whether she was correct or not, "The Places That Belong to You" was a beautiful song, and had it been included in the film, it would surely have been nominated for an Oscar. As it was, *The Prince of Tides* did garner seven nominations (although in another surprising slap in the face, Streisand didn't receive a single one of them), including one for James Newton Howard's score.

Moving On . . . America's Voice

1993 *Back to Broadway*
1993 *Duets*

In 1992, Barbra Streisand returned to the concert stage for the first time in six years. First, in September, Streisand volunteered to sing at a fund-raiser for Democratic presidential candidate Bill Clinton. Again, as they did with *One Voice*, the Hollywood Women's Political Committee sponsored the event, and it was Streisand's name that made the fund-raiser a sellout. With the enthusiasm that comes from a campaign which is on the way to victory, Streisand's performance was superb, prompting speculation that she was planning to launch a world tour. Two months later, Streisand was given the prestigious AIDS Project Los Angeles

(APLA) Commitment to Life Award and took part in the evening's entertainment. Streisand teamed with Johnny Mathis for a duet drawn from two *West Side Story* songs: "I Have a Love"/"One Hand, One Heart" and "Somewhere." By then, Bill Clinton had won the election, and an inaugural celebration was in the works for January 1993. When Barbra agreed to appear and sing, CBS Television decided to broadcast the inaugural as a special program. Of course, it didn't hurt that Aretha Franklin, Fleetwood Mac, Barry Manilow, Michael Jackson, Bill Cosby, and other top stars were also going to take part! However, when the inaugural celebration aired, it was Streisand's performance which was shown in its entirety and Streisand who had the honor of introducing the new president. It was during this show that Streisand also initially sang "Children Will Listen" from Stephen Sondheim's *Into the Woods*. That song—and the Mathis duet from APLA—were previews for Streisand's next album, a sequel to *The Broadway Album* called *Back to Broadway*.

Back to Broadway was Streisand's first album under her new contract with Sony Entertainment (Columbia Record's new parent company). The Sony deal was worth $60 million for Streisand, and it encompassed both her recording and film work. It was a reward for her longevity and loyalty to Columbia, but it would never have been so lucrative an offer if Sony did not believe in her ability to maintain her artistry and popularity throughout the nineties and into the next century. Her deal was equal to or greater than ones negotiated by Janet Jackson, Madonna, and Prince.

Streisand would deliver dividends for Sony almost immediately. Streisand's fiftieth album, *Back to Broadway*, was released in June 1993, and based on the success of *The Broadway Album*, record stores ordered thousands of copies. Not surprisingly, *Back to Broadway* shipped platinum. The first week it was eligible for the *Billboard* album chart, *Back to Broadway* debuted at number one . . . a first even for Streisand. Barbra was grateful for the approbation, and in a 1992 interview, she offered a reason for her overall success: "The people who have kept me a star for thirty-some years have done so because there's a truth to my work and that's what they get. And if I keep telling the truth, I can't get hurt."

Back to Broadway made news for more than its going to number one. Because of her involvement in the Clinton campaign and a much-publicized visit to Washington in which she was feted like a foreign dignitary by everyone from General Colin Powell and Attorney General Janet Reno, Streisand was under

"Children Will Listen" was released as a promo single for *Back to Broadway*— six months after the album was in the stores.

intense public scrutiny. Amazingly, many critics analyzing *Back to Broadway* accused Streisand of allowing her politics to influence her musical choices. And when she showed up at Wimbledon to watch tennis star André Agassi— with whom she may or may not have been having an affair—some reviewers wondered if her love life had affected her music.

The criticism was not only farfetched, it was negligent. It failed to recognize the quality of the material on *Back to Broadway* and Streisand's superb execution. Once again, it was the Sondheim works which gave the star an opportunity to shine brightly. "Everybody Says Don't" from *Anyone Can Whistle*, a fast-paced, driving tune, was reminiscent of "Don't Rain on My Parade," and Barbra's enthusiastic performance was a *Back to Broadway* highlight. For the album version of "Children Will Listen," Streisand asked Sondheim if there were a way to musically link the verses: in her performance

Barbra and Johnny Mathis finally got together, in song, with a *West Side Story* duet on *Back to Broadway*.

Unlike its predecessor, *Back to Broadway* boasted two major duets with top recording stars: the aforementioned "I Have a Love"/"One Hand, One Heart," which brought Johnny Mathis and Streisand together on disc for the first time, and "The Music of the Night" from Andrew Lloyd Webber's *Phantom of the Opera*. Michael Crawford, who had immortalized the role of the Phantom on stage, agreed to share the mike with Barbra on this number, even though it had become his signature song. The two had appeared together in *Hello, Dolly!* and, after renewing their friendship when Crawford was on Broadway, had discussed teaming up on a duet. Both duets were welcome additions to the album, and either would have been ripe for a music video or single release.

Lloyd Webber's newest work, *Sunset Boulevard*, a musical version of Billy Wilder's classic Hollywood drama, was opening in London just as *Back to Broadway* was debuting in America. To boost interest in the show, Lloyd Webber had contacted Streisand months before, asking if she would record material from the show for her next album. Barbra agreed to consider the possibility, and the composer sent her the entire score with a note that read "Take whatever you want." He appreciated the power of Streisand's mass appeal, as well as her keen musical taste: *Cats* benefited greatly from her recording of "Memory," and he hoped the same for *Sunset Boulevard*. Barbra chose two songs from the show, "As If We Never Said Goodbye" and "With One Look." The former was the better song, an internal monologue detailing the faded star's return to the studio and her emotional response. Streisand imbued the song with a quiet sense of awe about the wonders of moviemaking, a subject close to her heart. "With One Look," a showy, anthem-like number—the one probably intended to be a hit—was, in fact, released in England as a single. When Streisand recorded it, lyricist Don Black was blown away: "It was the highlight of my career hearing Barbra Streisand record one of my songs. She kept asking if her voice was okay as she hadn't sung for a while. To me, it sounded like liquid diamonds." Still, despite the gusto

for President Clinton, Barbra had a spoken bridge about parents and children. Sondheim understood exactly what Streisand wanted and unearthed quatrains which had been dropped from *Into the Woods* when it was in previews. And on the album's last cut, Streisand juxtaposed two songs from *Sunday in the Park With George*: "Move On" and "We Do Not Belong Together." With Sondheim's blessing and invaluable assistance, a classic medley was born: a piece not only intensely dramatic, but musically challenging. It was more of an aria than a song, and Streisand, the quintessential actress who sings, wrung every drop of emotional turmoil from the words as her voice carried the melody. It was a masterful recording, similar perhaps in technical difficulty and all-encompassing emotion to "A Piece of Sky" from *Yentl*.

in Streisand's performance, the material lacked the musical power of Lloyd Webber's more memorable works. The single was a marginal hit at best.

There were some discussions between Streisand and Sony about making a music video of "With One Look." Feature director Stephen Frears (*The Grifters, Dangerous Liaisons*) was consulted about filming a mini-drama which would incorporate scenes from the original Gloria Swanson –William Holden movie, with new footage of Barbra in full costume and makeup as Norma, singing the showstopper. It was an ambitious idea . . . and an expensive one. Reportedly, Sony felt it was too expensive, and the video never went beyond the talking stage.

Back to Broadway was Barbra Streisand's seventh number-one album. Ultimately, it did not have the staying power of *The Broadway Album*, nor has it sold as many copies. Perhaps the lack of a single release and a video in the United States hurt; *The Broadway Album* had both. Without those elements, awareness of *Back to Broadway* was limited to word of mouth and print advertisements. As the year came to an end, however, *Back to Broadway* began to climb back up the *Billboard* Top 200. The reasons were threefold: Christmas shoppers buying the album to give as a present; the excitement generated when Streisand announced her plans to appear in concert for two shows at the new MGM-Grand Hotel in Las Vegas on New Year's Eve and New Year's Day; and her inclusion in a new Frank Sinatra album called *Duets*.

For many years, Marty Erlichman had tried to find a project in which Barbra could be united in song with Frank Sinatra. But Sinatra had been out of the recording studio for many years, preferring to focus on concert work. In 1993, Charles Koppleman spearheaded a project to get Frank Sinatra back to the recording booth. The proposed album, called *Duets*, would team Sinatra with contemporary artists, ranging from instrumentalist Kenny G to Gloria Estefan to U2's Bono. In addition to current hot artists, a handful of legends were also asked to sing along with Frank: Aretha Franklin, Tony Bennett, and Barbra.

The recording sessions for *Duets* were unusual: Frank and the guest artist would not sing together. Each track would be recorded separately, Sinatra's first. In Barbra's case, her agreement to participate was contingent on her final approval of the duet once it was mixed. As with so many of her projects, Streisand demanded and got artistic control (although Sinatra also had the same veto power, since it was his album). Gershwin's "I've Got a Crush on You" was selected in part because it was a song Frank had previously recorded—which was the basis for the album. It was also intended for *Back to Broadway* but didn't make it into the final cut. Sinatra's original Nelson Riddle arrangement was dropped in favor of a new one by Pat Williams, and Streisand brought in David Foster to coproduce the cut with Phil Ramone. Singing along with Sinatra, Streisand was in excellent voice and created an atmosphere of intimacy between the two despite the fact that they were never actually singing in a studio together. Says Phil Ramone: "She has a magic that doesn't get touched until you get around her instincts. Her musical ability is all instinct. . . . I always tell Barbra, 'I go to school on you.' I always learn something brand new when I work with her. She's like a little girl who has the brights to ask,

(Above) Like these two photos, Streisand and Sinatra never actually got together for their duet "I've Got a Crush on You" from Frank's *Duets* album. Warner Bros.

'Why?' I tend to believe there's nothing she can't do. She has become mellower over the years. She's more compassionate about where other people are coming from. But her standards are twice as high. She never settles." *Duets*, despite mixed reviews, was an immediate hit, debuting at number two on *Billboard*'s Top 200.

The two MGM shows were a huge success, prompting rumors that Barbra would overcome her stage fright and do a worldwide concert tour in 1994. In March, Streisand's representatives announced that she had indeed decided to take her show on the road. When asked what had changed her mind about singing live, Barbra commented, "I honestly believed it was going to be just two concerts. But it was such a lovely experience—feeling the connection with the audience after all these years—that I decided to do a limited tour to express my admiration for the love and support I have received for such a long time." Streisand scheduled twelve dates in New York, London, Anaheim, San Francisco, Washington, and Detroit, with tickets selling for $50, $125, and $350. The media carped about the high prices, but Streisand fans didn't seem to mind; every seat in every arena was sold out within one hour of going on sale. Furthermore, the overwhelming demand for tickets caused Barbra to double the number of shows she had planned. In every venue she played, Streisand broke all existing box-office records, including $16.6 million for seven shows at Madison Square Garden in New York. In all, Streisand gave twenty-four concerts, grossing in the neighborhood of $65–$70 million . . . and that's not including what she will earn for the broadcast rights to a television version of the concert, a video release, as well as the Columbia Records album.

On May 17, 1994, Columbia Records released "Ordinary Miracles," a mini-CD single to promote Barbra's historic concert tour. The four-song disc included two versions of the title tune—a studio version and the live recording from the New Year's Day concert in Las Vegas—as well as "As If We Never Said Goodbye" from *Back to Broadway* and "Evergreen" from *One Voice*. "Ordinary Miracles" was written especially for Barbra by lyricists Marilyn and Alan Bergman and composer Marvin Hamlisch, the same team which created "The Way We Were." The Bergmans also wrote the concert script with Barbra, and Hamlisch acted as her conductor for the duration of the tour. Despite the enormous attention Streisand's tour was getting in the press and the positive response to the song each night she sang it, disc jockeys didn't take to "Ordinary Miracles." It didn't chart in *Billboard* and received limited airplay.

Barbra Streisand: The Concert 1994, as it was called, was videotaped as a television special and broadcast on August 21, 1994, on the HBO cable station. Columbia-TriStar Video planned to release the television special as a video in late 1994, and Columbia Records scheduled a multi-disc album version of *The Concert* for fall 1994, officially slating it as Streisand's fifty-first album for the label.

The Streisand Album Table Notes

The Streisand Album Table lists Barbra's albums, their release date, their highest placement on the *Billboard* Top 200 album chart, and their gold, platinum or multi-platinum certification.

The following albums were not included in the table because they were not charted in *Billboard* or they were not solely Streisand albums:

Pins and Needles

Harold Sings Arlen (With Friend)

The Owl and the Pussycat

Eyes of Laura Mars

Duets

The Streisand Album Table

Album	Grammys	Release Date	Top Spot	Weeks	Awards
Back to Broadway		June 1993	10	Ongoing	Gold, Platinum
Barbara Joan Streisand		Aug 1971	11	26	Gold
Barbra Streisand Album, The	Album of the Year; Best Female Vocal; Best Album Cover	Feb 1993	6	101	Gold
Barbra Streisand's Greatest Hits		Jan 1970	32	30	Gold, Multi-platinum (2M)
Barbra Streisand's Greatest Hits, Vol 2		Nov 1978	1	86	Gold, Multi-platinum (4M)
Barbra Streisand…& Other Musical Instruments		Oct 1973	64	16	
Broadway Album, The	Best Female Pop Vocal; Best Arrangement-Vocal	Nov 1985	1	50	Gold, Multi-platinum (3M)
Butterfly		Oct 1974	13	21	Gold
Christmas Album, A		Oct 1967	1		Gold, Multi-platinum (3M)
Classical Barbra		Feb 1976	46	14	
Collection: Greatest Hits & More, A		Oct 1989	26	25	Gold, Platinum
Color Me Barbra		Mar 1966	3	36	Gold
Emotion		Oct 1964	19	29	Gold, Platinum
Funny Girl (soundtrack)		Aug 1968	12	108	Gold, Platinum
Funny Lady		Mar 1975	6	25	Gold
Guilty	Best Pop Vocal by Duo or Group w/ Vocal	Sept 1980	1	49	Gold, Multi-platinum (5M)
Happening in Central Park, A		Sept 1968	30	20	Gold
Hello, Dolly!		Nov 1969	49	33	
I Can Get It for You Wholesale		April 1962	125	5	
Je M'Appelle Barbra		Oct 1966	5	29	
Just for the Record…(Boxed Set)		Sept 1991	38	16	Gold, Platinum
Lazy Afternoon		Oct 1975	12	20	Gold
Live Concert at the Forum		Oct 1972	19	27	Gold, Platinum
Main Event, The		June 1979	20	18	Gold
Memories		Nov 1981	6	106	Gold, Multi-platinum (4M)
My Name is Barbra	Best Female Vocal	May 1965	2	68	Gold
On a Clear Day You Can See Forever		July 1970	108	24	
One Voice		April 1987	9	28	Gold, Platinum
People	Best Female Vocal; Best Arrangement-Vocal	Sept 1964	1	84	Gold
Prince of Tides, The		Dec 1991	84	12	
Second Barbra Streisand Album, The		Aug 1963	2	74	Gold
Simply Barbra		Oct 1967	12	23	
Songbird		May 1978	12	27	Gold, Platinum
Star Is Born, A	Song of the Year, Best Female Pop Vocal	Nov 1976	1	51	Gold, Multi-platinum (4M)
Stoney End		Feb 1971	10	29	Gold, Platinum
Streisand Superman		June 1977	3	25	Gold, Platinum
Third Album, A		Feb 1964	5	74	Gold
Till I Loved You		Nov 1988	10	26	Gold, Platinum
Way We Were, The	Song of the Year	Jan 1974	1	31	Gold, Platinum
Wet		Oct 1979	7	26	Gold, Platinum
What About Today?		July 1969	31	40	
Yentl		Nov 1983	9	26	Gold, Platinum

4

In Others' Words

Fellow Singers and Stars

● "Whenever I want to reach back for one of them fine old tunes, I get in here and refresh my memory. But I also get Barbra Streisand. She can sing awhile, can't she? And the Beatles. It's music and the swing. Say what you like, Daddy, but she's outswinging every ass this year."—Singer-musician **Louis Armstrong**, 1969

● "Barbra fractures me. Even though our styles are different, we've been compared as having the best ears in the business in that we both sing perfectly in tune. *Funny Girl* knocked me to the ground. I would love to have had that part."—Singer **Karen Carpenter**, 1981

● "Meeting Barbra was one of the most memorable evenings in my life. I had brought her a song that I cowrote with Alan and Marilyn Bergman. I sang it for her, then we stayed up most of the night discussing vocal techniques, which was like taking a Ph.D. in music."—Singer **Melissa Manchester**, 1983

● "I think Barbra has one of the most beautiful voices in the history of pop, but her music doesn't mean as much to her as it once did. I think she wants to be a director; Barbra wants to be an auteur, she wants that respect. That's the main thing with her. She's a very lovely girl who has all sorts of tremendous gifts, but maybe she feels that she doesn't get any respect. This is a tough business. . . . Directors are the only people who get any respect in this town. The actors get a lot of money, but they don't get any respect."—Singer-actress **Bette Midler**, 1991

● "You certainly can't say 'fuck you' unless you can back it up with something. Barbra Streisand can't say 'fuck you' with her face or her body. She's got to say 'fuck you' with her voice and her talent."—Singer-actress **Cher**, 1988

● "Streisand is great with the big orchestra. She can really belt. I'm not like that. I like the simplest form of music. I would prefer singing with just a guitar or a piano. See, I have to sing into somebody's ear."—Singer-actress **Doris Day**, 1969

● "I've always credited Streisand with being my vocal coach, and I used to sound a lot more like her than I do now. I learned breathing from imitating her records."—Singer **Maureen McGovern**, 1984

● "Recently, I went to see Barbra sing. She's one lady I would have died to see and she performs so seldom that when I got the chance, I grabbed it. She was more than I expected. Just to see her . . . I admire her for lasting so long. It's the sort of career I want myself. I don't want to be Madonna, who will burn herself out. I'd like to perform for decades to come. Also, like Barbra, I'd like to do films."—Singer **Whitney Houston**, 1988

● "I made a promise that no matter where it was or how much it cost or what country it was in, that I would be there whenever Barbra Streisand sang in public again. . . . If it wasn't for Barbra, I wouldn't be doing what I'm doing."—Singer **Sheena Easton**, 1986

● "One of the most fantastic singers to come along in years. I like this kind of singer because she's trying to tell you something. If you don't get the message, you're a complete idiot. And she has musicianly quality—and sings in tune—let us not forget to include that!"—Singer **Carmen MacRae**, 1964

● "I can imagine the pressure she must have had when she was starting out, to change herself over. She either must have known things would be changing, or she must have had unbelievable confidence."—Actress **Sylvia Sidney**, 1979

● "I have all of her albums. Of course, I haven't told her that, but I do. I adore Barbra and if she

told me to come some place and lay face down in a mud pie, I would probably do it."—Actress **Sally Field**, 1986

● "I think the thing I admire most about Barbra is that she is a perfectionist. When it came to her performance, her singing, it had to be one hundred percent the way she thought it should be. . . . I found Barbra to be a very kind, generous and sweet person. Sincere in her work and her attitudes toward people."—Entertainer **Liberace**, 1980

● "I love her. We're very good friends. She's such an interesting, fabulously eloquent, perfectionistic woman. And I would love to work with her, with her directing me. I'd feel completely safe. I wouldn't have to take care of the physical [details]—the lighting, scenery, costumes—or even the emotional details. She would be there for me. You have to have a director you feel is there for you."—Actress **Shirley MacLaine**, 1991

● "Streisand is a tough cookie on screen and off. I like that in a woman and in Hollywood you need to be strong. I admire Barbra for her toughness and survival although I don't know how happy she is. The fear of not being liked is strong in a woman and if you show off other talents than beauty, you're called a bitch. If you want to be a woman who can express herself intellectually, you have to accept not being liked—especially in Hollywood. Barbra is an inspiration to all actresses who want to take charge of their careers and maybe later move behind the camera."—Actress **Sean Young**, 1989

● "*Funny Girl* is the ultimate showcase for a star. The music is beautiful and Streisand is magical. I'd love to be able to sing like Streisand. . . . These days I'm on a major Streisand binge. I prefer her sixties records, which are totally brilliant. My favorites are *The Third Album* and *A Happening in Central Park*."—Actress **Helen Slater**, 1990

● "I cannot remember any star as young as she is, possessing the stage presence, vocal control, and quality as well as the truly original style that is the mark of a great performer. As an actress and a singer she can be funny as well as touching, sing a song with strength and be seemingly nerveless. She learned early the most important and the rarest thing of all—not to be a carbon copy and to allow her own personality to emerge."—Pianist **Oscar Levant**, 1968

Working With Barbra

● "There is just not going to be another Barbra Streisand, now or ever. What she is, happens once. . . ."—*On a Clear Day* lyricist-librettist **Alan**

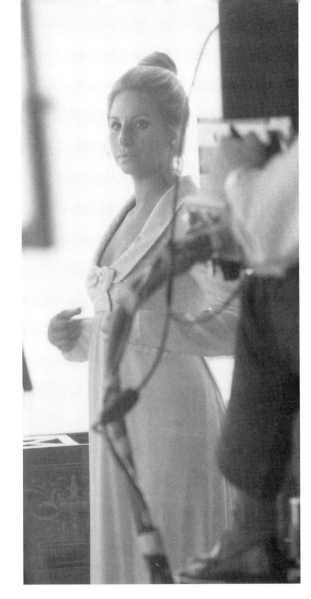

Jay Lerner, 1969

● "Barbra could do whatever she wants—and does. She could have been Joe Montana, Norman Schwarzkopf, Jonas Salk, Maggie Thatcher, or Barbra Streisand. I think she made the right choice."—*Funny Girl/The Way We Were* producer **Ray Stark**, 1991

● "She's a smart gal . . . very honest, very hep. She came to me one day and said, 'Jimmy, you know, they say I'm temperamental. I just want things to be right for me and I know what's good for me and what's bad.' Well, I think that's a wonderful trait. She protects herself . . . and she should."—*Funny Lady* cinematographer **James Wong Howe**, 1975

● "She used to be a waitress in a Chinese restaurant, then an usherette in a cinema. Now she has her own company. And she's just started. She's going to be responsible for her own pictures in the future."—*On a Clear Day* producer **Howard W. Koch**, 1969

● "She walked in [to audition] and just knocked me out. In those days, what Barbra looked like was not considered attractive. All this talk about her nose is nonsense; she actually has a lovely nose. It's the eyes that are a problem."—*The Way We Were* author **Arthur Laurents**, 1987

● "She's an absolute pro; I never saw any of that dragon-lady personality she's supposed to have. She was so much younger than the part had been written for, but I'm sure that gave Dolly a lot more life."—*Hello, Dolly!* composer **Jerry Herman**, 1986

"Barbra is an artist, one of those rare people who can do anything she wants. . . . Barbra thinks she's been held back because she's a woman, but she has done everything she's wanted to do."—Record executive **David Geffen**, 1991

● "She [is] a strange, strange girl. She has a sort of unusual attraction about her. It's not only her talent—which is enormous—but she has this extraordinary personality which comes through, even when you first meet her and talk to her. I think that she's far more friendly than her reputation would lead one to believe."—*For Pete's Sake* director **Peter Yates**, 1974

● "You know, she's a very sweet girl. It sounds a silly thing to say about Streisand. I have to tell you that I love her—there isn't anything I wouldn't do for her. I'm very moved by her in a peculiar way which I can't explain. I think that inside, when you get through all the fears, the insecurities and the defensiveness, she's a good person. One senses that in her singing and her performances. There's a goodness there that I'm touched by."—*The Way We Were* director **Sydney Pollack**, 1976

● "Like everybody else, I had read stuff about her. I thought, 'Holy God, I am going to be working with the bride of Frankenstein.' I was completely stunned to find out that she was a delight. But all the people who work closely with Barbra have been with her thirty years. She inspires great loyalty. Her birthday came . . . What amazed me was the number of flowers she received from her ex-boyfriends. She keeps up with them. They like her. She likes them. The notes they sent were lovely, really lovely. Like Jon Peters . . . I didn't think there were that many roses alive in New York."—*The Prince of Tides* author **Pat Conroy**, 1992

● "We became friends during *The Way We*

Were. She's honestly brilliant and people don't like that in a woman."—Actress **Sally Kirkland**, 1990

● "Barbra Streisand is a very real person, not an icon at all. She's very straight and doesn't lie. The thing Barbra's great at is stamina. She doesn't leave until it's done. You think you know people who work hard—then you see Barbra."—*The Prince of Tides* actress **Kate Nelligan**, 1991

● "I was a kid when I did that role [in *All Night Long*] with her. She's a very beautiful woman. There's a glow about her. When you're in her presence, it's very special."—Actor **Dennis Quaid**, 1990

● "In a strange, offbeat way she's physically attractive. God, I think there's a lot of similarity between her and Sinatra—they're too bright to be fooled. They don't want double-talk or crap. They go right for the throat. Life is too complicated, time too precious. Elizabeth Taylor is the same way. But Elizabeth developed her frankness through years and years of listening to it all; Barbra by her very nature is that way."—Producer **Richard Zanuck**, 1969

● "That she is a great artist is known to the world. She is also a passionate and compassionate humanist, a social activist who brings the same intelligence and commitment to the totality of her life."—Lyricist **Marilyn Bergman**, 1992

Memorable Close Encounters

● "She's very extraordinary. She is one of the real phenomenons of today. My favorites are Bea Lillie and Billie Holliday, and she's the only one I've heard to equal them."—Author **Truman Capote**, 1963

● "When I first met Barbra in acting class, she was fifteen. But there was nothing remotely adolescent about her, even then. She's grown, of course. Her taste is better; she's seen more, done more, lived more. But all her qualities were there to begin with. She already knew her mind."—Barwood president **Cis Corman**, 1968

● "I have fallen in love with Miss Barbra Streisand. I just sat there with my mouth open."—Actress **Bette Davis**, 1966

● "[When I was in *Drat, the Cat* on Broadway in 1967] I was totally fascinated with her. I asked Elliott how she did her makeup. I vocalized to her albums. Jon never had heard of her when I took him to the Hollywood Bowl to see her. Isn't life bizarre? But I believe in karma and cosmic connections."—Singer-actress **Lesley Ann Warren**, Jon Peters's ex-wife and Elliott Gould's costar in *Drat, the Cat!*, 1977

● "Erasmus High School, 1956: I was the golden boy, she was the outcast. We were seated next to each other, alphabetically, for the geometry Regents test that I was about to fail for the third time. Being caught cheating meant immediate expulsion. I had little to lose as I couldn't graduate without passing this test, but she was an 'A' student with everything to lose. Nonetheless, she permitted me to copy her answers, and I passed. Thanks, Barbra Streisand. You're a real mensch."—Erasmus Hall High School alumnus **Everett Robins**, 1992

● "As soon as I heard her sing, my intuition told me that the kid had a terrific set of pipes and a natural style. She was a new, fresh talent. And despite her looks—or lack of them—she would someday have to be reckoned with as a great star. So I started putting her on my TV show."—Talk show host **Joe Franklin**, 1978

● "She was just getting ready to leave [a coffee shop] so I felt I wouldn't be intruding. I said:

On the set of *The Owl and the Pussycat* with director Herbert Ross *(left)* and producer Ray Stark.

'Excuse me, I just wanted to tell you how much I've always admired your work.' She didn't want to know. She looked up at me with a please-go-away look and nodded thanks, rather ungraciously. So I turned and left. She'd no idea who I was, of course, not that it would have made any difference. I suppose it must be tiresome having people come up like that, but it isn't hard to be gracious. I think the only reason I did it was because I saw her in *Funny Girl* when I was in school and that was what determined me to be an actress."— Actress **Lisa Eichhorn** (Barbra replaced her in *All Night Long*), 1981

● "Barbra Streisand, who struck me as being ugly at first, gradually cast her spell over me. I fell madly in love with her talent and her personality. The feeling was mutual for four months—the time it took for shooting the picture."—*Funny Girl* costar **Omar Sharif**, 1976

● "None of us could get in the Actors Studio. We'd always try, and flunk, but we'd always go there when they had projects. Barbra had a funny reputation then because she was younger than us, maybe seventeen or something. . . . I had seen her do some project on stage at the Theatre Studio, and I remember this funny-looking girl sitting cross-legged onstage. And she had nothing to do, she had a very small part, she didn't have any lines. But by some magic wave of her wand, she was making everybody look at her. That was the first time I saw her act. I thought she was interesting. Anyone who, without seeming to do anything, could make people look at her was somehow interesting."—Actor **Dustin Hoffman**, 1976

● "First, I learned that everything I had heard about Barbra Streisand was absolutely true. The ultimate professional, she worried over every camellia in the garden, every word she uttered and, even more, every word Jon Peters uttered. But she is such a talent, and in truth, so vulnerable, that I would forgive her anything. She obviously felt the same way, because we did another interview with her nine years later—and she worried just as much.—ABC-TV interviewer-anchorwoman **Barbara Walters**, 1988

● "I'm twenty-five years old, this dork. I was standing on the set [of *The Way We Were*] and [Barbra] turns to me and asks, 'Are you afraid of me?' I really didn't understand what she meant. I told her, 'The only one around here who should be afraid is you, because I'm really good at this.' I was smiling, kidding, and she laughed. Then after a take, she turned to me and said, 'Hmm . . . you

Barbra's leading man in *Funny Girl*, Omar Sharif, found working with her an affair to remember.

might be right!' "—Actor **James Woods**, 1989

● "I'd talk to my father a great deal so it was almost like I knew her. I would do it [the photography] the way he did it. He used to talk about her a lot. He'd say how soft she was; how fast she would pick things up; how she'd ask why aren't you doing this, why did you do that? He said most of the times she was right. And he'd been doing it for what—forty years? She's a very intelligent lady. *The Way We Were*—hell, I was very apprehensive. It was a big movie. Naturally, I wanted to do good because my father had worked with her so much."—*The Way We Were* cinematographer **Harry Stradling Jr.** 1976

Unconventional, Unforgettable

● "The girl not only has a magnificent talent, but she is beautiful, too. The point is that Barbra Streisand has an unconventional face. In another way, mine is unconventional, too. But now the unconventional is accepted. . . . She looks like no one else and her unconventional face is all lighted up by her magnificent talent."—Actress **Audrey Hepburn**, 1964

● "She was always a little extra special and a little extra sensitive and a little . . . the word different isn't even the right word, it wouldn't be fair to her. But she was in a separate place. She was some-

A great moment in *Hello, Dolly!*: Streisand and Louis Armstrong singing the title song.

thing special."—*What's Up, Doc?* arranger **Artie Butler**, who attended Erasmus Hall High School with Barbra, 1986

● "My favorite actress? Barbra Streisand's wonderful. I take vicarious pride in her accomplishment with *Yentl*. It moves me to think of the tenacity and talent it took to get it done as well as she did."—Actress **Piper Laurie**, 1984

● "Barbra is my love. She could have felt like an ugly duckling, but she's smart and she's positive. She worked with herself—and she is. When she sat for me, she wanted to do her own makeup, so we compromised. We did it the first day, and she did it the second. She's so smart! She picked up all kinds of tricks to use the second day!"—Fashion photographer **Francesco Scavullo**, 1981

● "There are people who aren't regarded as terrific looking, but who become beautiful once you find out that they are talented, interesting human beings. Barbra Streisand is a good example. I think she's gorgeous."—Actor **Daniel J. Travanti**, 1982

● "Barbra is one hell of a sexy lady. I can say that I've known thousands of women, but Barbra was one of the best. Unequaled. She is shrewd, strong, clever, and direct. She was equally direct making love. We had some great times together and I shall never forget her."—Actor **Don Johnson**, 1989

● "I wouldn't want to be a young actress in

Anne Francis blamed Barbra for her part being severely cut in *Funny Girl*.

Dennis Quaid *(right)* was Barbra's lover and Gene Hackman's son in *All Night Long.*

films now. I think of Barbra Streisand in comparison, and what she did with *Yentl.* She has to buy the story, has to convince Singer that she's the one to play it, she does an absolutely spectacular job and for some reason she's passed over at the Oscars—which was wrong. Now she's got to start all over again with the next project from scratch."—Actress **Esther Williams**, 1984

Barbra kidding around with director Peter Yates while filming *For Pete's Sake* in the New York subways.

The Minority Opinion

● "I happen to despise Barbra Streisand as a performer. In fact, everything I know about her makes me despise her. [But] it offended me when John Simon started writing about her nose. I don't think Streisand's nose the least bit unattractive, and I don't think it has anything to do with her act."—Director **Robert Altman**, 1981

● "I had only one unpleasant meeting with Barbra Streisand during the entire five months of *Funny Girl,* but the way I was treated, it was a nightmare. It was like an experience out of *Gaslight.* From the beginning, it was like, 'What was I doing here?' "—Actress **Anne Francis**, who accused Streisand of cutting her out of *Funny Girl,* 1967

● "On one level, she is a great talent. When she performed, she was unbelievable. Offstage she was somebody else. Very disagreeable, with no charm or humor. . . . The girl doesn't joke. You're always uncomfortable with her because she's basically a dull girl."—*My Name Is Barbra, Two* record producer **Robert Mersey**, 1985

5

Streisand on Film:
The Best . . . and the Rest

In 1967, Barbra Streisand stepped off a plane at Los Angeles Airport with one goal in mind . . . to become a movie star. She was in Hollywood to make the film version of her Broadway success *Funny Girl*, and she had two additional musicals lined up—*Hello, Dolly!* and *On a Clear Day You Can See Forever*. Her childhood dream of movie stardom was within her grasp, and with the same determination and commitment to excellence she had displayed in her drive to make it to the top of the recording industry, on Broadway, in nightclubs and concerts, and on the small screen, she was ready to conquer the film world.

A year and a half later, as the rave reviews and box-office receipts rolled in for *Funny Girl*, there was little doubt Streisand had indeed captured Hollywood. And in the years since *Funny Girl*, she has sustained her film stardom and built on her success. Streisand has become one of the most enduring movie stars of the post-studio era, and one of the most recognizable box-office stars in the world.

Since her auspicious, Oscar-winning debut, Barbra Streisand has made fourteen more films. While fifteen movies in twenty-seven years may seem like an insubstantial body of work compared to other stars, Streisand has traveled a road which is uniquely her own. She was primarily a singer-actress when she came to Hollywood . . . on a par with Julie Andrews and Liza Minnelli; today, Barbra Streisand is still an actress who sings, but she's also a director, a scriptwriter, a producer, a composer, and the head of a film production company. She literally has no peer among today's women in film, and few men in the film industry are as all-encom-

passing in their work. As Streisand has grown as a filmmaker, the movies she creates have become more and more personal. And, consequently, Streisand has taken more and more time "turning her visions into reality." And unlike other top moviemakers like Barry Levinson, Oliver Stone, Robert Redford, Warren Beatty, et al., Streisand is the only one who has maintained a thriving recording career simultaneously.

Whether foolish or wise, Barbra Streisand has tried to do everything. And as time goes by, it is evident that she has, more often than not, succeeded.

To rate the quality and success of Streisand's film work, a methodology has been been devised to weigh the overall impact of a film. Not only a film's critical approbation, but also other variables which are of value are included in this formula, i.e., box-office appeal, fan reaction, and historical perspective. Each film will be rated on these four criteria, with an assignment of from zero to twenty-five points for its success in each of these categories. A movie which was a box-office hit, a critical success, loved by Streisand fans, and is now regarded as a seminal Streisand film, could score a perfect 100 points. In the end, all fifteen Streisand films will be ranked, in order to ascertain which are truly "the best."

Funny Girl
COLUMBIA PICTURES, 1968

Starring: Barbra Streisand as Fanny Brice; Omar Sharif as Nick Arnstein; Kay Medford as Rose Brice; Anne Francis as Georgia; Lee Allen as Eddie Ryan; Walter Pidgeon as Florenz Ziegfeld

Production: Directed by William Wyler; Produced by Ray Stark; Screenplay by Isobel Lennart; Musical Numbers Directed by Herbert Ross; Music by Jule Styne; Lyrics by Bob Merrill; Director of Photography, Harry Stradling; Production Designed by Gene Callahan; Costumes Designed by Irene Sharaff; Edited by Maury Winetrobe and William Sands

In her first film, Streisand would win the Oscar as Best Actress.

"I'm a bagel on a plate full of onion rolls!" — Barbra as Fanny in *Funny Girl.*

We're very much alike. Like Miss Brice, I find it hard to take advice from anyone. . . . I knew that I would do Fanny justice by being true to myself. Funny Girl is about me. . . it just happened to Fanny Brice earlier.
—BARBRA ON FANNY BRICE

More than any other picture, *Funny Girl* holds a special place in the Streisand filmography. It is the only screen adaptation of a Broadway musical which had originally featured Streisand as its star. It is also her film debut. Going in, loyal fans, seasoned movie critics, and even uninitiated filmgoers were tipped off by the media to expect something special.

And when the movie premiered on September 18, 1968, Oscar-winner William Wyler's direction, Herbert Ross's choreography, Jule Styne and Bob Merrill's score, and Ray Stark's overall production were indeed top drawer. The one major question which hung over the film concerned Barbra Streisand: Would she be able to duplicate her Broadway, recording, and television success on the silver screen? Would the dimensions of the big screen prove to be a sort of Mt. Everest in her climb up the show business ladder? Was she truly the first superstar—a term created to describe Streisand's multimedia stardom?

"Sadie, Sadie, Married Lady."

When Streisand began filming *Funny Girl*, she had thousands of questions about moviemaking, and while her zeal was viewed in some Hollywood corners as impudence, within the company, Streisand was earning respect and admiration. Wyler, no stranger to working with great actors and actresses, liked Streisand's energy and never considered her a temperamental star. "Women like Bette Davis and Barbra Streisand have a tremendous amount of spirit and vitality. Girls like that are difficult in the same way as I am difficult: they want the best. They're demanding on everyone, including themselves. . . . Barbra was wonderful, full of ideas and always questioning everything, every detail about making movies. I admire her perfectionism . . . of course we had disagreements, but always because we wanted the picture to be marvelous. She was wonderful really."

Streisand was stung by the talk in Hollywood about her trying to direct the director. It was blatantly untrue, yet the rumors persisted. Years later, she still couldn't understand why they were so pervasive. "I had opinions and I think people weren't used to women with opinions in the sixties, when I made *Funny Girl*. I adored William Wyler, I adored Harry Stradling, my cameraman. And I was shocked by what I read in the papers . . . that I was telling Harry how to light. Harry was a genius. Harry lit my first four pictures."

On *Funny Girl*, no one worked harder than Barbra; she was fearless in her determination to do whatever was necessary to make the picture a hit. Producer Ray Stark surrounded her with Oscar-winning professionals like costume designer Irene Sharaff (who had also been with the Broadway production) and cinematographer Harry Stradling. Early footage of costume and lighting tests were viewed immediately to determine how Streisand would look with her eyes thirty feet wide. People anticipated her performance, expecting it to be captivating and exciting, brimming with vibrancy and power; but there were doubts about how she would look in wide-screen Technicolor. Without a doubt, the answer was clear in the first scene. When Barbra stepped in front of the mirror and looked at her image, she quipped, "Hello,

Barbra was supposed to be an ugly ducking in *Funny Girl*; instead, she looked gorgeous.

The romance between Nick and Fanny was doomed, and audiences loved it.

Gorgeous!" It wasn't a lie. Streisand was gorgeous. *Funny Girl* dialogue referred to Fanny as an ugly duckling, but the close-ups showed the actress playing the role to be anything but. In *Billboard's* 1983 special issue, *The Legend of Barbra Streisand*, Herbert Ross—who had worked on *I Can Get It for You Wholesale* with Barbra and was assigned to stage the musical numbers for the film—remembered sitting next to her as she watched those first dailies: "She was terrified; it was the first time she'd ever seen herself on film. Well, on screen, she looked a miracle. How could anyone have known that her skin was going to have that brilliant reflective surface, that she would look radiant?" With the help of Harry Stradling's artistry, Barbra Streisand was more beautiful on celluloid than on stage or television. Film lighting accentuated her positives and could be manipulated to eliminate her negatives.

Funny Girl was the kind of mythic hit novelists write about in show-biz fiction. Streisand was canonized by most film critics as the greatest thing to hit the big screen since Judy Garland. Pauline Kael wrote in the *New Yorker*: "Barbra Streisand arrives on screen when the movies are in desperate need of her. The timing is perfect. There's hardly a star in American movies today. . . . The end of the movie, a long single take, is a bravura stroke, a gorgeous piece of showing off, that makes one intensely, brilliantly aware of the star as performer and of the star's pride in herself as performer. The pride is justified."

The positive news about *Funny Girl* outshone any lingering controversy about Streisand's supposed temperament. Columbia Pictures was ecstatic when the good reviews translated into big box-office numbers. As a road-show release—wherein filmgoers purchased tickets in advance for specific dates (as when attending a play or stage musical)—*Funny Girl* was one of the top releases of 1968 and ran through 1969, when Columbia put the picture into wide release and pointed up Streisand's Oscar for Best Actress (in a tie with Katharine Hepburn for *The Lion in Winter*).

Streisand's fans were expecting nothing less than a home run from the star. After all, by that

Director William Wyler and Barbra filming the opening scenes. They enjoyed a close friendship while shooting the movie and in years after.

time, Barbra had been remarkable in her ability to capture the spotlight, galvanizing the public with not only her voice but also her persona. On Broadway, in *I Can Get It for You Wholesale* and *Funny Girl*, she was seen as one of the greatest stars of the Great White Way. On television, her one-woman specials, *My Name Is Barbra* and *Color Me Barbra* in particular, were ratings and Emmy winners. Musically, her albums and concert appearances set records. When the Streisand fans saw Barbra onscreen for the first time, she simply lived up to their wildest dreams. *Funny Girl* would help to create more Streisand fans, as would many of her subsequent films.

Twenty-five years after its release, *Funny Girl* is remembered as one of the best film musicals of the late sixties, in an era when big-budget disasters like *Doctor Dolittle, Star!,* and *Camelot* were more commonplace than hits such as *The Sound of Music* or *Oliver!* Streisand's is also regarded as one of the finest screen debuts ever. No other movie star had had so perfect a vehicle to show off her talents. That she delivered such a gangbuster performance only enhanced her reputation. For most viewers today, *Funny Girl* is regarded as perhaps Barbra Streisand's best film, certainly her best traditional musical. It was nominated for eight Academy Awards, including Barbra's for Best Actress. It was a major surpise when on the night of April 16, 1969, there was a tie in that particular category (only the second tie in Oscar history).

Accepting the award from Ingrid Bergman, a noticeably touched Barbra had the perfect line to speak as she took hold of the golden statuette and addressed the millions of viewers: "Hello, Gorgeous!" She was understandably proud of her accomplishment and said in her acceptance speech that she was honored to share the prize with Hepburn. Years later, she reflected on how strong a year 1968 was for actresses. "When I was nominated for the Academy Award for best acting, there were five fabulous performances. I couldn't tell you mine was the best. I mean, Katharine Hepburn was great . . . and Joanne Woodward [*Rachel, Rachel*] was great. Vanessa Redgrave [*Isadora*],

Barbra Streisand's first musical number in *Funny Girl*, "I'm the Greatest Star."

Patricia Neal [*The Subject Was Roses*] . . . there were five great performances. . . . I wish they would just give plaques, say 'These are the best performances of the year.' "

Ratings:

Critical Approbation	23
Fan Reaction	25
Box-Office Appeal	22
Historical Perspective	25
Total Score	**95**

The display for the road-show engagement of *Funny Girl* at the Criterion Theatre in New York.

Streisand created a ruckus when she was cast as Dolly Levi.

Hello, Dolly!
TWENTIETH CENTURY-FOX, 1969

Starring: Barbra Streisand as Dolly Levi; Walter Matthau as Horace Vandergelder; Michael Crawford as Cornelius Hackl; Marianne McAndrew as Irene Malloy; E. J. Peaker as Minnie Fay; Danny Lockin as Barnaby Tucker; Tommy Tune as Ambrose Kemper; Louis Armstrong as Orchestra Leader

Production: Directed by Gene Kelly; Written for the Screen and Produced by Ernest Lehman; Associate Producer, Roger Edens; Dances/Musical Numbers Staged by Michael Kidd; Music and Lyrics by Jerry Herman; Director of Photography, Harry Stradling; Production Designed by John De Cuir; Costumes Designed by Irene Sharaff; Edited by William Reynolds

Originally, the matchmaker was not a particularly glamorous character to me. But I began to enjoy using the part of me that I said I'd rather not use, but knew would work for Dolly. . . . I have very little in common with Dolly, who fixes people up and lives other people's lives. I do share the fun she gets in bargaining and buying and can understand her experience as a woman who has loved and lost. A woman can be any age for that.
—BARBRA ON DOLLY LEVI

The film version of Broadway's *Hello, Dolly!* was marred by controversy from the beginning. Concurrent with Streisand's arrival in Hollywood in 1967, the news broke heralding Barbra as Twentieth Century-Fox's choice to play Dolly in the film version of the smash hit. Streisand was chosen instead of Carol Channing, who had originated the role, and who, in fact, had beaten Barbra for the Tony Award in 1964 as Best Actress in a Musical. In the role of Dolly Levi, a part considered matronly and far more mature than her twenty-seven years, Streisand left herself open to intense criticism. For starters, she seemed completely miscast. True, she would have no trouble singing the Jerry Herman score; but could Streisand make audiences believe she was a man-hungry, matchmaking, forty-something widow in turn-of-the-century New York? There were many, many doubters. Then there was the old problem of recasting the film version of a successful play rather than simply having the stage stars re-create their roles. But Ernest Lehman, producer of *Dolly!*, decided against giving such a plum musical role to Channing, who in his estimation

At twenty-seven, Barbra was much younger than most of the actresses who played Dolly Levi, and probably sexier as well.

Costume tests for Irene Sharaff's outfits.

the *Hello, Dolly!* shoot. While filming in Garrison, New York (doubling for Yonkers in the movie), Streisand and Matthau had a row on the set. Although it would later be characterized as a simple actors' spat over lines, news reports swirled that Matthau had humiliated Streisand, claiming he had "more talent in my farts than you have in your whole body." The Brooklyn girl responded with equal (if more polite) venom, suggesting her costar clean out his mouth with a bar of soap. The referee in the middle of all this was Gene Kelly, who did his best to calm his high-priced talent and get them back to work. With great diplomacy and charm, Kelly managed to do just that, and there were no other incidents. In 1983, Streisand recalled the blowup and the whole idea that she was trying to be the director: "I had an idea about something I thought would be funny involving a scene with a wagon. I said, 'What do you

had no movie box-office pull. Furthermore, he was not the only Hollywood executive who considered Channing a larger-than-life personality, one which did not translate well onto film. Whether Streisand said yes to *Dolly!* or not, Carol Channing wasn't going to play the role. Still, the Hollywood buzz preferred to paint Streisand in a negative light, as if she had purposely slighted Channing by taking the part. Whatever the circumstances, the aura surrounding *Hello, Dolly!* cast Barbra in a defensive posture: she would have to prove to critics and audiences alike that she could pull off the role of Dolly Levi.

Streisand also had to prove to her *Dolly!* director, Gene Kelly, that all the Hollywood gossip alluding to her being a temperamental star was just that—gossip. "I came into this picture with my dukes up because I'd heard [Barbra] might be uncooperative. But she's the most cooperative actress I've ever worked with," said Kelly in 1968. "She'll try anything to be good. There has never been any friction between us . . . and I predict there never will be." That was not the case with Walter Matthau, her leading man.

Controversy seemed to be the watchword for

Michael Crawford was hardly the seductive Phantom of the Opera when he played opposite Barbra in *Hello, Dolly!*

No expense was spared on *Dolly!* Even Barbra's trailer was overproduced.

think of this?' and people started to laugh. But all of a sudden, Walter Matthau closed his eyes and started screaming: 'Who does she think she is? I've been in thirty movies and this is only her second, the first one hasn't even come out yet, and she thinks she's directing? Who the hell does she think she is?' I couldn't believe it. I had no defense. I stood there and I was so humiliated I started to cry, and then I ran away. And what came out in the papers was Walter

Before making it big on Broadway as a performer/director/ choreographer, Tommy Tune *(left),* was Barbra's dance partner in *Hello, Dolly!*

Matthau complaining about Barbra Streisand."

Matthau had his version of the story, which he shared in a *Chicago Tribune* interview in 1974: "I tried very, very hard to be civil, but it's extraordinarily difficult to be civil to her. See, she's a soloist, and she likes to tell the conductor when the flutes come in, when the violins come in. When she 'acts,' she likes to tell the director when the other actors should come in. She pretends as though she's asking, but she's overstepping her boundaries. She should simply be the instrument of the director, and not be the conductor, the composer, the scene designer, the costume designer, the acting coach, et cetera. Unfortunately, that's what happens when people become stars before they learn their craft."

Kelly concurred more with Barbra's recollection than Matthau's. In Clive Hirschhorn's biography of him, Kelly said, "Barbra wouldn't do anything to anyone deliberately. Whatever Walter claims she did, like stepping on his lines or telling him what to do, was done out of sheer ignorance or insecurity. She's not that kind of person. She's ingenuous and unsophisticated, and hard as it may be to believe, naive. She is definitely not a girl who 'does things' to people."

Once the film wrapped, there were still more problems with the picture, more controversy. Because of an agreement with David Merrick, the film version of *Dolly!* could not be released until the Broadway production closed. A savvy theatrical producer, Merrick kept *Dolly!* running with innovative recasting: he hired Pearl Bailey to play Dolly backed with an all-black cast. In 1968, Merrick lured Ethel Merman (for whom the musical had been written in the first place) out of semiretirement to star in the show. Fox was forced to shelve *Hello, Dolly!* for a year until Merrick finally relented and allowed the film to open while Merman's production was still running.

When Streisand's *Dolly!* opened on December 17, 1969, it was greeted with many excellent reviews. Though some critics carped about the elephantine production, Barbra's obviously too-young Dolly, and Gene Kelly's "old-fashioned" direction, the picture was still, for the most part, well received—especially Barbra. Vincent Canby in the *New York Times* wrote: "*Hello, Dolly!* is not invulnerable to criticism, but I suspect that Barbra Streisand is. At the age of twenty-seven, and for the very good reason that she is one of the few, mysteriously natural, unique performing talents of our time, she has become a National Treasure. Casting her as Dolly Levi is rather like trying to display

Legendary song-and-dance man Gene Kelly guided Barbra through *Dolly!*

There was no chemistry between Barbra Streisand and Walter Matthau.

Yellowstone National Park in a one-geyser forest preserve. It doesn't really work, but most people probably couldn't care less." In the voting for the New York Film Critics Awards, Streisand came in second as Best Actress. Commercially, however, *Dolly!* had a tremendous burden to bear. The film wound up costing Fox nearly $20 million, a huge sum for that time. If the picture didn't pull in the kind of box office *The Sound of Music* did, it would probably never see a profit. *Dolly!* was not quite the success *The Sound of Music* was, but it did make some money. At best, it was a modest hit—hardly what Fox had anticipated.

To the growing legion of Streisand fans, *Hello, Dolly!* was a perfectly acceptable follow-up to *Funny Girl.* While the picture lacked the romantic pull of Streisand's debut, it did showcase the star in another musical . . . one as lavish and colorful as the great, classic MGM musicals in which Gene Kelly had starred. In many ways, Streisand was showcased in song and dance sequences like a latter day Judy Garland. For example, "Put on Your Sunday Clothes" builds to the moment where Streisand sings "All aboard!" in a manner very reminiscent of Garland in the "Atcheson, Topeka, and Santa Fe" number from *The Harvey Girls.* And when she sings "Love Is Only Love" (written for the movie), Barbra as Dolly moves around her

Daisy Gamble discovers she's something special in *On a Clear Day*.

On a Clear Day You Can See Forever
PARAMOUNT PICTURES, 1970

Starring: Barbra Streisand as Daisy Gamble/Melinda Tentrees; Yves Montand as Dr. Marc Chabot; Jack Nicholson as Tad Pringle; Larry Blyden as Warren Pratt; Bob Newhart as Dr. Mason Hume; John Richardson as Robert Tentrees

Production: Directed by Vincente Minnelli; Produced by Howard W. Koch; Screenplay and Lyrics by Alan Jay Lerner; Music by Burton Lane; Director of Photography, Harry Stradling; Production Designed by John De Cuir; Contemporary Clothes Designed by Arnold Scassi; Period Costumes Designed and Created by Cecil Beaton; Edited by David Bretherton

It was a really interesting piece about reincarnation and this kind of Jewish, Brooklyn girl who, in another life, was an English woman. . . . The two parts I play come close to my schizophrenic personality: the frightened girl as compared to the strong woman in me.
—BARBRA ON DAISY AND MELINDA

Everything about *On a Clear Day You Can See Forever* spelled success for Barbra Streisand . . . everything except the final execution. *Clear*

apartment, turning on the gaslight lamps, one by one. In *Meet Me in St. Louis*, director Vincente Minnelli had staged a scene very like this one with Garland and costar Tom Drake.

Fans were generally wowed by the film. Looking back, *Dolly!* still shines as a glorious production, full of gorgeous color and spectacular sets and decor. But the lack of chemistry between Streisand and Matthau is palpable, and the supporting cast is adequate at best, but certainly not memorable.

Ratings:

Critical Approbation	19
Fan Reaction	23
Box-Office Appeal	16
Historical Perspective	18
Total Score	76

The infamous black-sequined, see-through pajamas Barbra wore to the 1969 Oscars were actually designed by Arnold Scassi for her to wear in *On a Clear Day*.

Director Vincente Minnelli created a wonderful flashback for Melinda in a Dickensian orphanage.

Cinematographer Harry Stradling was once again asked to shoot the film, having become Barbra's favorite cameraman. Their relationship had grown into a mutual admiration society. "She's one of the greatest talents I've ever worked with," said Stradling at the time. "She knows photographic quality—what's good and what's not good. She knows what height the camera should be and just where it should be placed for her close-ups—and she's learned all this during the short time she has been in pictures. . . . The contours of her face give her a rare beauty. She's just a very wonderful, really brilliant woman."

The task of playing Streisand's leading man, the doubting psychiatrist who is turned off by Daisy Gamble but who falls in love with Daisy's past incarnation of Melinda Tentrees, was given to French actor-singer Yves Montand. Reportedly, Richard Harris and Louis Jourdan (who was in the stage version initially) were considered, but Montand was selected after a cordial meeting with Streisand. The two were considered a strong combination, but that

Day had been a modestly successful Broadway show; it had even produced a couple of hit songs—the title tune and "What Did I Have I Don't Have Now." The story no doubt appealed to Streisand, dealing as it did with a modern, New York woman who through hypnosis relives a past life as an elegant English lady. The duality of playing a commoner and a noble-woman would become a theme in Streisand's film work, and *Clear Day* offered perhaps the most striking dichotomy of any of her film characters.

With *Clear Day*, Streisand was also given creative input by producer Howard W. Koch, something she had had little of in her previous two films (despite rumors to the contrary). Therefore, when asked whom she would like to direct the picture, Streisand told Koch she'd always admired Vincente Minnelli, most especially his Oscar-winning musical *Gigi*. *Clear Day* creator-lyricist Alan Jay Lerner had written the screenplay and collaborated on the score for *Gigi*, and had great affection for Minnelli. Minnelli was signed, and as with her first two films, Barbra would be surrounded by all-star, veteran, behind-the-camera talent. Cecil Beaton, who had designed the costumes and sets for *Gigi*, was enlisted to do the period decor for *Clear Day*, and Barbra's choice for the task of creating her modern costumes was Arnold Scassi.

Jack Nicholson had yet to become a star, let alone a superstar, when he played Barbra's ex-stepbrother.

In an elegant Cecil Beaton costume for *On a Clear Day*, Barbra shows off her rarely photographed right profile.

notion would be dispelled once the production began. Although dynamic in his French films, Montand struggled in his few forays into American cinema. In 1960, he costarred with Marilyn Monroe in *Let's Make Love*, failing to create any onscreen sparks with the sex god-

As Daisy, Barbra had a modern, "groovy" outfit for every change of scene.

dess although they were having an offscreen affair. There was even less chemistry between Montand and Barbra.

But Barbra did have chemistry with her director. As filming commenced, Streisand and Minnelli developed a close friendship, one which carried over after the picture wrapped. In 1974, when Minnelli wrote his autobiography, *I Remember It Well*, he recalled working with Barbra: "I listened to what [she] suggested, and implemented some of her suggestions. I found her creative and bright, and we got along beautifully. When the picture ended, Barbra, having noticed that I take only cream in my coffee, presented me with an antique silver coffee service, the sugar bowl missing. On the coffee pot was inscribed, 'To Vincente, whom I adore . . . Love, Barbra.' On the creamer: 'You're the cream in my coffee.' It remains one of my great treasures."

It was while working on *Clear Day* that Barbra was awarded the Oscar for *Funny Girl*, and the producers were certain their film would benefit from her success. But Paramount Pictures was undergoing changes which would radically affect the future of *Clear Day*. Musicals were coming under severe criticism, primarily because of their big budgets. While a film like *Funny Girl* was a financial blockbuster for Columbia, *Hello, Dolly!* was something of a bust for Fox. Around Hollywood, the failed musicals—*Star!*, *Doctor Dolittle*, *Paint Your Wagon*, *Goodbye, Mr. Chips*—had studios rethinking their commitment to the genre. Like these other pictures, *Clear Day* was originally scheduled to be a road-show attraction, a marketing plan which was lucrative only if the film in question was perceived by the public to be worthy of an advance ticket purchase. It would be shown with an intermission; there would be an overture; souvenir programs would be sold in the lobby . . . it would be a special experience. All of this would rate a ticket buyer plunking down four dollars in advance.

Minnelli's original cut for *Clear Day* was nearly three hours long, which would not have been problematic if Paramount had gone ahead with the Easter road-show release. But

Paramount pulled a switch and decided to give the picture a general release. It recut the picture, against Minnelli's wishes, trimming it to 129 minutes. With little fanfare, *Clear Day* was released on June 17, 1970 . . . to mostly positive reviews. In fact, some of Streisand's personal notices were superb. *New York Times* critic Vincent Canby gushed over her, saying in his conclusion, "Talent such as hers will not break when tested; it becomes enriched."

Good reviews, however, did not translate into good box office. Perhaps influenced by the changing mood of the country in 1970—a time when flower power, Vietnam protests, and civil disobedience were becoming prevalent—a lavish, traditional musical like *Clear Day* seemed out of place. The modern sequences—with Daisy modeling a dazzling, chic outfit in every new scene—were dated as soon as the film premiered. It was the period sequences, the story of Melinda's life and death, which made the movie fly. But overall, the imbalance between Streisand's characters caused the picture not to work.

To loyal Streisand fans, *Clear Day* was an

Marc and Melinda dance together in a fantasy.

As Melinda, the guttersnipe turned elegant lady, in *On a Clear Day*.

unqualified winner, presenting to the star an abundance of material to be brought to life. The film was not only beloved at the time but remains a big favorite. It is also the only time, so far, that Streisand has costarred with two-time Oscar–winner Jack Nicholson. To those beyond the Streisand fandom, *Clear Day* has not aged nearly as gracefully. It is regarded as an interesting, flawed motion picture distinguished only by Minnelli's direction and Streisand's inspired performance in the period sequences.

Ratings:

Critical Approbation	23
Fan Reaction	24
Box-Office Appeal	9
Historical Perspective	10
Total Score	**66**

The Owl and the Pussycat
COLUMBIA PICTURES, 1970

Starring: Barbra Streisand as Doris Wadsworth/
Waverly/Washington/Wellington/Wilgus; George Segal
as Felix Sherman; Robert Klein as Barney; Roz Kelly as
Eleanor; Allen Garfield as Dress Shop Proprietor

Production: Directed by Herbert Ross; Produced by Ray
Stark; Screenplay by Buck Henry; Based on the play by
Bill Manhoff; Music by Richard Halligan; Performed by
Blood, Sweat & Tears; Directors of Photography, Harry
Stradling and Andrew Laszlo; Production Designed by
John Robert Lloyd; Edited by John F. Burnett

*For the first time, I'm doing without wigs,
hairpieces, dyes . . . it's just going to be me.
The me that's natural and very today.*
—BARBRA ON DORIS

After three blockbuster musicals, Barbra
Streisand planned a change of direction in her
screen career. Her fourth film would not be a
musical. In fact, Barbra wouldn't sing a note,
therefore testing whether audiences would have
any desire to see Streisand without benefit of
her golden vocalizing. Bill Manhoff's successful
two-character Broadway play *The Owl and the
Pussycat* was raucous and romantic, and as
translated to the big screen by writer Buck

Romance blossoms for Felix and Doris in *The Owl and the
Pussycat.*

Streisand as Doris, an actress and a model, and don't call her a
hooker.

Henry, the story was also bawdy, sexy, and
boldly provocative. There was even a nude
scene for Streisand. It was a daring move for the
Oscar-winner, placing her in a potentially make-
or-break situation. After all, in Hollywood, where
you're only as good as your last film, Streisand
was coming off of two less-than-spectacular
movies. If *The Owl and the Pussycat* was a dud,
would Barbra Streisand be labeled box-office
poison? Would she be relegated to appearing
onscreen only when she sang? It was a possibility, to be sure; but in retrospect, Barbra's move
away from the musicals and into mainstream
films was one of the wisest of her entire career.

Ironically, producer Ray Stark had signed
Streisand to a three-picture deal when he chose
her for the film version of *Funny Girl*. In fact,
he wouldn't let her have *Funny Girl* without the
commitment to do two more projects for his
company. But by 1968, Streisand was committed to *Hello, Dolly!* and *On a Clear Day*. Stark
wasn't thrilled. He sued Streisand for breach of
contract, claiming she had taken other work
while refusing the projects he'd offered her.
Before *Dolly!* had finished filming, Streisand set-
tled the dispute by agreeing to do *The Owl and
the Pussycat*, a property Stark had once envi-

sioned for Elizabeth Taylor and Richard Burton!

Onstage, Alan Alda had created the role of Felix opposite Diana Sands's Doris. For the film, Stark considered casting Sidney Poitier as Streisand's leading man. However, in Manhoff's play, racial differences between Felix and Doris are never explored. The casting of a black actress (Sands) against a white actor (Alda) was completely random. It was decided to drop the racial angle entirely, and George Segal was chosen as Barbra's romantic interest. In what was essentially a two-character piece, Segal and Streisand carried the film, and it was the comic chemistry they shared which made it work. Buck Henry adapted Manhoff's play, adding wicked humor and dropping much of the business which had bogged down the second act of the play. His script included hilarious bits for both Barbra and George: Felix's re-creation of a typical evening of television fare enacted through the glass of a fish aquarium, and Doris's near-violent reaction to Felix's short story, which began with these words: "The sun spit morning into Julian's face."

Unlike her two previous leading men—i.e., Matthau and Montand—Barbra had a terrific rapport with George Segal, and he was impressed with his leading lady: "There's a reason for all the excitement she generates. She's fantastic. I think there's Brando and there's Barbra. She has an unerring instinct; she's a natural phenomena. There's no acting; she is. And I think that's the same with Brando."

The Owl and the Pussycat broke the mold for Streisand. It established her as a comedienne: "the latest of our girls—our Normands, Lombards, Harlows, Blondells, Monroes," wrote Jack Kroll in *Newsweek*. And just as important, it established Streisand as a sexually alluring screen entity. Her subsequent success in love stories like *The Way We Were* and *A Star Is Born* was predicated on the notion—introduced in *Funny Girl* and solidified in *The Owl and the Pussycat*—of Streisand's sexual desirability.

Finally, the bottom-line results for *The Owl and the Pussycat* told the most important, immediate story: the picture was a big hit for Columbia Pictures. It proved to the movie exec-

The poster for *The Owl and the Pussycat* showed Barbra in Doris's modeling outfit. The *New York Times* and other newspapers refused to run the ad until the hands and heart were airbrushed out.

utives that in an era when female film stars seemingly were unable to establish any consistent box-office appeal, at least one woman appeared to be bankable. This bankability, established with *Funny Girl* and reaffirmed with *The Owl and the Pussycat*, paved the way for her continued preeminence in the motion-picture business throughout the seventies and eighties and into the nineties.

Playing Doris, the New York hooker with the

George Segal and Barbra had great chemistry in *The Owl and the Pussycat*.

Doris tries go-go dancing to make a living after she's evicted from her apartment.

Owl and the Pussycat by today's standards, there's little about the film which seems so provocative. However, it remains as funny today as it was when it was released. If anything, the picture succeeds as one of the better romantic comedies of the seventies, devoid of the topicality which mars many films from that time period. Although Segal and Streisand would only do one picture together, this one collaboration holds an allure similiar to that of Spencer Tracy and Katharine Hepburn's comedy *Pat and Mike*. It would have been interesting to have seen them reunited onscreen in another comedy, but for a number of reasons, that has yet to occur.

Ratings:

Critical Approbation	22
Fan Reaction	22
Box-Office Appeal	20
Historical Perspective	21
Total Score	**85**

In *The Owl and the Pussycat*, Barbra posed for sexy leather photos which were used to illustrate Doris's one porno film, *Cycle Sluts*.

proverbial heart of gold, Streisand opened the eyes of filmgoers who imagined her as perhaps another Julie Andrews or Audrey Hepburn. Doris was vulgar, crude, and in many ways low-class. She had a foul mouth and was blatantly aggressive when presented with a sexual situation. But Streisand's performance went beyond the superficial. She gave Doris a subtext of sweetness and vulnerability. She was a character who desperately wanted love and affection, and in the bookish, repressed writer Felix Sherman—played to perfection by George Segal—Doris found a man who could give her all that and become her mentor as well. It was a switch on the *Pygmalion* story, and under Herbert Ross's direction, *The Owl and the Pussycat* worked like a charm.

Fans had little trouble accepting Streisand in a racy comedy like *The Owl and the Pussycat*. While Barbra's nude scene (which was ultimately dropped because she thought it distracted from the comedy of the scene) and the R rating were shocking at the time, the film was truly a traditional romantic comedy. Looking at *The*

What's Up, Doc?
WARNER BROTHERS, 1972

Starring: Barbra Streisand as Judy Maxwell; Ryan O'Neal as Howard Bannister; Madeline Kahn as Eunice Burns; Austin Pendleton as Frederick Larrabee; Kenneth Mars as Hugh Simon

Production: Directed and Produced by Peter Bogdanovich; Screenplay by Buck Henry, David Newman, and Robert Benton; From a story by Peter Bogdanovich; Director of Photography, Laszlo Kovacs; Production Designed by Polly Platt; Music Arranged and Conducted by Artie Butler; "You're the Top" by Cole Porter; Sung by Barbra Streisand; Edited by Verna Fields

> *What interests me is how so many people liked it. I was embarrassed to do that film. I thought it was infantile humor.*
> —BARBRA ON *DOC*

After she took over a year off, Streisand's next film was a surprise. *What's Up, Doc?* was not one which had been developed and nurtured. In fact, it was a happy accident. Streisand's ex-husband Elliott Gould had begun filming a movie for Warner Brothers called *A Glimpse of Tiger*. Gould had creative differences with director Anthony Harvey, and the production was shut down. Within weeks, Warners announced that Streisand was going to take over the role; Gould's role would be rewritten for her. Having just seen a preview of *The Last Picture Show*, Streisand suggested Peter Bogdanovich direct. She was also anxious to do a straight drama. But Bogdanovich had other ideas. "I read the script and I didn't want to do it. It was kind of a comedy-drama with social overtones," said Bogdanovich. "But I told [Warner president] John Calley I'd love to do a picture with Barbra. 'Let's do a screwball comedy,' I said. I saw Barbra as sort of a Carole Lombard. . . . " Reeling a new story off the top of his head during a meeting with Warner executives, Bogdanovich sold them on his improvisation, which was, in many ways, just a variation on the 1938 Howard Hawks classic *Bringing Up Baby*. Barbra wasn't convinced—she had wanted to do a drama—but she was taken by Bogdanovich's energy and enthusiasm. In Streisand's career, *What's Up, Doc?* would turn out to be perhaps her most

Barbra and Ryan O'Neal were perfect comic foils in *What's Up, Doc?*, Bogdanovich's screwball comedy.

serendipitous, fortuitous film project.

Cast as the bumbling bespectacled musicologist Howard Bannister, whose life is turned upside down when he meets outgoing college student Judy Maxwell at a convention in San Francisco, was Ryan O'Neal. At the time, O'Neal was considered a capable, attractive dramatic actor, an Oscar nominee for *Love Story*, but he had never done comedy. Still, O'Neal was sexy, cute, and the complete antithesis of his leading lady. Would opposites attract onscreen?

Bogdanovich liked to demonstrate how to do scenes, here stepping in for O'Neal.

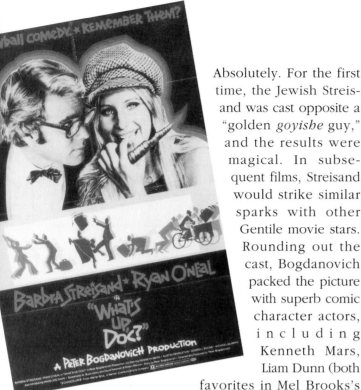

Absolutely. For the first time, the Jewish Streisand was cast opposite a "golden *goyishe* guy," and the results were magical. In subsequent films, Streisand would strike similar sparks with other Gentile movie stars. Rounding out the cast, Bogdanovich packed the picture with superb comic character actors, including Kenneth Mars, Liam Dunn (both favorites in Mel Brooks's comedies), and Madeline Kahn, in her film debut as Howard's repressed, controlling fiancée Eunice. Kahn nearly stole the picture from Streisand and O'Neal.

Doc was filmed in Hollywood and on location in San Francisco, and the mood was very up. Streisand and O'Neal were dating at the time, and their romantic scenes benefited from their offscreen rapport. The positive feelings extended to the large supporting cast as well. Actor-director Austin Pendleton was interviewed in 1989 and recalled his experience on *Doc*, in particular working with Streisand: "I never felt awestruck by Barbra because she's so natural, so real, so down-to-earth, a real mensch." Nevertheless, those ever-present rumors of temperament

dogged Streisand even on *What's Up, Doc?* In 1983, she told Gene Shalit on *The Today Show* that she had been horrified when it was reported at the time that she had stormed off the *Doc* set demanding a new bathtub. True, a new bathtub was needed, but it wasn't because of anything Barbra required. The one in the set was too low for the bubble-bath scene Bogdanovich envisioned.

Bogdanovich was riding high during the filming of the picture; he was basking in the glory of his acclaimed second feature, *The Last Picture Show.* Streisand and Bogdanovich were a winning combination, even though the actress clashed with the director about the film's comedy. Trying to recreate the elegant slapstick and romantic energy of the classic screwball comedies of the thirties, Bogdanovich often resorted to acting out scenes for his stars. O'Neal and Streisand did as he wished, but Barbra was sure the film wasn't funny. She told her director the picture wasn't going to work. Fortunately for

(Above) "A screwball comedy, remember them?" Millions did and they all went to see *What's Up, Doc?*

Doc was filled with character actors such as Austin Pendleton *(center)* and Kenneth Mars *(behind Barbra).*

Barbra as Judy Maxwell.

of Cole Porter's "You're the Top" over the credits and a snippet of "As Time Goes By" within the film. Streisand fans enjoyed the comedy and Barbra's chemistry with her leading man, but her look in *Doc* was also a revelation. As Judy, the playful college student, Barbra wore off-the-rack clothes and her hair long and parted down the middle, and her complexion shone with a healthy tan. It was a natural, youthful, and sexy look—far more realistic than her coiffed, costumed college kid in *Clear Day*.

What's Up, Doc? was a charmed project. Everything about it clicked. It made a lot of money, was enjoyed by most critics, and was loved by the fans, and, looking back, it still holds up very well.

Ratings:

Critical Approbation	22
Fan Reaction	25
Box-Office Appeal	24
Historical Perspective	23
Total Score	94

Streisand, she was wrong. Bogdanovich succeeded in creating a modern screwball comedy, one that was an immediate hit. A year after *Doc* was released, Barbra was still immune to its charms: "I hated it with a passion. What interests me is how so many people like it. I was embarrassed to do that film. I thought it was infantile humor and not one-sixteenth of the film that it was trying to emulate [*Bringing Up Baby*]. I only agreed to work with Bogdanovich because I had liked *The Last Picture Show* so much. But it was a disappointing experience."

Doc was released in Easter of 1972, going straight to the top of the box-office chart. Audiences welcomed the G-rated comedy, which included at least a couple of moments of Streisand singing—a fabulous version

What's Up, Doc? climaxed with a madcap chase through San Francisco.

Up the Sandbox
FIRST ARTISTS, 1972

Starring: Barbra Streisand as Margaret Reynolds; David Selby as Paul Reynolds; Ariane Heller as Elizabeth; Terry/Garry Smith as Peter; Paul Benedict as Dr. Beineke; Jane Hoffman as Mrs. Yussim; Jacobo Morales as Fidel Castro

Production: Directed by Irvin Kershner; Produced by Irwin Winkler and Robert Chartoff; Screenplay by Paul Zindel; Based on the novel by Anne Richardson Roiphe; Director of Photography, Gordon Willis; Production Designed by Harry Horner; Music by Billy Goldenberg; Edited by Robert Lawrence

There's a part of me that longs to stay home and be with my child, to discover the best butcher shops and bakeries, to feed the people I love. But there is another part of me that needs a form of expression other than bearing children, just as there is another part of Margaret that feels love is not enough. She'd like to go back to school, to write, to find where she belongs without putting herself into a niche. She doesn't want to be just a housewife or just a career woman.
—BARBRA ON MARGARET

Barbra Streisand realized very early in her career that to do the projects she wanted to do,

Barbra *(here with David Selby)* was more natural and restrained as Margaret in *Up the Sandbox*, a film she loved. It failed at the box office.

and to be the architect of her professional legacy, creative control was essential. In her negotiations with Columbia Records in 1962, she traded financial perks for total artistic control of her albums, and it would prove to be a key to her success. When agreeing to a $5 million deal with CBS for a series of television specials, again Streisand (and her chief adviser, personal manager Martin Erlichman) insisted on control of her product and ownership as well. She created a company called Ellbar (a blend of Elliott—as in Gould—and Barbra) to produce the shows and to control the rights for their future broadcast. Like her record contract, the television deal would show her to be a savvy, farsighted businesswoman.

When she came into the motion-picture business, Streisand did not have the luxury of that kind of control. She discovered that to take artistic responsibility for her work, and to acquire power over her product, would be an arduous task. In her first five films, she was simply a working actress. She had no intrinsic creative input, other than her choice of Minnelli to direct *Clear Day*, beyond what the producers and directors deigned to give her. Because of her eleventh-hour heroics with *What's Up, Doc?*—filling in for Elliott Gould when *A Glimpse of Tiger* fell apart—she was given par-

Margaret discovers Fidel Castro has a secret in *Up the Sandbox.*

ticipation points as well as her salary for the film, but a piece of the action was only one aspect of the power she was looking to attain.

Streisand, however, saw that if she was to be in control of her own movie destiny, if she was going to set the course for her future, she had to be in the driver's seat. She had seen how Ray Stark operated, wielding his contract with her like a hammer, forcing her to comply to the terms of the deal. She wanted to be free from the yoke of such obligations and took steps to do just that. In 1969, Streisand teamed up with Sidney Poitier and Paul Newman to form a company called First Artists Productions. Their goal was to produce and star in films which they would develop and nurture for themselves. They would be able to create their own work and not have to sit back and wait for a producer to come to them with an offer. It was a major step forward in the direction of independence.

Up the Sandbox was Barbra's initial release for First Artists. She was in reality the executive producer of the movie but relinquished the film credit and gave producers Irwin Winkler and Robert Chartoff responsibility for many aspects of the production. Streisand, however, did develop the project, Anne Richardson Roiphe's novel about a New York housewife torn between her desire to stay at home with her husband and children and her desire to pursue a life outside the house. To compensate for her conflicting feelings, Margaret fantasized a life filled with adventure and wild imaginings. When Margaret discovers she's pregnant, she is uncertain whether to have another baby (and be even more rooted in family life) or to have an abortion and take the opportunity to get beyond the four walls of her home. Roiphe's book was bold and telling, taking readers into the inner world of a typical, modern American woman. It appealed to Streisand in a variety of ways—especially since she was at the time the mother of a young child and was trying to balance her home life with work.

Unlike either *The Owl and the Pussycat* or *What's Up, Doc?*, *Sandbox* was not a flat-out comedy. It was much more of a drama, with some humorous elements: it mirrored real life.

An elaborate fantasy sequence shot in Africa was by and large cut from the final release print.

Streisand chose Irvin Kershner to direct, as his past work on films like *Loving* and *A Fine Madness* indicated he was well suited to the subtle blend of drama and comedy which *Sandbox* would need in order to succeed. Filming in New York and using many stage actors—including David Selby as Streisand's leading man—added a level of realism to the project. Selby had recently starred Off-Broadway in an acclaimed Vietnam war drama called *Sticks and Bones*, but his greater claim to fame was his role as Quentin Collins in the Gothic daytime drama *Dark Shadows*. "I had the break of working with Barbra Streisand, and the misfortune to be her husband—the villain of the piece—in her least popular film," Selby recalled in 1983. "I wouldn't have traded the experience. We were both at our peak, and she was very maternal, with kids all around her. . . . Some people felt I was intimidated opposite [her], but I wasn't. I was just being quiet and observing a lot. Actually, I looked at her as *Funny Girl*, so I had no trouble liking

One of Margaret's fantasies lands her in the park sandbox.

her. She was delightful."

Kershner also worked closely with cinematographer Gordon Willis. He wanted to enhance the film's realism with natural lighting, the antithesis of the glamour photography used in Barbra's previous movies. Remarkably, Willis's lighting resulted in the most striking photography of any Streisand film, and she never looked more beautiful. "I did lots of photographs and tests on her, and then I got this different visual quality on film," explained Kershner after the picture was completed. "She looks different in *Up the Sandbox*. Then as I got to know her, I found that there were personality elements that I had never seen in any of her previous work. And I encouraged these elements. What came across, after all, was a softness and a sweetness and a femininity. Then when we wanted to pull the plug and let the other out—let that strident thing out—the contrast was very pronounced. I think she has an enormous range. I think she could do anything."

To guide Roiphe's novel to the screen, Kershner brought in the Pulitzer Prize–winning playwright Paul Zindel (*The Effect of Gamma Rays on Man-in-the-Moon Marigolds*) to do the screenplay. Unfortunately, the delicate balance *Sandbox* tried to achieve, the blending of reality

and fantasy, drama and comedy, never coalesced. As the shoot progressed, Streisand realized the film was in trouble and discussed the problems with Kershner. The director was candid with Barbra: the script had not been ready when they began filming. He had hoped they would be able to work out the difficulties during production. Barbra was stunned: why didn't he just tell her the script needed more work before they began? Kershner had been told by people around Barbra (nobody was specifically named) that if he had done that, she would have pulled out of the picture. Barbra said that was simply not true, and Kershner conceded he should have trusted her. Streisand learned a valuable lesson based on this experience. In future film projects, especially ones as important to her as *Yentl* and *The Prince of Tides*, production would not commence until Barbra was sure the script was ready to roll.

Despite a moving, winning performance by Streisand, *Sandbox* was judged by critics to be a film with noble aspirations which failed to materialize on screen. The fantasy sequences were often triggered by subtle, nearly sublimi-

Streisand's obvious love of children is very evident in the film.

Barbra as Margaret Reynolds.

nal signals which were not picked up by most viewers. While the film boasted some memorable sequences, the finale was vague and unfocused. Filmgoers walked out of the theatre not knowing exactly what to make of the ambivalent ending. So while Barbra was admired for her effort to bring *Sandbox* to the screen and was recognized for her illuminating, thoughtful performance, the movie was not a success.

The box office was even worse; *Sandbox* could barely draw the die-hard Streisand fans. Among the fans, *Sandbox* fared only slightly better than it did with the public at large. It was a difficult film to digest on a single viewing, and yet it wasn't the type to automatically rate return visits. It would take the advent of home video, many years later, for Streisand fans to appreciate the qualities of *Up the Sandbox*. Home video also gave *Sandbox* a chance to be rediscovered from a historical perspective. The subtleties were easier to see when you could watch the film more than once. The fantasies, which were deemed to be the big selling point for the film (the print ads—playing on the success of *What's Up, Doc?*—boasted "What's Barbra up to? Up the revolution? Up the Zambesi River?") were not the strength of the picture at all. It was Kershner's cinema-verité look at domestic life, the camera focusing on the small, everyday moments between a mother and a child, a husband and wife, which were magical. *New York Daily News* critic Rex Reed voiced the kind of

glowing criticism Streisand earned for *Sandbox*: "Barbra has always fused in her work opposing elements of show biz razzmatazz and recognizable femininity in the girl-next-door. But there is a new vulnerability in her work here, a touching sweetness that makes you want to know the character instead of the actress. The maturity, depth and the vision she has achieved as a woman and as an actress are really joyous to observe."

Sandbox today is regarded as one of Streisand's unheralded gems. Its stock has risen with time, becoming something of a cult favorite. And it is still one of Streisand's. She never fails to mention *Sandbox* as a film of which she is very proud: "I liked *Up the Sandbox*. That was my statement about what it means to be a woman. It's what I wanted to say and I'm glad I said it even if it didn't make a nickel."

Ratings:

Critical Approbation	21
Fan Reaction	18
Box-Office Appeal	8
Historical Perspective	22
Total Score	**69**

Margaret shuts her mother up in *Up the Sandbox* by shoving her face in a birthday cake.

114

The Way We Were
COLUMBIA PICTURES, 1973

Starring: Barbra Streisand as Katie Morosky; Robert Redford as Hubbell Gardiner; Bradford Dillman as J. J. Jones; Patrick O'Neal as George Bissinger; Lois Chiles as Carol Ann; Viveca Lindfors as Paula Reisner; Murray Hamilton as Brooks Carpenter

Production: Directed by Sydney Pollack; Produced by Ray Stark; Screenplay by Arthur Laurents, based on his novel; Director of Photography, Harry Stradling Jr.; Production Designed by Steven Grimes; Costumes Designed by Dorothy Jeakins and Moss Mabry; Music by Marvin Hamlisch; Lyrics by Alan and Marilyn Bergman; Sung by Barbra Streisand; Edited by Margaret Booth

I fell in love with it instantly.
—BARBRA ON *THE WAY WE WERE*

Arthur Laurents met Barbra Streisand in 1962 when he was directing the musical *I Can Get It for You Wholesale*. It was Streisand's first Broadway show, and Laurents found her to be undisciplined, opinionated, brutally honest, perpetually late, and immensely talented. Ten years later, Laurents wrote the treatment for a film with Streisand in mind. It was called *The Way We Were*, and when Striesand read the

Barbra as Katie Morosky in *The Way We Were.* She came to a costume party as her favorite Marx brother, Harpo.

Streisand and Redford, in *The Way We Were,* were magical together, especially in the classic last scene.

breakdown, she knew that it was a film she wanted to make. She called Ray Stark, who was producing the movie, and told him it was a go.

It's not surprising Streisand was so enthusiastic about *The Way We Were.* The love story of Katie Morosky—a strong-willed, left-wing-liberal, Jewish ugly duckling—and Hubbell Gardiner—an all-American WASP jock with a perfect smile, a modicum of writing talent, and no moral convictions—was compelling, complex, and an emotional powerhouse. Even though the treatment was a mere few scenes, Streisand recognized in Katie the kind of character she could play better than anyone else in Hollywood. Laurents actually based the character on a woman he had known in college, but since he wrote it with Streisand in mind, there were custom-made features which excited her.

Of course, casting Streisand was only one-half of the equation in the making of a successful love story. Who would play Hubbell was the next great challenge of *The Way We Were.* Director Sydney Pollack had read *The Way We Were*, and to him only one actor could bring the right blend of superficial guile and inner angst to Hubbell Gardiner—Robert Redford. Redford, however, didn't care for the script. He felt the role of Katie was rich and well drawn but that Hubbell was a cipher, that there was no character to play. Streisand was in agreement with Pollack about Redford, but Ray Stark grew impatient waiting for the actor to decide. He was ready to go with Ryan O'Neal in the role and told Pollack either to sign Redford or O'Neal would get the part. Redford finally relented. He trusted in Pollack (with whom he had previously worked on three films) to bring the script up to speed, to improve the Hubbell character, and to build more conflict into the breakup of Katie and Hubbell.

There were extensive rewrites by Laurents, and the likes of David Rayfield and Francis Ford Coppola were brought in to work on the screenplay as well, much to Laurents's displeasure. In time, the characters of Hubbell and Katie became more balanced: a key scene was

Katie Morosky, a character screenwriter Arthur Laurents wrote especially for Barbra.

added in the second half of the film delineating the differences between the couple. By the time Streisand and Redford began shooting, *The Way We Were* had taken shape. And then something amazing happened: onscreen, Streisand and Redford were dazzling. Their differences—his cool, her heat; his detached aloofness, her visceral passion; his model good looks, her unconventional beauty—created a magic which can only be labeled "chemistry." Pollack and Stark knew they had the makings of a hit.

In September 1973, *The Way We Were* was previewed in San Francisco, but the first showing wasn't the smash Pollack and company had expected. In fact, it was a flop; audiences were disappointed with the picture. Preview cards indicated the movie fell apart somewhere in the second hour. Before the second preview later that same night, Pollack and editor Margaret Booth were in the projection booth cutting eleven minutes out of the movie. The new version worked brilliantly, and if the plot points about the Hollywood blacklist were left on the cutting room floor, audiences didn't seem to care. What mattered most, the cards revealed, were Redford and Streisand and the way they were in the movie.

When *The Way We Were* opened a month later, reviews varied: some critics loved the glossy, old-fashioned love story; others were put off by the lack of depth given to the politi-

When FDR dies, Katie loses her composure and then nearly loses Hubbell.

cal themes. Overall, though, most critics were enthusiastic. Streisand garnered nearly unanimously excellent notices, and she received her second Academy Award nomination as Best Actress. But the 1973 Oscar was given to Glenda Jackson for the comedy *A Touch of Class*. Redford's fears that his role would seem subordinate to Streisand's were realized when critics overwhelmingly called *The Way We Were* her film. A month after *The Way We Were* was released, though, Redford's next film, *The Sting*, was in theatres, and Redford was the top movie star in the country, with two box-office smashes. He was nominated for an Academy Award as Best Actor . . . but for *The Sting*, a clever period comedy, rather than for his work in *The Way We Were*.

One of the many special features of *The Way We Were* was the title song, sung by Streisand, which went to number one on the *Billboard* pop chart. It became the biggest song of the year and won not only the Oscar for Best Song (and another for Best Original Score) but also the Grammy for Song of the Year. The success and recognition of the song was part of the

Before filming, Barbra and Bob posed for some romantic publicity photos for *The Way We Were*.

In college, Katie was cursed with frizzy hair. But when Hubbell meets her years later in New York, he notices her new hairdo. "I have my hair ironed," she explains to him. "Does it hurt?"

movie's popularity, helping it to become one of the top films of 1973. Box office for it was so good that *The Way We Were* was credited with bailing Columbia Pictures out of a near-catastrophic slump at that time.

There was little doubt among Streisand fans—the die-hard and the pedestrian—that *The Way We Were* was fabulous. If anything, the character of Katie Morosky won Streisand more fans. In the same way Streisand was born to play Fanny Brice, she was also perfectly cast as Katie. But Streisand did more with the character than simply look the part and say the words. She gave Katie the kind of vulnerability and emotional depth which made her eminently sympathetic. Sitting in the darkened theatre, watching Katie tentatively undress and climb into bed with a sleeping Hubbell, one watched Streisand enact a range of feelings in a very few minutes onscreen which illuminated all the character's swirling emotions: her desires, her fears, her audacity, and, ultimately, her humiliation. It was just one scene in a film filled with many highlights, but it is the one which may best encompass the totality of her understanding of the character and her

Some things just aren't funny to Katie.

ability to share those feelings with the viewer.

Looking back, *The Way We Were* is now even more revered than it was in 1973. It seems that every year on Valentine's Day, magazines prepare a list of movies to rent to share with someone you love. Invariably, *The Way We Were* is the one film from the seventies which is always mentioned. Even critics who were once parsimonious in their praise of *The Way We Were* today employ revisionist history and find qualities in the film they didn't see the first time around. Without a doubt, the positive, historical view of *The Way We Were* has grown significantly.

Ratings:

Critical Approbation	20
Fan Reaction	25
Box-Office Appeal	24
Historical Perspective	25
Total Score	94

For Pete's Sake
COLUMBIA PICTURES, 1974

Starring: Barbra Streisand as Henrietta Robbins; Michael Sarrazin as Pete Robbins; Estelle Parsons as Helen Robbins; William Redfield as Fred Robbins; Molly Picon as Mrs. Cherry; Vivian Bonnell as Loretta; Louis Zorich as Nick; Richard Ward as Bernie

Production: Directed by Peter Yates; Produced by Martin Erlichman and Stanley Shapiro; Executive producer, Phil Feldman; Screenplay by Stanley Shapiro and Maurice Richlin; Director of Photography, Laszlo Kovacs; Production Designed by Gene Callahan; Music by Artie Butler; Song by Artie Butler and Mark Lindsay; Sung by Barbra Streisand; Edited by Frank P. Keller

You see, it's the kind of part I've always wanted, an intelligent, refined, sophisticated woman of the world.
—BARBRA ON HENRIETTA,
WITH TONGUE-IN-CHEEK

Pete and Henrietta Robbins, a young Brooklyn couple in *For Pete's Sake*.

In theory, following the dramatic success of *The Way We Were* with a light romantic comedy seemed like a good idea. However, where *The Way We Were* offered Streisand a chance to explore a character and grow as an actress, *For Pete's Sake* was little more than a domestic sit-com.

For Pete's Sake was a throwback to the movies Doris Day had made in the sixties—*Pillow Talk, The Thrill of It All, The Glass Bottom Boat,* and others. Henry (Henrietta) Robbins is a loving, happy homemaker who wants nothing more in life than to see her husband Pete succeed. Living in Brooklyn, Pete works as a cab driver, and Henry does odd jobs from the home, and together they struggle to put him through college. When Pete wants $3,000 to invest in the commodities market—he has a surefire tip about July pork bellies—Henry

"Zany Barbra" boasted the ads for *For Pete's Sake.* Zany meant riding a bull through the streets of Brooklyn.

Henri tries to reason with an unimpressed mobster.

goes to a loan shark to get him the money. When she can't repay the loan, her contract is sold to a variety of underworld types, and at each turn, Henry gets into more and more crazy shenanigans. All in all, *For Pete's Sake* strained to be humorous, rarely becoming more than just plain silly.

For Pete's Sake, which was originally called *July Pork Bellies* (then *For the Love of Pete*), was the first film produced by Martin Erlichman, Streisand's personal manager. Peter Yates, who had previously directed the Redford comedy *The Hot Rock* and Steve McQueen's action thriller *Bullitt,* came aboard to helm the picture. Yates had doubts about taking on the job, primarily centered on Barbra, having heard all the gossip about how difficult and temperamental she was. "I wanted to meet her to find out whether the stories [about her] were true. And I found they weren't, and indeed throughout the whole picture I found they weren't." To add realism and color to the movie, locations were scouted in Brooklyn. It would be Streisand's first official return to her hometown, and the publicity machine was wound up to make the most of it. But what the producers didn't count on was the overwhelming response Streisand's mere presence on the streets would create. The two-week shoot was cut back to one when the crowds proved to be too noisy and unruly.

For Pete's Sake was released in the summer of 1974, and with the high-voltage appeal Streisand was producing at that time, it was an immediate success. Most reviewers felt it was an innocuous comedy and basically critic-proof. Many simply gave it a pass and wrote it off as forgettable summer fare. But if the reviewers took little notice of For Pete's Sake, the same could not be said of audiences. In box-office receipts, if not a blockbuster, For Pete's Sake was a winner. To Streisand fans, For Pete's Sake was easy to take, and after the Sturm und Drang of The Way We Were, it wasn't unwelcomed. But the title song for the film was a throwaway for Barbra, and as a leading man, Michael Sarrazin was hardly in Redford's, Segal's, or even Yves Montand's class. In all, Streisand was the draw, and for most fans, that was plenty.

There's little about For Pete's Sake that has improved with time. It's still regarded as an innocuous, romantic comedy, with Streisand the main asset (or deterrent, depending on how one feels about her). Perhaps the only thing

time has done for the film is to make it seem more dated. Henry's willingness to debase herself in order to give Pete his chance was beginning to be an antiquated notion in 1974. With the perspective of twenty years, it now seems asinine. Feminism and political correctness would have reworked the comedy of For Pete's Sake in 1994, to be sure.

But more than that, For Pete's Sake is hardly the kind of film Barbra Streisand claims she wants to do. She has always had aspirations to do the classics—Shakespeare, Ibsen, Chekov—and while that is perhaps unattainable in todays's film market (unless you work with Kenneth Branagh), the record reveals Barbra has wasted film opportunities on throwaway entertainment like For Pete's Sake. Had it been an isolated case, it wouldn't matter much, but The Main Event falls into the same category as For Pete's Sake: formulaic comedies with only Streisand to recommend them.

With her Jon Peters-designed wig, Barbra had a fresh new look in For Pete's Sake.

Ratings:

Critical Approbation	16
Fan Reaction	20
Box-Office Appeal	20
Historical Perspective	14
Total Score	70

(Above) The poster promised madcap merriment. July Pork Bellies just wouldn't fly as a title.

120

Funny Lady
COLUMBIA PICTURES, 1975

Starring: Barbra Streisand as Fanny Brice; James Caan as Billy Rose; Omar Sharif as Nick Arnstein; Roddy McDowall as Bobby; Ben Vereen as Bert Robbins; Carole Wells as Norma Butler

Production: Directed by Herbert Ross; Produced by Ray Stark; Screenplay by Jay Presson Allen and Arnold Schulman; Director of Photography, James Wong Howe; Production Designed by George Jenkins; Costumes Designed by Ray Aghayan and Bob Mackie; Original Songs by John Kander and Fred Ebb; Music Arranged and Conducted by Peter Matz; Edited by Marion Rothman

> *She was a tough character and I tried to underplay so it would be truthful and real. She was a woman who was really successful and didn't have to yearn anymore. . . . The script is about really learning to accept ourself. . . . My Fanny Brice syndrome is ending. I think I'm younger now than I was then.*
> —BARBRA ON FANNY

James Caan was much more handsome and virile than the real Billy Rose, but in *Funny Lady*, he had the right style for Barbra.

Barbra pulled out all of her best schtick to play Fanny Brice one more time in *Funny Lady*.

In December 1965, Ray Stark announced that Barbra Streisand would star in the film version of *Funny Girl*. What Stark did not reveal in the press release was that he had also tied up Streisand for three other pictures. Streisand was a golden goose for Stark, proving herself a top box-office draw in the Rastar pictures *Funny Girl, The Owl and the Pussycat*, and *The Way We Were*. Stark and Streisand were a winning combination, and Ray knew it. So did Barbra, but she was eager to make her own films. When she worked as a hired actress, she wanted to be the one to choose "when," "if ever," and "in what project."

In 1974, Barbra Streisand was becoming more involved in developing her own projects. But Ray Stark hovered in the background, reminding her that she owed him one more movie, and that he had just the picture to bring their association to a slam-bang finish: a sequel to *Funny Girl* called *A Very Funny Lady*. Streisand was not impressed. She told Stark, in no uncertain terms, that it would take litigation to make her do a sequel.

Barbra's rendition of "Am I Blue?" was played for comedy, a takeoff of Fanny Brice's hit "He Hasn't a Thing Except Me."

edge, although it was also unfocused and meandering. But as far as his depiction of Fanny was concerned, Schulman's script showed the comedienne as tougher, more acerbic, more mature, and definitely not the wide-eyed, desperate kid she was in Isobel Lennart's *Funny Girl.* Schulman's script deglamorized romance: unlike Fanny's idyllic, fairy-tale courtship with Nick Arnstein, her marriage to Billy Rose was very much a pairing of two people who were too much alike. They couldn't pretend with each other; they recognized the best and worst of what they were in each other's eyes. Billy and Fanny understood and liked each other, but love and marriage was something they rarely found time for when they were husband and wife.

Streisand was intrigued by the screenplay, but she encouraged Stark to develop the material, to incorporate more of the real Fanny Brice, not just the version she had played in *Funny Girl.* Jay Presson Allen, the scenarist who had

Streisand's reaction was not too surprising. She had lived and breathed Fanny Brice for over two years onstage and for another year while making the movie. Streisand felt she had done *Funny Girl* and done it very, very well. What was left to say about Fanny that hadn't already been covered in *Funny Girl?*

Stark, one of the shrewdest producers in Hollywood—as well as Fanny Brice's son-in-law—had the answers for Streisand. He persuaded her to read Arnold Schulman's script, which dramatized Fanny's relationship with her third husband, songwriter-producer Billy Rose. Schulman's screenplay had a hard, wryly comic

Amid the yelling and screaming, Fanny and Billy found a little time for love.

Water wings and all, Barbra joins the water ballet for one of Herb Ross's more elaborate musical numbers.

Stark and company chose macho James Caan, fresh from his Oscar-nominated performance in *The Godfather*. Although Caan physically was all wrong for the role, his leading-man good looks were right when paired with Streisand. Caan also possessed an acceptable singing voice and could play the piano. Rounding out the cast was Omar Sharif, who was asked back in a cameo reprising his Nick Arnstein characterization.

As the film began shooting, a problem developed with cinematographer Vilmos Zsigmond. When Columbia executives, producer Stark, and director Ross viewed the rushes, the film looked dark and realistic. Zsigmond was trying to light the musical numbers the way they actually looked on stage in the thirties. Columbia demanded a change, and Zsigmond was replaced by the venerable James Wong Howe, coaxed out of retirement, and he brought the requisite splashy color and bright lights to the photography. He and Streisand hit it off—as she did with most cameramen, interestingly

The film's musical highpoint was Fanny's bitter look at her life: "How Lucky Can You Get?"

adapted the film version of *Cabaret*, was assigned to work on the screenplay. *Funny Lady*, as the script was now called, came together quickly, and Barbra agreed to do the film. She rationalized that she could show how Fanny had changed because of her marriage to Nick, and this time out, she could play her more like Fanny really was, rather than as an extension of Barbra Streisand. But it is more than likely that Streisand's greater motivation was to fulfill her contractual obligation to Ray Stark.

Herbert Ross, who had filmed the musical numbers for *Funny Girl* and directed Streisand in *The Owl and the Pussycat*, was assigned to direct the sequel; *Cabaret* songwriters John Kander and Fred Ebb signed on to write original songs for the film musical, and some Billy Rose songs would round out the score. To play Rose, the diminutive producer-songwriter-showman,

Fanny's most famous character was Baby Snooks, which she played on radio for many years.

enough—and Wong would eventually be an Oscar nominee for his work on *Funny Lady*.

Streisand also had a very good relationship with her costar, James Caan, then at the height of his popularity. Caan had a reputation for being pugnacious, in the same way Barbra had a reputation for being temperamental. Going in, the potential for fireworks between the two stars definitely existed. "You don't play with Streisand . . . you work your ass off. We worked very well together . . . and I mean worked hard. I liked her despite the stories the tabloids tried to spread. She's an interesting and ambitious woman—there should be more ladies like that in the world," Caan said in 1979.

Stark was determined to give *Funny Lady* a strong send-off. A live television special was planned at the Kennedy Center in Washington to benefit the Special Olympics, with Streisand appearing in concert with Caan. The special gave audiences a chance to see Streisand singing live for the first time in years . . . and anticipation for the film was very high. The fans were not disappointed. *Funny Lady* may not have had the romantic pull of *Funny Girl*, and the score lacked the original musical's hits, but it had a strong performance by Streisand and

lots of songs for her to sing. The critics were mixed in their opinions—many welcomed her in this character; but there were detractors, like the *New Yorker*'s Pauline Kael, who suggested Streisand had completely lost touch with the actress she aspired to become.

Box-office results were very strong, placing *Funny Lady* among the more successful films of 1975, although nowhere near the monster hit of the year, *Jaws*. With time, *Funny Lady* has shown its flaws. The production is bright and peppy, although there is little dramatic weight to the film. But *Funny Lady* has aged badly. Streisand's performance seems superficial and strained. Sadly, *Funny Lady* begs the question first voiced in *On a Clear Day*: "Why is the sequel never the equal? Why is there no encore?"

Ratings:

Critical Approbation	18
Fan Reaction	20
Box-Office Appeal	20
Historical Perspective	14
Total Score	**72**

A Star Is Born
WARNER BROTHERS–FIRST ARTISTS, 1976

Starring: Barbra Streisand as Esther Hoffman; Kris Kristofferson as John Norman Howard; Paul Mazursky as Brian Wexler; Gary Busey as Bobby Ritchie; Joanne Linville as Freddie Lowenstein; Vanetta Fields and Clydie King as The Oreos

Production: Executive Producer, Barbra Streisand; Produced by Jon Peters; Directed by Frank Pierson; Screenplay by John Gregory Dunne & Joan Didion and Frank Pierson; Based on a story by William Wellman and Robert Carson; Director of Photography, Robert Surtees; Production Designed by Polly Platt; Musical Concepts by Barbra Streisand; Edited by Peter Zinner

I wanted to explore relationships today, the role-playing today as opposed to that of the thirties and the fifties. . . . I don't believe in radical feminism, just in women, women taking hold of their own strength. It's very interesting in the liberation of women like Esther that they're not afraid to confront a male society; the women in the past [versions of A Star Is Born*] were very passive. I wanted Esther to want everything. That's what women want today, I think. They want families and careers—it's not one or the other.*

—BARBRA ON ESTHER

Barbra was ecstatic when she won an Oscar for writing "Love Theme From *A Star Is Born.*"

Barbra learned to play guitar for *A Star Is Born*, but cut the nails on only her right hand to do so.

There is no film in Barbra Streisand's filmography more controversial than *A Star Is Born*. There is also no other Streisand film more commercially successful. To this day, though, the notion persists that *A Star Is Born* was the worst thing Barbra Streisand ever did. In many ways, it was just the opposite.

In 1974, Streisand met Jon Peters. The ensuing romance between them was intense and all-consuming. Soon enough, Barbra and Jon were doing everything together. With her penchant for becoming obsessed with her work, involving him in these projects was a way to share more and more of her life with him. And Jon was anxious to expand his horizons. He wanted to test his acumen in the moviemaking business, and he was up front and honest about his desires. Their first collaboration was Barbra's album *ButterFly*. While not a huge hit for Barbra, it was not a disaster or a joke. But while they were working on that Streisand project, another, bigger one was bubbling under the surface.

Beginning in July 1973—before Barbra and Jon were a couple—a remake of the Hollywood classic *A Star Is Born* was developed by Joan Didion and John Gregory Dunne, setting the lovers in the modern world of rock 'n' roll. The finished script was called *Rainbow Road*, and the writers envisioned James Taylor and Carly

After John Norman's death, Esther performs at his memorial concert.

Simon in the starring roles. However, since neither of these talented singer-songwriters had any substantive film experience, it was highly unlikely they'd fit Hollywood's idea of casting. So the script began to circulate among Tinsel Town's top talent, and, naturally, Barbra Streisand was one of the first to see it. She didn't like it and sent it back to her agent. The screenplay then went from star to star all around town.

By the time Jon Peters saw a copy, it was dog-eared and coffee-stained. He had no idea Barbra had seen and rejected the script. With his enthusiasm for what the film could be, he sold her on his vision of the film. It was thanks to Jon that Barbra agreed to do the movie; her production company, Barwood Films, acquired the rights. Streisand would be executive producer of the film, and Peters would produce it.

Jon and Barbra began putting the picture together in earnest, starting with the screenplay. They were naive and brazen in the way they approached screenwriters, suggesting their personal love story be incorporated into the film. Often their energy and enthusiasm were off-putting. They went through a series of writers—including Didion and Dunne, and Jonathan Axelrod—and the original director, Jerry Schatzberg, dropped out soon after Streisand

and Peters jumped in. Barbra recognized in the midst of all this revolving-door activity that the ultimate responsibility for the film would rest squarely on her shoulders. If the film flopped, Jon wouldn't be blamed—it would be Barbra who took the hit. Furthermore, she would be criticized for more than merely making a bad movie; in this instance, she would be accused of allowing her heart to rule her head. Therefore, she took on more and more creative responsibility. She began to study the guitar so she could play it in the film, and worked on a musical score for the film, turning to composer Rupert Holmes (who had just worked with her on the album *Lazy Afternoon*) to write songs for it. If Barbra Streisand's name was going to be on the film as executive producer, then Barbra Streisand was going to take charge.

However, before the film could be given the green light by Warner Brothers, the screenplay had to be readied. All the versions combined still didn't add up to a finished product. It was at this juncture that Jon and Barbra became aware of Frank Pierson, who had just done a brilliant script for Al Pacino's *Dog Day Afternoon*. He was contacted to do a quick rewrite on *A Star Is Born*, but "in a moment of wild ambition," Pierson agreed to work on the script under one condition . . . that he could direct the film. Streisand was skeptical: Pierson

Esther Hoffman is introduced in *A Star Is Born* as one of a singing group called The Oreos.

In hair and makeup tests for *A Star Is Born*, Barbra considered blond frizzy hair instead of red.

had very limited experience as a director—a 1970 British picture called *The Looking Glass War* and the 1971 television movie *The Neon Ceiling*. Could he handle a film as difficult as this one, with a live concert sequence and more location shoots than studio sets? Pierson said he could do it, and Jon Peters was willing to take a chance on him; after all, Peters himself was a first-time producer. Streisand countered Pierson's condition with one of her own: he could direct only if he was willing to collaborate fully with the producers, i.e., Barbra and Jon. Pierson agreed, and the deal was done.

It was only during the subsequent weeks of filming that Streisand would discover that Pierson never intended to collaborate. He didn't care for Streisand's input, and when she tried to discuss scenes with him, she found him to be without ideas. After having worked with experienced directors like William Wyler, Vincente Minnelli, and Sydney Pollack, Streisand sensed that Pierson was in over his head. Peters and Streisand considered firing him but instead decided to stick it out.

While it was clearly a smart move to cast Barbra as the up-and-coming star, it was nearly as important that the right man be cast as the fading rock star. Streisand and Peters considered Elvis Presley, but when they saw Presley in Las Vegas, it was all too evident that he was in no shape to make a movie. If anything, he was too much like John Norman Howard, the character they wanted him to play. A far more savvy choice for the role was Kris Kristofferson, an actor and songwriter who was virile, handsome, and very talented.

Filming was difficult and complicated on *A Star Is Born*, especially the staging of a live concert at Sun Devil Stadium in Tempe, Arizona. The all-day shoot coincided with a real concert—put on by the film company—which was attended by 60,000 people, and a press junket for newspapers and magazines coast to coast was held to capture all the moviemaking excitement. The pressures of the day were overwhelming for the principals, most assuredly for Streisand, who had to deal with her fear of singing live as well as the details of shooting scenes. At one point, while filming scenes of John Norman Howard on stage, Kristofferson and Peters got into a shouting match; unfortu-

Recognizing that the love story would be a major selling point for the film, Streisand and Kristofferson posed in a variety of romantic combinations.

When Esther's career takes off, she gets her own television special — *My Name Is Esther.*

nately, it was within range of an open microphone. The press heard every angry word, and if the buzz for *A Star Is Born* wasn't already bad enough, the results of the concert only made the scuttlebutt worse.

Fortunately for Jon and Barbra, there were good things which came out of the Tempe shoot. The concert footage was magnificent: vibrant, realistic, and dramatic. When the studio viewed the rushes, whatever lingering doubts they had about Streisand and Peters's "$6 million home movie" were dismissed. It was clear *A Star Is Born* was a quality production. Included in the location rushes were scenes of Streisand in concert. She appeared before the crowd, and without revealing her own nervousness, nor the tumult going on behind-the-scenes, Barbra thrilled fans with renditions of "The Way We Were" and introduced two new songs from *Star*, "Evergreen" and "The Woman in the Moon." The audience response was overwhelmingly positive.

When the film wrapped—on time and under budget—*A Star Is Born* was still considered a doomed project, if one listened to Hollywood gossip. It was being called "Barbra's folly." Still, Peters and Streisand felt they had the makings of a hit. Frank Pierson had six weeks to deliver his director's cut, but it would be Streisand who would have the final one. When she finally got the film in her hands, she went to work on the editing. If there was, in Barbra's career, a defining moment in which she realized she wanted to be a film director, this may have been it. She was able to put the picture together, but it was not her vision. She was limited by Pierson's choices of which shots to print, which angles to shoot, and when the shot was right. It all came down to the director's point of view, and she was hampered by the lack of vision she felt Pierson brought to the film. In the end, *A Star Is Born* was compromised by the lack of collaboration between the director and the producers. It is only speculation, but given her quality work in *Yentl* and *The Prince of Tides*, one can only imagine what *A Star Is Born* might have been if Barbra had simply chosen to direct the film at the start.

Pierson's final contribution to *A Star Is Born* was an attempt to sabotage the opening. Six weeks before the scheduled release, Pierson published in *New York* and *New West* magazines

Film director Paul Mazursky (*An Unmarried Woman*) appeared as Brian, John and Esther's manager.

Just as Barbra and Jon Peters had built their home in Malibu, onscreen in *A Star Is Born* John and Esther create an adobe love nest in the Arizona desert.

an article called "My Battles With Barbra and Jon." The behind-the-scenes exposé about the filming of *A Star Is Born* was a clever calculation by Pierson. He took credit for whatever was good in the film while dishing out blame for the flaws to Streisand and Peters. The coverage was exactly what the film did not need, especially since "Evergreen" was climbing up the radio charts. Streisand and Peters countered with a live interview from the New York premiere party at Tavern on the Green, with Geraldo Rivera, to be broadcast on ABC televi-

On the set, Paul Mazursky, Joanne Linville, and Kris Kristofferson *(back to camera)* consult with the executive producer.

sion's *Goodnight, America*. With Kristofferson by their side, Barbra and Jon did their best to put forth a positive image of the film.

It was probably too late to persuade the critics. When *A Star Is Born* was reviewed the next day, it was given the worst notices of any Streisand film ever. Most reviewers did not look at the movie objectively, choosing instead to critique Streisand and Peters's involvement in the picture. In between the personal gibes and attacks, the picture was ridiculed. Some of the criticism was warranted, but much of it was not.

Despite all the negatives attached to the production of the film, and disregarding the overwhelmingly bad notices, audiences were anxious to see *A Star Is Born*. In addition, the curiosity was not reserved for the opening weeks alone. Remarkably, Streisand's faith in the audience's appreciation of the film that she and Jon had tried to create was rewarded. Viewers seemed to appreciate the movie, warts and all. Streisand fans, by and large, loved *A Star Is Born*, and the film won her thousands of new fans. The soundtrack album went to number one in the country, as did the single "Evergreen." So did the movie. Despite all the turmoil, Streisand and Peters delivered a money-making film, and the bottom line in Hollywood, ultimately, is box office. It wasn't Frank Pierson who was credited with the commercial success of *A Star Is Born* . . . it was Barbra and Jon.

For Kris Kristofferson, the experience turned out to be a major turning point. He stopped drinking after seeing the picture and has been sober ever since. In 1980, he looked back: "I feel an overwhelming gratitude and indebtedness to Barbra. I think she put together a real good thing for me. While we were making the film, though, there was a lot of fighting going on. I was trying to protect the integrity of the music part of it, and she was protecting her vision of the film. I'm sure that a lot of the communications were complicated by the fact that I was drinking a quart-and-a-half of tequila a day. But I'm real proud of the work that I did in it. When we finished the film, she gave me a little antique silver pillbox that I carry with me. She

The producers of *A Star Is Born* were joyous and relieved at the film's wrap party.

inscribed on it, 'A superstar is born. Let it be an easy birth. Love, Barbra.' And I thought at the time, 'Well, you're crazy. Why are you doing this to me because we were fighting all the time.' But it was an indication of her being able to look above and beyond the individual battles at what was [really] going on."

Today, the talk in Hollywood is about making another remake of *A Star Is Born*, this time a black version, possibly starring Whitney Houston and Denzel Washington. While it is still automatic, à la Pavlov's dog, for critics to call Streisand's *A Star Is Born* a debacle—one need only look at the television listing the next time it's televised—there would be no consideration of another *A Star Is Born* if Barbra's had not been such a popular success. The 1976 *Star* is not revered as are the 1937 Fredric March–Janet Gaynor and the 1954 Judy Garland–James Mason versions, but it is now more clearly seen as a film which touched the public with its strong performances and memorable music. To this day, *A Star Is Born* stands as Barbra Streisand's most popular picture.

Ratings:

Critical Approbation	5
Fan Reaction	25
Box-Office Appeal	25
Historical Perspective	12
Total Score	67

The Main Event
WARNER BROTHERS–FIRST ARTISTS, 1979

Starring: Barbra Streisand as Hillary Kramer; Ryan O'Neal as Eddie "Kid Natural" Scanlon; Paul Sand as David; Whitman Mayo as Percy; Patti D'Arbanville as Donna Rochester; James Gregory as Leo Gough; Richard Lawson as Hector Mantilla

Production: Producers, Barbra Streisand and Jon Peters; Directed by Howard Zieff; Screenplay by Gail Parent and Andrew Smith; Production Designed by Charles Rosen; Director of Photography, Mario Tosi; Music Score by Michael Melvoin; "The Main Event"/"Fight" written by Paul Jabara and Bruce Roberts and Bob Esty; Sung by Barbra Streisand; Edited by Edward Warschilka

Actually, I wanted to make a film reminiscent of the screwball comedies. They were about relationships. They weren't sentimental about love.
—BARBRA ON *THE MAIN EVENT*

Following the ordeal of *A Star Is Born*, Barbra was spent. The experience had been painful and exhilarating, arduous and exciting, intimidating—and liberating. It's no wonder that she retreated from work (for a while) and rested on the laurels she had earned for *A Star Is Born*.

Barbra as Hillary Kramer. "You know, the lady from Beverly Hills who lost all her money."

But as she began thinking about a new movie, Streisand had one compelling commitment still hanging over her head: she owed First Artists one more picture. If she did not get started on a project of her own choosing by a particular date, the corporation would assign her one. Streisand had *Yentl* in development, but as she would discover over the next few years, while attempting to get that film off the ground, there was tremendous resistance to Barbra's "little movie."

A comedy seemed to be in order, especially following the emotional drama of *A Star Is Born*, and Streisand began to think about what

Barbra decided to use her workouts in Gilda Marx's gym for a scene in *The Main Event*. The head between Barbra and Paul Sands is that of Roslyn Kind, Barbra's sister.

Barbra and Ryan continued their mutual admiration society when they reteamed for *The Main Event*.

kind of comedy she wanted to do. After viewing such vintage screwball comedies as *His Girl Friday*, Streisand liked the idea of examining the battle of the sexes in a modernized eighties version. Apparently, she liked screwball comedies much better in 1979 than she did in 1972. *What's Up, Doc?* screenwriters Robert Benton and David Newman vividly recalled a screening with Peter Bogdanovich before filming began where both Streisand and O'Neal were skeptical about the charms of *Bringing Up Baby*—or the prospect of trying to fit their images into roles modeled after Katharine Hepburn and Cary Grant.

Perhaps time had softened her view, because in 1979, she was very interested in doing a screwball comedy. Writers Gail Parent and Andrew Smith had penned an original screenplay for MGM, called *Knockout*, about a businesswoman who owns the contract on a boxer, and when she is wiped out by an unscrupulous accountant, all she has left is the pugilist. The script went into turnaround (Hollywood lingo for being put on the shelf) and ended up as a Barwood project. Streisand worked with Smith and Parent on the screenplay, having them inject more of her own personal philosophy about men and women into the story. And plenty of in-jokes were added, such as making the

The film's final clinch. Over the credits, Barbra's vocal of the title song proved to be a real knockout!

Streisand character, Hillary, the owner of a perfume company called Le Nez ("the nose" in French). Barbra then turned to her former *Doc* costar, Ryan O'Neal, to play the washed-up prizefighter. Barbra knew Ryan had once been an amateur boxer and had recently lost the starring role in *The Champ*, a remake of the thirties Wallace Beery–Jackie Cooper weeper, to Jon Voight. O'Neal was happy to have the chance to work with Barbra again, especially since their off-camera relationship had grown into an enduring friendship.

With Streisand and O'Neal and a screenplay, all *The Main Event* (as it was now renamed) needed was a director to bring it all together. For the first time in her career, Streisand was faced with the realization that she was not about to hand over a film she had nurtured and prepared, with full intention to follow through to fruition, without the assurance that the director would be her collaborator. As she learned from *A Star Is Born*, promises are made to be broken. Director Frank Pierson, on that film, had agreed to work with Streisand and Peters, only to renege on their understanding and stab them—as well as the entire project—in the back with his poison-pen article. The answer to Barbra's dilemma seems obvious in retrospect: direct the film yourself. But this was a leap Streisand was not yet ready to take in 1979.

Instead of taking the reins herself, she turned to Howard Zieff, an experienced comedy director (*House Calls* and *Slither*, among others).

Filming commenced on *The Main Event* without incident, although the script remained in a state of flux. Parent and Smith were kept on standby, often writing new scenes with Streisand the night before shooting. Still, there was a positive, happy atmosphere on the film, and press reports from the set said good things, as opposed to the bile which seeped from *A Star Is Born*. Streisand and O'Neal renewed their mutual-admiration-society memberships, and Zieff was accepting of the producers' [Jon's and Barbra's] efforts to inject their ideas into the picture. "Her company was backing the movie, and she had a concept she wanted carried out," Zieff recalled after the film was finished. "That's one kind of directing, as opposed to being an auteur. It was a box-office comedy, her reteaming with Ryan O'Neal. One thing about Streisand, she does make it into a family, and her enthusiasm is infectious, although few can match her stamina."

One of the sillier notions in *The Main Event* was Hillary's attempt to instruct Kid Natural on the pugilistic fundamentals.

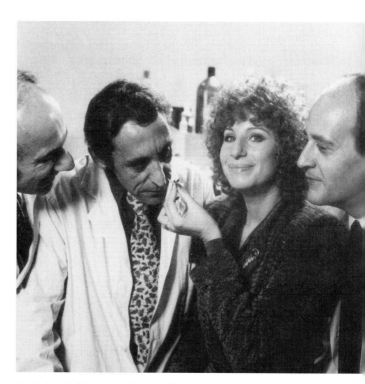

Opposites attract in *The Main Event* — Long Beach boxer Kid Natural and Beverly Hills exec Hillary Kramer.

As the head of Le Nez Perfume, Hillary had the best nose in the business.

To elevate the commercial prospects for the film, Peters encouraged Streisand to sing a theme song over either the opening or closing credits. He also lobbied Warner Brothers to release *The Main Event* during the lucrative summer season and garnered a hefty advertising budget to promote the film.

Once *The Main Event* was in the can, Streisand felt the film lacked a key element: a scene to explain the changed dynamics in Hillary and Eddie's relationship after they make love. Over the objections of Zieff and others, she and Ryan O'Neal went back to the studio to shoot the new scene, and Streisand directed it herself. The sequence was hardly a masterwork, but it was a nice, satiric turn on the traditional "morning after" scene. In two recent comedies, *When Harry Met Sally . . .* (1989) and *Boomerang* (1992), directors have dealt with modern attitudes about the morning after, but from a decidedly masculine perspective. Streisand's take in *The Main Event* was from the feminine point of view and was funny in an

entirely different way.

The final touch was the music. To take advantage of the disco craze which was at the height of its popularity, songwriters Paul Jabara and Bruce Roberts came up with a hard-driving dance tune, "The Main Event." It was then combined with Jabara and Bob Esty's campy vamp called "Fight." The medley was recorded by Streisand and placed over the film's climactic finale.

The Main Event opened big in 1,100 theatres nationwide. The song was filling the airwaves, and the movie was an audience winner. The critics, however, were decidedly mixed about Streisand and O'Neal's comic battle of the sexes. As she had suffered with *A Star Is Born*, Barbra was reviewed as much for her activities off-screen as on. Every single one of her physical features seemed to be under scrutiny: hair, nails, tanned complexion, even her rear end. And jabs at her appearance often were accompanied by a disturbing trend toward disrespect. Were critics picking Streisand apart because of what they saw on the screen, or were they being influenced by the notion that she was seemingly invulnerable to their criticism?

It did not seem to matter to viewers. *The Main Event* was one of the most popular films of the year. It did excellent box office, and at the time, it seemed as though Barbra was critic-proof. Streisand fans were generally pleased with a new comedy from her, but there was, along with it, a sense of disappointment. Having waited for three years since *A Star Is Born*, fans found *The Main Event* a lightweight follow-up. For an actress who spoke eloquently about her desire to stretch and grow, *The Main Event* seemed like a formulaic product, one not much more advanced than *For Pete's Sake*. And in retrospect, it was a step backward for Streisand.

There is an old show business story about a great actor who is dying. As he is drawing his last breath, a colleague kneels down and asks him, "Are you all right?" The actor opens his eyes and says, "Yes. Dying is easy. Comedy is hard." Comedy is also hard to come by in Hollywood. Streisand is a gifted, natural comic actress. She can take even subpar comedy and make it seem funny. *The Main Event* was not the comedy Barbra Streisand hoped it would be, but she and Ryan O'Neal did make it seem funny.

With twenty-twenty hindsight, there is no denying that *The Main Event* was a good move commercially: it made a lot of money. However, this is all that it was; it plays like a sitcom—a screechy one at that—and the screwball aspirations Streisand had for the picture are only achieved on the most superficial level.

Ratings:

Critical Approbation	10
Fan Reaction	18
Box-Office Appeal	20
Historical Perspective	10
Total Score	58

All Night Long
UNIVERSAL, 1981

Starring: Gene Hackman as George Dupler; Barbra Streisand as Cheryl Gibbons; Dennis Quaid as Freddie; Kevin Dobson as Bobby Gibbons; Diane Ladd as Helen Dupler; William Daniels as Richard Copleston

Production: Directed by Jean-Claude Tramont; Produced by Leonard Goldberg and Jerry Weintraub; Screenplay by W. D. Richter; Director of Photography, Philip Lathrop; Production Designed by Peter Jamison; Costumes Designed by Albert Wolsky; Music by Ira Newborn and Richard Hazard; Edited by Marion Rothman

I put on a blond wig and I went to a country-western bar in the Valley [in California]. I put on ridiculous clothes and many jewels and all this. . . . And as soon as I walked in the door, I heard someone say, "Oh, hi, Barbra!" And I thought, "I don't believe this! Now they think I have this lousy taste!"
—BARBRA ON HER PREPARATION FOR CHERYL

Perhaps stung by the criticism she received for *A Star Is Born* and *The Main Event*, Streisand was determined to commit herself to a film project with which she felt truly connected. There is a story conveyed in Karen Swenson's book on Streisand's career, *The Second Decade*, which clearly illustrates the impetus that lead her to begin preproduction on *Yentl* in earnest. While shooting *The Main Event* in Big Bear, California, she and Jon Peters got into an argument about the picture. Barbra remarked that she hated what she was doing (*The Main Event*) and that she should be making *Yentl*. Peters told her she would never make that film and instead they would work on something else. With fire in her eyes, Streisand told Peters she would make *Yentl* no matter what. She finished *The Main Event*, and with the same determination she had had when she began her career, Streisand launched into the intensive research and preproduction of *Yentl*.

While working on *Yentl*, Streisand's agent, Sue Mengers, was monitoring the progress of her husband, French director Jean-Claude Tramont, who was making his first American film, *All Night Long*. Things were not going

well. Tramont was unhappy with his leading lady, a young actress named Lisa Eichhorn. After three weeks of filming, it was clear to Tramont that Eichhorn and Hackman had no chemistry and that the film was in serious trouble. Lisa Eichhorn was fired from *All Night Long*, and in a surprising turn of events, Sue Mengers's top client, Barbra Streisand, was announced as her replacement. It was the first time Streisand had ever stepped into someone else's role, one which was clearly supporting, and speculation in Hollywood was that she was trying to do Sue and Jean-Claude a favor.

The part of Cheryl Gibbons was subordinate to Hackman's George Dupler, but befitting a

star with her box-office draw, Streisand would receive a salary of $4.5 million, plus fifteen percent of the gross, for twenty-four days of work. It was a staggering sum—more than any other movie star was getting at that time.

The money was surely flattering to Barbra, but more significantly, she knew it was important to change the critics' perception of her. And by taking part in a project which was not of her own design with an actor as admired as Gene Hackman, perhaps Streisand would prove to the media that she was not an egotistical self-promoter.

Cheryl was a departure for Streisand, very unlike other characters she had played. She created the part from the outside in, using the look of Cheryl—the blond bouffant hairdo, the lavender cigarettes, the omnipresent gold jewelry—to inform her persona. Although she was a late replacement to *All Night Long*, Streisand had little trouble becoming part of the company. Kevin Dobson, who played her husband Bobby in the film, was expecting the Barbra Streisand he had read about in gossip columns, the temperamental diva. "I don't understand how Barbra got such a bad reputation," said Dobson in 1981. "She's an artist, she's creative and was very willing to share. . . . She's a doll. She's been really delightful. My experience with her has been rewarding to the point where we sit down together and create, talk about the part and how to make it better. Let me tell you, she's all right."

Director Tramont and W. D. Richter did not rework the movie to make it a Barbra Streisand film. On the contrary, the starring role remained Gene Hackman's, and Streisand happily let him have the spotlight. The story was George's, not

With blond wig and a touch too much jewelry, Barbra created her version of Cheryl Gibbons from the outside in.

(*Above*) The poster for *All Night Long* promised audiences a wacky Barbra Streisand comedy. Sadly, that was not what the film was at all. *Barbra Quarterly*

In *All Night Long,* Gene Hackman and Barbra were quite charming together, although most people didn't get to see it.

Even if the film had had a great ad campaign, its appeal could not be changed. *All Night Long* did not click with audiences. Many Streisand fans were baffled by Barbra's character and unamused by the Richter screenplay. Critics were mixed, but a few went out of their way to appreciate Streisand's efforts to be part of the ensemble as opposed to overpowering the film with her superstar persona. With little positive word of mouth, mixed criticism, unfocused advertising, and nonexistent promotion by the stars, *All Night Long* disappeared very quickly. It stands as the poorest showing ever for a Streisand film.

Over time, there has been little change in opinion regarding *All Night Long.* It remains the

Cheryl's, and Streisand knew that from the start. Hackman was coming back from a three-year-long, self-imposed retirement from the screen. "We all had a good time," he told *After Dark* in March 1981. "Barbra and I had a real rapport, and I think the chemistry worked for us." The *All Night Long* shoot continued to be pleasant and uneventful . . . until the last few days. A strike by the Screen Actors Guild forced the production to close down before filming was completed. Three months passed before the stars could be brought back and the film wrapped.

All Night Long opened not with a bang but with a whimper. And in the brief weeks it stayed in circulation, it was an utter failure. Universal's marketing department seemed unsure of what to do with the film: the first print advertisement was bland and without imagination, simply listing the stars' names and the film's credits on a fire-engine-red background. The revised advertising campaign was a cartoon rendering of Streisand as a Marilyn Monroe-like vixen, sliding down a fire pole into the waiting arms of Quaid, Hackman, and Dobson. The poster suggested a madcap comedy along the lines of *What's Up, Doc?* or *For Pete's Sake,* perhaps. But there wasn't anything brassy and raucous about *All Night Long.* It was a subtle comedy, with a very European tone. In the same way that *Up the Sandbox* was sabotaged by its advertising, so, too, was *All Night Long.*

Shades of Zany Barbra? In *All Night Long,* Cheryl gets around the Valley on a Vespa.

Barbra took over the role of Cheryl Gibbons when the director decided Lisa Eichhorn wasn't working out.

did *Yentl* and proved to Mengers (among others) that she was not crazy to have wanted to make the film, she and Sue rekindled their friendship. However, they never resumed a professional relationship.

Ratings:
Critical Approbation	10
Fan Reaction	12
Box-Office Appeal	8
Historical Perspective	10
Total Score	40

strangest and quirkiest Streisand comedy, one which fortunately never hurt her career. The problems with the film may have been in miscasting Streisand as Cheryl, but that was a decision which originated from the producers and Universal Pictures. There was one significant casualty in the *All Night Long* affair: Streisand and Mengers dissolved their professional relationship after this film. Speculation was that Streisand resented Mengers expecting her customary ten percent agent's cut of Barbra's salary. But if, as some columnists suggested, Streisand had taken the role as a favor to Mengers—to bail out her husband's troubled film—then was it appropriate for Sue to expect payment? Mengers, interviewed years later in the *Los Angeles Times*, revealed the true nature of her split with Streisand: Mengers was dead set against Barbra doing *Yentl*. After Streisand

Shooting on a cool California night, Barbra bundled herself up in a blanket.

Yentl

MGM-UA, 1983

Starring: Barbra Streisand as Yentl/Anshel; Mandy Patinkin as Avigdor; Amy Irving as Hadass; Nehemiah Persoff as Papa; Steven Hill as Reb Alter Vishkower; Allan Corduner as Shimmele

Production: Produced and Directed by Barbra Streisand; Executive Producer, Larry De Waay; Screenplay by Jack Rosenthal and Barbra Streisand; Based on the Short Story "Yentl, the Yeshiva Boy" by Isaac Bashevis Singer; Director of Photography, David Watkin; Production Designed by Roy Walker; Music by Michel Legrand; Lyrics by Marilyn and Alan Bergman; Edited by Terry Rawlings

Yentl is like me. I'm like Yentl. She existed. I didn't invent her, but I do serve the material. In the Yeshiva of Brooklyn in Williamsburg, whether the teacher called on me or not, I'd always answer. I'd ask "Why?"—like Yentl.
—BARBRA ON *YENTL*

At the age of forty, Barbra Streisand finally got her little film *Yentl* to the screen.

From the time Barbra read Isaac Bashevis Singer's short story "Yentl, the Yeshiva Boy," she was inexorably tied to the material. She had an affinity for the character of Yentl, an understanding of the girl's unusual predicament, and

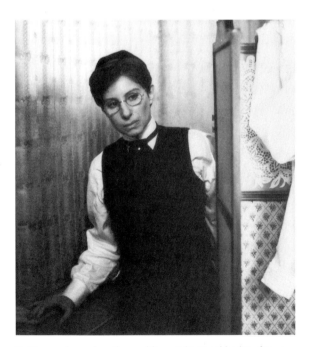

Getting undressed on the wedding night, Yentl had to figure out how to avoid sleeping with the bride.

a vision of what the story could be on film. More than any other project with which she had been associated, *Yentl* was her baby. She risked much more than money and time in her quest to bring this story to the screen: she put her reputation on the line. Creating *Yentl* called upon everything Barbra Streisand had learned in her years of filmmaking, employed all her known talents—decor, design, music, and acting—and forced her to develop new ones. Streisand was so committed to *Yentl* that everything else in her life was put on hold. *Yentl* became Streisand's magnificent obsession, so fierce was her determination and so unquenchable her desire to realize her dream. And in the end, she created a magnificent film . . . one which changed the world's perception of her forever, and more importantly perhaps, one which truly changed her.

It all began in 1968 when producer Valentine Sherry sent Streisand a copy of Singer's short story. Barbra had just finished filming *Funny Girl* and had two other films lined up, but she was so enamored of "Yentl, the Yeshiva Boy" that she told her manager she had found her next project. Ironically, it would take the star fifteen years to get the picture into theatres. In 1971, Streisand's publicist issued a press release announcing Barbra would star in a movie called *Masquerade*, based on Singer's short story "Yentl, the Yeshiva Boy." Ivan Passer was slated to direct, and Singer and Passer would write the screenplay. But *Masquerade* never materialized as described. Then, in 1975, a nonmusical stage version of the story, called *Yentl*, was presented on Broadway starring Tovah Feldshuh in the lead; it was a minor success. Still, no film version was forthcoming. For whatever reason, Barbra Streisand didn't seem able to get *Yentl* off the ground. She continued talking about this little film she wanted to do called *Yentl*, but the more she talked about it, the more it seemed like a pipe dream.

As time went by, three key factors lead to Barbra Streisand finally deciding to make *Yentl* and direct it herself: her experience as executive producer on *A Star Is Born*, her frustration with the kind of material she was being offered, and her coming to terms with her feelings about her father's death. Taking responsibility for *A Star Is Born* and seeing that film to fruition, Streisand discovered she had the ability and the desire to be a filmmaker. Moreover, after working first

On "his" wedding day, Anshel married Hadass to make Avigdor happy, as Yentl became even further enmeshed in a web of lies.

with Frank Pierson on *Star* and then Howard Zieff on *The Main Event*, Streisand felt she was as capable of directing as were they. As she contemplated the production of *Yentl*, Streisand realized the story was too important to her to trust to just any director. If she couldn't convince a topflight director to make this film with her, then she would make it on her own. At one point, she approached Milos Forman, who had won an Oscar for *One Flew Over the Cuckoo's Nest*. After hearing Streisand's ideas about *Yentl*, Forman told her what she probably already knew: she should direct the film herself.

In 1977, Barbra Streisand was the top female box-office star in the world. But rather than being at a point in her career where she was being deluged with great scripts, Streisand was frustrated. The material she was seeing did not excite her. In the midst of filming *The Main Event*, she wondered why she was making an inconsequential comedy when she could be making *Yentl*. As she neared her fortieth birthday, Barbra Streisand realized she could no longer wait for perfect roles to fall into her lap. She was squandering her opportunities. She had read *Yentl* all those years before and still had a passion for the material. As it said in the Talmud, "If not now, when?" Rather than wait for something better, Streisand decided it was

For *Yentl*, Barbra created the image of a good, loving, and wise father, then cast Nehemiah Persoff to play the part.

Donning her papa's tallis, Yentl dreamt of studying the Talmud like the yeshiva boys she saw all around her.

time to finally bring *Yentl* to the screen.

Streisand envisioned *Yentl* as a film with music. It would not be a traditional musical: the songs in *Yentl* would be voice over and would comment on the action. In 1980, she began working with Alan and Marilyn Bergman and Michel Legrand on the score for *Yentl*. Their collaboration would shape the film. It was a unique working experience, with the songwriters having the luxury of the star-producer-director standing by to try out any idea they came up with. Streisand took this incubation period a step further: she would enact scenes from the proposed film with all of them taking part. Some of the scenes were even videotaped so Streisand could get an idea of how it should be filmed.

As she became more and more immersed in preproduction for the film, Streisand traveled to Europe to scout locations. She dressed in the costume of a yeshiva boy and had coproducer Rusty Lemorande take home movies of her on the streets of Prague. The trip convinced her that filming *Yentl* on location in Europe was essential. Amazingly, once Stresand had committed to directing *Yentl*, she was fearless about the idea of shooting away from Hollywood studios, far from home with a foreign crew. She was also unfazed about making the film a musical, despite the fact that musicals are more difficult to do and more expensive. As *Yentl* progressed, Streisand would not be paralyzed by the challenges she faced; she would instead become empowered.

Perhaps Streisand's greatest challenge with *Yentl* was getting a studio to agree to finance the picture. Despite her proven box-office appeal and her track record as a responsible producer (*Up the Sandbox, A Star Is Born*, and *The Main Event*), Streisand was turned down by many studio heads. Columbia and Warner Brothers, two companies which had made an awful lot of money on Barbra Streisand films, said no to *Yentl*. Ultimately, Streisand convinced MGM-UA to green light the film, and in June 1981, official preproduction began on *Yentl*.

Streisand cast Broadway star Mandy Patinkin as Avigdor and Amy Irving as Hadass. Neither offered much box-office draw, but Streisand was working with only a $14.5 million budget. It was her name above the title which would bring in the crowds. While she may have preferred a top star for her leading man, the reality was that she couldn't afford a Michael Douglas or a Richard Gere. Gere, in fact, told Streisand he would only do the film on the condition that Streisand either direct or star—one or the other, not both. With Patinkin, Streisand did not have to choose, nor did she have to come up with a multimillion-dollar salary. And with Mandy she got an up-and-coming actor with just the kind

Yentl found saying goodbye to Hadass more emotional than she had imagined.

As a director, Streisand wanted to use the elements . . . even if it meant sloshing through the rain.

of passion and intensity the role called for. Veteran character actor Nehemiah Persoff was chosen to play Yentl's papa, and Steven Hill was cast as Hadass's father.

As her leading lady, Streisand selected Amy Irving. But Irving didn't really want to play just "another sweet, young thing." Once Irving met with Streisand, and Barbra gave Amy an inkling of the depth she saw in the Hadass character, she was sold on doing the film. Irving's performance would earn her an Academy Award nomination, and the experience of watching Streisand work gave her a unique perspective on the star: "I admire Barbra greatly. I've always been a fan of hers, but I got to know her as a fantastic human being with a great talent, lots of warmth and intelligence. But I wouldn't want to change places with her. . . . I honestly believe that stardom is very limiting and highly overrated."

The *Yentl* production set up shop in London, building sets at the Lee International Studios. Streisand rehearsed the company for two weeks, then principal photography began. But the bulk of the shoot was done on location in Czechoslovakia with a crew of Czech technicians. Throughout the shoot, Streisand dealt with the rigors of directing, acting, and producing as if she were born to it. There were no extraordinary delays, the production stayed

close to budget, and the novice director seemed to have great command of the material. The cast and crew were charmed by Streisand, and their affection for her made the production take on a family atmosphere. The one complaint heard on the set was that Streisand's commands as director weren't loud enough: they asked her to speak up! "She did everything but play the janitor," said Steven Hill, reflecting on Streisand's multiple jobs on *Yentl*. "She's a perfectionist. You'd do one scene over and over until you were climbing the walls, but then it was right. She exercised incredible control. I suspect that if she let it get out of control, everything would have collapsed. But it never did."

Once the film wrapped, the *Yentl* company had a party to celebrate the shoot. Streisand gave each crew member a silver necklace with a small charm of a book. On the back of the book was the inscription "Thank you. Love, Barbra." Streisand's gratitude extended beyond what the crew had done on the set. The cast and crew,

There's something Streisandesque about singing out on the bow of a ship, you know?

So, tell me, where is it written? Yentl can't help asking why.

unbeknownst to Streisand, had sent a letter to the British press in defense of her. They had been stung by the rumors the tabloids were printing while the production was in London. The letter read:

> The undersigned are currently working on the film *Yentl*, which is directed by and stars Barbra Streisand. Because she is subjected to so much adverse press, we thought it might interest you to know that during the last three months of rehearsal and filming, she has completely captivated us all. Though undoubtedly a perfectionist, in her dealings with everyone—producers, camera, sound, electrical crews, props, wardrobe, makeup, hairdressers, stage-hands, actors, extras, stand-ins—she has shared jokes, chats, and pleasantries each and every day. She appears to have no temperament, her voice is scarcely heard on the set, her smile is seen constantly. We have all worked with directors and stars who are the complete antithesis of Barbra Streisand, but whose antics don't reach the newspapers. This letter is entirely unsolicited, and is the result of our collective affection.

It was signed by the entire company and was only printed in one trade publication. It became one of Barbra Streisand's most prized possessions.

Postproduction on *Yentl* involved the complicated task of editing the film and perfecting the soundtrack. Streisand stayed in London, working diligently on both. Steven Spielberg—who was also in England working on *Indiana Jones and the Temple of Doom*—had dinner with Streisand on a few occasions, and the two film-makers discussed their pictures. When Spielberg saw *Yentl*, he called it perhaps the best directorial debut since Orson Welles's *Citizen Kane*. MGM-UA was enthusiastic about *Yentl* as well, and the film was scheduled for a holiday release. It was positioned as a major Oscar contender.

On November 16, 1983, *Yentl* premiered in Los Angeles and New York. Streisand received many glowing reviews, complimenting her production, her performance, her singing, and especially her direction. There were detractors, though, and their reviews accused Streisand of creating a vanity production. The *New York Times* suggested that Streisand had designers create special yarmulkes (skullcaps) for her to wear in the picture. But the positive notices out-

A movie triangle unlike any other: Avigdor loves Hadass, Hadass loves Anshel, and Anshel loves Avigdor . . . only Anshel is really Yentl.

Barbra's passionate singing was one of *Yentl's* greatest assets. This number "Papa, Can You Hear Me?"

"Directing is a great job for someone who likes to make decisions," said Barbra. Here the director consults with cinematographer David Watkin on the set of *Yentl*.

shone the negatives, and the film was listed as one of the best of the year on some critics' lists. However, the most vocal of the negative responses to the movie came from Isaac Singer. In an interview with himself in the *New York Times*, Singer ripped Streisand and the movie. He said his character did not sing and Streisand had taken too many liberties with his story, especially allowing Yentl to begin a new life at the end of the film by sailing to America and resuming life as a woman. In Singer's story, Yentl maintains the charade and wanders from yeshiva to yeshiva, continuing to study as a man.

Fans were undeterred in their appreciation and admiration for *Yentl*. It was an unqualified triumph in their view, and Streisand had taken a significant step forward in her development as an artist. The box-office results for *Yentl* were good if not spectacular. Studio heads who had turned down the project because they believed it lacked commercial appeal were probably shocked that the picture made as much money as it did. For a film with a decidedly ethnic appeal, *Yentl* may not have garnered the box-office receipts of *Fiddler on the Roof*, but it exceeded those of other Jewish-themed films like *The Chosen, Hester Street, The Frisco Kid,* and *The Jazz Singer.*

Yentl received six Golden Globe nominations, winning two: Best Director and Best Picture (Comedy or Musical). Streisand was ecstatic and surprised by the wins, and her acceptance speech was heartfelt and touching. Within weeks, however, a controversy occurred when *Yentl* received five Academy Award nominations. Although Streisand was eligible in no less than four categories—acting, direction, screenplay, and best picture (as producer)—she was shut out. The fact that Streisand was so clearly the auteur of the film made it seem to many that the Academy's refusal to recognize her efforts was a direct slap in the face. An official protest was launched on the night of the Oscars, and a picket line greeted stars as they got out of their limousines at the Dorothy Chandler Pavillion. Streisand admitted that she was disappointed to be overlooked but took

After telling Avigdor the truth, Yentl receives her first kiss.

vel, after the fact, at Barbra Streisand's great leap into the unknown—when she set out not only to produce and star in *Yentl*, but also to write and direct it. We could use a little more of that kind of audacity today." Canby's retrospective appreciation was not unique, and when Streisand lived up to the promise she showed as a director in *Yentl* with *The Prince of Tides*, her stock rose dramatically in the perception of both the public and the critics.

Ratings:

Critical Approbation	22
Fan Reaction	25
Box-Office Appeal	19
Historical Perspective	22
Total Score	88

great pride in the nominations the film did receive: Best Supporting Actress–Amy Irving; Best Original Film Score; two for Best Song ("Papa, Can You Hear Me?" and "The Way He Makes Me Feel"), and Best Art Direction. It won for Best Score, and stepping up to the podium, Marilyn Bergman spoke for her husband and Michel Legrand. She thanked the Academy, then thanked Barbra Streisand whom they felt deserved the lion's share of the credit for *Yentl*.

Had *Yentl* been an isolated, one-time-only project for Streisand, it would have been an interesting anomaly in her career, similar to perhaps her classical album. But *Yentl* was not a lark. It was a turning point. By choosing to direct and proving that she was very good at it, Streisand set a new course for her future. Before her career is through, Barbra Streisand will be as well known for her film directing as she is for her acting. And it was *Yentl* which opened the door and revealed a new facet in Streisand's multidimensional career.

On a broader level, the perception of Streisand changed dramatically because of *Yentl*. Even critics who did not like the film were impressed by her effort and her commitment. In 1986, Vincent Canby reflected in the *New York Times* on Streisand's accomplishment by comparing it to the films *Wildcats* and *Just Between Friends*. He wrote: "It makes one mar-

This sequence on the Charles Bridge in Prague was an impressive achievement for a first-time director.

Nuts

WARNER BROTHERS, 1987

Starring: Barbra Streisand as Claudia Draper; Richard Dreyfuss as Aaron Levinsky; Karl Malden as Arthur Kirk; Maureen Stapleton as Rose Kirk; James Whitmore as Judge Stanley Murdoch; Eli Wallach as Dr. Herbert Morrison; Robert Webber as Francis MacMillan; Leslie Nielsen as Allen Green

Production: Directed by Martin Ritt; Produced by Barbra Streisand; Executive Producers, Teri Schwartz and Cis Corman; Screenplay by Tom Topor and Darryl Ponicsan & Alvin Sargent; Based on the Play by Tom Topor; Director of Photography, Andrzej Bartkowiak; Production Designed by Joel Schiller; Music by Barbra Streisand; Edited by Sidney Levin

Claudia is honest, sometimes shockingly honest; but the truth is all she has and she refuses to give it up. This movie is not only about a courtroom case, it deals with the mystery of appearances. . . . We focus on the difference between conventional appearances and inner truth. People are not always simply what they seem to be. . . . The truth is not always polite. I found the lack of social etiquette, the directness, the honesty, absolutely engaging and refreshing. That's what I love about Claudia. Without fear of the consequences, she tells it like it is!

—Barbra on Claudia

The role of Claudia in Tom Topor's successful Off-Broadway play *Nuts* was among the most sought-after by Hollywood actresses. There simply weren't that many great parts for top female movie stars, and *Nuts* had a great one. The story of Claudia—a well-educated, high-priced hooker from a good family who kills a john in self-defense and then has to endure a competency hearing to prove she is able to stand trial for her crime—was at one time earmarked for Bette Midler, with Mark Rydell directing. Other actresses were in the hunt as well, including Susan Sarandon and Debra Winger. Streisand joined the fray when she began exploring film projects after her hiatus following *Yentl*.

Barwood Films was able to option the property, and Streisand teamed with Rydell to prepare the film for production. Topor worked on

Levinsky finds this sexy picture of Claudia when going through her apartment.

the screenplay, as did top-notch scenarists Darryl Ponicsan (*Cinderella Liberty*) and Alvin Sargent (*Ordinary People*). Because the role of Claudia was so demanding, Streisand chose not to direct the movie, but she would produce and

Barbra was only producing *Nuts* but was still curious enough to double-check what director Martin Ritt had in mind for a shot.

star; therefore, her influence was very great. At some point, Rydell reluctantly decided to back out of the project. Streisand then turned to veteran Martin Ritt, who had directed *Hud, Norma Rae, Sounder*, and *The Great White Hope*, among others, to helm *Nuts*.

Claudia Draper was the most

than Streisand, as well as top billing. With a budget of nearly $25 million from Warner Brothers, producer Streisand opted to go with Dreyfuss (who asked

openly sexual, vulgar, and hard-edged character Streisand had ever played. She was more brazen than Doris in *The Owl and the Pussycat*, because beneath Claudia's angry exterior was a well of deep, unspeakable pain; Doris did not have that kind of subtext. Claudia's vulgarity was a weapon, and she used her sharp tongue to lash out defensively at the world. For Streisand, who had almost always played characters closer to her own persona, Claudia was a reach. She would have to open up emotionally to reveal Claudia's pain, to allow the audience to get beyond her crust. Fortunately, she was up to the challenge. The shtick and mannerisms which had been so distracting in some Streisand films—*The Main Event* and *Funny Lady*, for instance—and threatened to limit her ability to grow as an actress, were no part of Claudia.

Richard Dreyfuss was chosen to play Aaron Levinsky, Claudia's reluctant attorney who becomes a vigilant seeker of the truth as the story unfolds. Dustin Hoffman and Streisand had talked about him playing the role initially, but reportedly, Hoffman wanted more money

for considerably less than Hoffman) and filled the remaining cast with Oscar-winning veterans—Maureen Stapleton and Karl Malden—and brilliant character actors—James Whitmore, Eli Wallach, Leslie Nielsen, and Robert Webber.

Nuts filmed some location scenes in New York, including the final sequence depicting

The film's cast included Oscar winners Streisand, Richard Dreyfuss *(seated right)*, Maureen Stapleton, and Karl Malden *(top left)*, and James Whitmore, Eli Wallach, and Robert Webber *(far left)*. Everyone in the cast was gray, except Barbra!

(Above) For *Nuts* Streisand posed for these graphic black-and-white pictures depicting Claudia behind bars.

Claudia's liberating exit from the courthouse. To accomplish those few minutes onscreen, traffic was stopped in lower Manhattan for half a day. New Yorkers were unimpressed with the lights and cameras, but the sight of Barbra Streisand was something else. Crowds lined the sidewalks and office workers hung out of windows to catch a glimpse of her. The few New York scenes added needed verisimilitude, despite the expense and difficulties, because the rest of *Nuts* was very stagebound—most of the action took place in courtrooms. Filming progressed in Hollywood, and *Nuts* was on time and on budget as the production wrapped.

As with Zieff and Pierson, Streisand's only problems with Martin Ritt came after the film had been completed. Ritt presented Streisand with his cut of the picture, but as in *A Star Is Born* and *The Main Event*, Barbra had final cut. Although Ritt knew this going into the project, it did not stop him from complaining about her version of the picture. He probably should have

"I'm a knockout...." Streisand practices her left for a scene.

reserved judgment until after the reviews were filed. Many critics listed *Nuts* as one of the best films of the year, and Streisand was considered a shoo-in for an Oscar nomination. In fact, Streisand and Dreyfuss were given uniformly excellent notices. The film reviewers who had problems with *Nuts* harped on the fact that the movie was too stagebound; others felt the material—which had been so controversial when *Nuts* played Off-Broadway in the seventies—seemed predictable and pedestrian in 1987. To this vocal minority, Claudia's revelation that her stepfather had repeatedly sexually abused her as a child was the fodder from a typical television movie. Overall, however, *Nuts* was given more critical picks than pans.

The film was released in time for Thanksgiving 1987. Considering that it was rated R (for adult themes and language) and that the plot was extremely dramatic, it was hardly holiday entertainment. And the forbidding, angry photograph of Streisand on the poster was anything but inviting. In fact, *Spy* magazine satirized the image in their "Separated at Birth" gag: Barbra's ferocious image was paired with a shot of Ron Perlman in full make-

Shooting in New York, Streisand was up to the challenge of playing Claudia.

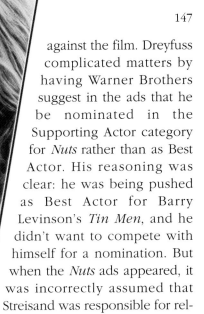

up as the beast from the television series *Beauty and the Beast*. But *Nuts* was considered an Oscar-worthy film, and Warner's thinking was to position it late in the year to keep it high in Academy voters' minds. The studio's other major release that season was Steven Spielberg's *Empire of the Sun*, which was as serious in tone as *Nuts*. While both films were definitely high quality and garnered good notices, neither could generate the kind of box-office appeal Warner expected from Streisand and Spielberg. *Nuts* failed to generate the receipts *Yentl* had, and that was considered not only subpar for Barbra but a failure.

The box office may have improved if *Nuts* collected a few Oscar nominations, and predictions were that Streisand and Dreyfuss were a good bet for Best Actress and Actor. However, the heavy promotional campaign to remind Academy voters about *Nuts* seemed to work

against the film. Dreyfuss complicated matters by having Warner Brothers suggest in the ads that he be nominated in the Supporting Actor category for *Nuts* rather than as Best Actor. His reasoning was clear: he was being pushed as Best Actor for Barry Levinson's *Tin Men*, and he didn't want to compete with himself for a nomination. But when the *Nuts* ads appeared, it was incorrectly assumed that Streisand was responsible for relegating Dreyfuss to the lesser category. In the end, Dreyfuss's strategy backfired totally: he wasn't nominated for either film. And *Nuts* was shut out. Streisand's performance, which was one of her most dynamic and moving, was passed over. Apparently, the negative backlash from the Academy she had experienced with *Yentl* was not a fluke.

The quality of Streisand's performance has not diminished with time, and if anything, the modest success of *Nuts* is seen as an enigma. Why didn't it do better at the box office? Why wasn't it nominated for a few Oscars? 1987 was an odd year: the one drama which captivated the public was *Fatal Attraction*, a far more fantastic one than *Nuts* or *Empire of the Sun*. The big winners all around were comedies, like *Three Men and a Baby* and *Good Morning, Vietnam!* Perhaps *Nuts* was simply a case of bad timing.

Ratings:

Critical Approbation	20
Fan Reaction	23
Box-Office Appeal	12
Historical Perspective	20
Total Score	75

Streisand confers with director Martin Ritt.

The Prince of Tides
COLUMBIA PICTURES, 1991

Starring: Nick Nolte as Tom Wingo; Barbra Streisand as Dr. Susan Lowenstein; Blythe Danner as Sallie Wingo; Kate Nelligan as Lila Wingo Newbury; Jeroen Krabbé as Herbert Woodruff; Melinda Dillon as Savannah Wingo; George Carlin as Eddie Detreville; Jason Gould as Bernard Woodruff; Brad Sullivan as Henry Wingo

Production: Directed by Barbra Streisand; Produced by Barbra Streisand and Andrew Karsch; Coproducer, Sheldon Schrager; Executive Producers, Cis Corman and James Roe; Screenplay by Pat Conroy and Becky Johnston; Based on the Novel by Pat Conroy; Director of Photography, Stephen Goldblatt; Production Designed by Paul Sylbert; Costumes Designed by Ruth Morley; Music by James Newton Howard; Edited by Don Zimmerman

As an actress, I was intrigued by the concept of the wounded healer I play in the film. I have encountered so many in the medical profession and other fields who spend their days helping other people, but are unable to cope with their own problems. Susan Lowenstein is enormously compassionate and nurturing to her patients, yet she goes home to an abusive husband and her own dysfunctional family.
—BARBRA ON LOWENSTEIN

Barbra related to the character of Dr. Susan Lowenstein, the wounded healer, in *The Prince of Tides*.

Following *Nuts*, Barbra was uncertain about her next film project. In development was *The Normal Heart*, Larry Kramer's searing play about the beginning of the AIDS epidemic, but there were difficulties with Kramer about the script. Since *The Normal Heart* wasn't ready to go into production, Streisand began to think about other properties. Sydney Pollack, Robert Redford, and Barbra had all discussed a sequel to *The Way We Were*, but a script had yet to be written which satisfied all three principals. Redford's production company, Wildwood Pictures, had optioned Pat Conroy's bestseller *The Prince of Tides*, and he was considering that as a future film. In 1988, Barbra became aware of the novel when Don Johnson, whom she was dating, brought it to her attention. It was a florid, sprawling, and intensely dramatic novel, and Streisand was immediately taken with it.

Conroy's novel tells the story of the dysfunctional Wingo family as told through the charac-

Shooting in the streets of Greenwich Village, Barbra had no problems asking New Yorkers to move their cars or help her with the film. *All About Barbra*

ter of Tom, a high-school football coach whose marriage is falling apart, when he receives word that his twin sister, Savannah, has tried to commit suicide. He travels to New York City at the request of Savannah's psychiatrist, Dr. Susan Lowenstein, to help uncover the root cause of her problems. Tom remembers those childhood memories that Savannah has blocked out, including the one incident which tore the family apart. As they get to know each other, Susan Lowenstein, who is also unhappy in her marriage, and Tom become aware of their mutual attraction. They develop a close rapport—in part because Tom begins coaching her son, Bernard—and eventually Tom and Susan fall in love. Their relationship is liberating for a while, but in the end Tom's wife, Sallie, asks him to come back to her. Tom is unable to leave his family and Southern life behind forever, and he and Susan break up.

As she had done with Katie Morosky in *The Way We Were*, Streisand recognized Lowenstein as a perfect fit for her. She wanted to do the film and approached Redford about their teaming

Pat Conroy suggested that Barbra cast her son, Jason Gould, as Lowenstein's son, Bernard.

Lowenstein and Tom Wingo's romance offers them both a chance to start one.

once again, this time for *The Prince of Tides*. Redford agreed to consider the possibility, and together they began to adapt the material. A first draft of the screenplay by Conroy—which amazingly had excised all the flashbacks from the novel—was rejected by Streisand. She had many ideas about how the novel could be successfully brought to the screen and felt that the flashbacks were essential to the telling of the story. At a certain point, Redford conceded that Streisand had a greater passion for the book than he did, and in a remarkably generous gesture he signed over the rights to her.

With Redford out of the project, Barbra's immediate concern was finding the perfect actor to play Tom, the central character in the story. It wasn't simply a case of finding a leading man to complement Barbra Streisand. In Conroy's novel, the Susan Lowenstein role was crucial but secondary to Tom: he was the one

Streisand was criticized for having too many schmaltzy moments between Wingo and Lowenstein, but moviegoers loved the romantic scenes.

who carried the weight of the story (in much the same way that Katie carried the story in *The Way We Were*). For a time, she had discussions with Warren Beatty. Beatty and Streisand had always wanted to work together but had never found the right film. But Beatty was just getting his long-awaited big-screen version of *Dick Tracy* into production, a film he had been developing for over a decade, and he wouldn't be available for a while. Kevin Costner was considered a viable choice for the role and certainly a box-office draw, but like Beatty, Costner didn't have an opening in his schedule. He went from *Dances With Wolves* directly into *Robin Hood: Prince of Thieves*, followed by *JFK*.

Streisand found her Tom Wingo when she saw Nick Nolte in the Sidney Lumet film *Q & A*. Although nearly unrecognizable in the film—he had dark brown hair and a bushy walrus mustache, was excessively overweight, and had high lifts in his shoes to make him stand not only two inches taller but with a tendency to lean forward—Nolte had the presence and power needed for Tom. Nolte was very interested in doing *The Prince of Tides*, and he was anxious to work with a woman. He wanted to explore the emotional qualities a female filmmaker brings to a project, as opposed to a male. To fit her image of Tom Wingo, Barbra had

Nolte lose thirty pounds and return his hair to blond. Nolte next went to work on perfecting the South Carolina Low Country accent. As a director, Streisand found Nolte to be very much her kind of actor: he did extensive research and was happy to work as long and as hard as she wanted. Nolte appreciated his director's tenacity in bringing authenticity and the essence of Conroy's book to the screen: "One thing about Barbra: there is not going to be a leaf unturned. We spent many days before we shot discussing masculinity, femininity, women, men, relationships, love, mothers, fathers. . . . She has an extreme amount of talent and in the early days she probably had to fight to exhibit that talent. She is one of the few females in her position. She's spent a long time in a man's world, which has given her a certain kind of toughness."

Rounding out the company, Streisand chose Blythe Danner as Tom's wife, Sallie; Melinda Dillon as Savannah; Jeroen Krabbé as Herbert, Susan's husband; and George Carlin as Eddie Detreville. There were two major castings which were somewhat controversial. Barbra decided to have Kate Nelligan play Lila Wingo, Tom's mother, in both the flashbacks as well as the present-day scenes. As Streisand explained, she couldn't find two actresses who could play the younger Lila and older Lila as well as

Nelligan could play them both.

For the part of Lowenstein's teenaged son, Bernard, Streisand cast her own son, Jason Gould.

The Prince of Tides filmed location scenes in Beaufort, South Carolina, as well as New York City. Streisand was more confident and contented directing this time around than she had been on *Yentl*: she never had to be asked to speak louder. Behind-the-scenes footage revealed a loose, happy set . . . and an affectionate one. Director of photography Stephen Goldblatt revealed a fact about Streisand that most people would never believe: "Barbra is never happier than when surrounded by twenty sweaty film technicians."

Columbia Pictures had considered, at one point, releasing *The Prince of Tides* for Christmas 1990. But in deference to Streisand—who wanted more time editing the film—studio

Streisand's direction resulted in Oscar nominations for both Nick Nolte and Kate Nelligan.

The Prince of Tides was shot on location in Beaufort, South Carolina, to capture the evocative scenes described in Pat Conroy's bestseller.

chief Frank Price announced *Tides* as a September 1991 release. But it soon became apparent to Columbia that *Tides* was too good to be released as anything but their prime 1991 Christmas film. It was a sure bet for Oscar nominations—along with Beatty's *Bugsy*—and perhaps the studio's strongest potential box-office lure. Even though a benefit premiere had already been scheduled in New York City, Columbia Pictures switched *The Prince of Tides* opening from September to December 25, 1991.

Fortunately for Columbia, the Hollywood buzz remained wholeheartedly positive about *The Prince of Tides*. Only film critic Caryn James of the *New York Times* took a cheap shot at Streisand and the film: in a fall preview section which listed the upcoming film releases, she depicted *The Prince of Tides* as "another *Hudson Hawk*, a vanity production." Frank Price took offense to her characterizing *Tides* as a bomb (which *Hudson Hawk* was) and asserted the studio's faith in both Barbra Streisand's direction and the film. By the time Christmas Day came around, Columbia's faith was rewarded. The critics were nearly unanimous in their praise of *The Prince of Tides*. For her direction, Barbra received even better notices than she

Lowenstein and Tom begin their relationship as doctor and surrogate patient; then they become friends and, later, lovers.

had for *Yentl*. As critic Janet Maslin pointed out in the *New York Times*: "*The Prince of Tides* marks Ms. Streisand's remarkably good job of locating the story's salient elements and making them come alive on the screen." Barbra's performance as Lowenstein also garnered praise (and too much concentration on the length of her nails), but the lion's share of acting honors were heaped on Nick Nolte. *The Prince of Tides* was a watershed film for Nolte, giving him the kind of recognition he had never before garnered. Kate Nelligan was also cited as one of the film's best assets; and in his biggest film role to date, Jason Gould was given excellent reviews. Not one word suggested he had been miscast or given the part only because of his connections to the director. Considering the critical brickbats hurled at Sofia Coppola when her father cast her in *The Godfather, Part III*, Barbra and Jason were treated to only bouquets of flowers.

The wonderful reviews were gratifying for Streisand, but she was also anxious that *The Prince of Tides* do well commercially. For an actress who had been the most bankable female star for a decade, she was not unaware of the

modest box-office results for her films in the eighties: *All Night Long* was a bomb; *Nuts* performed less than spectacularly; and only *Yentl* was a moderate success. In order to continue to

Coach Tom Wingo rekindles his love of teaching by coaching Bernard in the finer points of football.

have artistic freedom and control her film destiny, it was important for Barbra that *The Prince of Tides* exceed *Yentl's* box-office total and preferably compete as one of the top films of the year. Streisand did her part, doing dozens of interviews and appearing on television to promote the film. When she was asked why she was willing to talk, she revealed that she had not spoken to the media when *Nuts* came out and it probably hurt the picture.

With Streisand (as well as Nolte, Nelligan, and Jason Gould) promoting the film, the positive advance word, the excellent film reviews, and a romantic movie poster, *The Prince of Tides* should have opened strong. It did. And it continued to be one of the top films at the box office throughout the holiday season. With the additional boost provided by seven Oscar nominations, *Tides* nearly doubled *Yentl's* box office and became Barbra's second most successful film of all time. Streisand fans were ecstatic about *The Prince of Tides*. It was a worthy second directorial effort, following her debut with *Yentl*, and it was a film as passionate and vibrant, although set in a completely different time and place. *Tides* also had Barbra playing a romantic role in perhaps her best love story since *A Star Is Born*.

The seven Academy Award nominations for *The Prince of Tides* included Best Picture, Best Actor (Nick Nolte's first), Best Supporting Actress (Kate Nelligan), as well as art direction, musical score, cinematography, and screenplay adaptation. In yet another surprising omission, Barbra Streisand was not selected for either her acting or her direction. The morning after the nominations were announced, the media wondered how a film could be picked as one of the five best pictures without the director being recognized? (There was a similar occurrence in 1990: Penny Marshall's *Awakenings* was nominated as Best Picture, but her direction was overlooked.) Rather than focus on the negative, Streisand expressed pride in the nominations the film did receive and even attended the Academy luncheon honoring nominees, since she was the film's producer and, therefore, the person who would collect the Oscar if *Tides* won Best Picture. If Barbra was hungry for the approbation of her peers, she received it when her work for *The Prince of Tides* was recognized by the Directors Guild of America. Streisand's DGA nomination marked only the third time in its history that a woman had been cited. Although she did not win, Streisand felt the nomination itself was a great honor.

Though *The Prince of Tides* didn't win a single Oscar, its reputation has only improved in the few years that have passed. It was a superb adaptation of a well-loved novel, a rare occurrence in the past decade. And for Barbra Streisand, the overall glad tidings the film engendered only improved her stature in the film community. With time, the reputation of *The Prince of Tides* will undoubtedly gain luster.

Ratings:

Critical Approbation	22
Fan Reaction	25
Box-Office Appeal	24
Historical Perspective	21
Total Score	**92**

The Best of the Best . . . and the Rest Ratings

Film	Box-Office Ranking	Score
Funny Girl	5	95
What's Up, Doc?	3	94
The Way We Were	6	94
The Prince of Tides	2	92
Yentl	7	88
The Owl and the Pussycat	11	85
Hello, Dolly!	9	76
Nuts	10	75
Funny Lady	8	72
For Pete's Sake	12	70
Up the Sandbox	14 (tie)	69
A Star Is Born	1	67
On a Clear Day . . .	13	66
The Main Event	4	58
All Night Long	14 (tie)	40

Box-Office Status and Oscar Success of Streisand Films

Film	Year	Box Office*	Oscar Nominations/Victories
A Star Is Born	1976	$37,100,000	4/1 (Best Song)
The Prince of Tides	1991	$36,100,000	7/0
What's Up, Doc?	1972	$28,000,000	0
The Main Event	1979	$26,400,000	0
Funny Girl	1968	$26,325,000	8/1 (Best Actress)
The Way We Were	1973	$22,457,000	6/2 (Best Song, Best Score)
Yentl	1983	$19,630,000	5/1 (Best Song Score)
Funny Lady	1975	$19,313,000	5/0
Hello, Dolly!	1969	$15,200,000	7/3 (Sound, Art Direction, Score)
Nuts	1987	$14,100,000	0
The Owl and the Pussycat	1970	$11,645,000	0
For Pete's Sake	1974	$10,662,000	0
On a Clear Day . . .	1970	$5,350,000	0
Up the Sandbox	1972	$4,000,000	0
All Night Long	1981	$4,000,000	0

*According to *Variety*, this figure reflects domestic film rental, i.e., that portion of box-office ticket-sale grosses remitted by exhibitors to the film's distributor.

6

Family Ties

arbra Streisand has always been a very private celebrity. Although she is one of the world's most famous personalities, she has guarded her personal life vigorously, judiciously revealing only those aspects of her past and present relationships which come to bear on her professional life. With *Yentl*, for example, Barbra was exploring her feelings toward her father, Emanuel Streisand. To explain ideas within the film, what drew her to the material, her motivations, and the choices she had made as a director, Barbra opened the door to her past. By dedicating the film to her father ("and all our fathers"), she begged the questions, and within her own boundaries, she supplied the answers.

But more often than not, Barbra Streisand's personal life—especially involving her immediate family—is a closed book. It is occasionally the subject of gossipy speculation, when writers or reporters attempt to uncover the "real" Barbra. (No interviewer has ever had the opportunity to know Streisand well enough to find the real Barbra, and chances are, if and when she is revealed, it will be Streisand herself who writes the book.) When Mike Wallace interviewed Barbra on *60 Minutes* in November 1991, it was his persistent questions about her mother which pierced Barbra's self-protective armor of control. Wallace reduced Streisand to tears by telling her that Diana Kind had said that Barbra was incapable of being close to the people who love her. Barbra admitted that she had no idea why her mother had said that.

It is difficult to comprehend the complexity of Barbra's relationship with her mother; she was the main force in the launching of Barbra's career, but only in the most negative way. Diana Kind never believed in her daughter. She never thought Barbra was pretty enough or had enough talent to make it in show business. Barbra was always pragmatic about her mother's lack of encouragement, turning it into a plus rather than a minus: "My mother egged me on. The more she said I'd never make it, that I was too skinny, the more determined I got. . . . I'm thankful to my mother. My desires were strengthened by wanting to prove to [her] that I could be a star."

In 1969, soon after Barbra had won the Oscar for *Funny Girl*, her mother reflected on her daughter's desire to go into show business, telling the *New York Times*: "I thought it would be a terrible fiasco." Diana learned with time that Barbra was too determined, too intelligent, and too talented not to achieve the goals she had set for herself. By 1983, Diana had more perspective on her daughter: "Barbra is like her father in many ways. She, too, is always striving for knowledge." Emanuel Streisand was a man of many great accomplishments, even though he died much too young at age thirty-five. He was the assistant superintendent of schools at the Elmira Reformatory in New York; graduated from New York University; earned a PhD in education from Columbia University; wrote a doctoral thesis in psychology (analyzing the mother-son relationship between Diana and Sheldon). In school, he was Phi Beta Kappa; a member of the debate team, the chess club, the math club; and was interested in drama and fencing. He was also a lifeguard and dreamed

Even under pressure of shooting her first film, Barbra always tried to spend time with Jason.

someday of moving to California and becoming a writer.

When asked to speculate about what her father would have thought of Barbra's theatrical plans, Diana told the *Ladies Home Journal*: "I hate to think. Of course, he would idolize her, but he would have been as alarmed by her going into show business as I was." Nearly thirty years later, Diana Kind still seems mystified that Barbra's gambit paid off. In 1993, while appearing on *20/20*, Barbra related that when informing her mother of the $20 million salary the MGM–Grand Hotel was giving her for just two New Year's concerts, Diana had asked, "Why would they pay you so much money to sing?"

Diana Kind's amazement at Barbra's accomplishments is perhaps rooted in her own frustration. Like Barbra (and Diana's younger daughter, Roslyn Kind), Diana has a beautiful voice, and as a young woman, she considered a career in music. Her voice is a lyric soprano, and in her prime, according to her daughters, she sounded like Jeanette MacDonald. But Diana was too

Barbra's sister, Roslyn Kind, and mother, Diana Kind.

It was Diana's doubt and skepticism that pushed Barbra to prove herself. The Randy Emerian Collection

frightened to pursue a show business career, opting for a more traditional role as a wife and mother. In a 1991 interview, Barbra candidly spoke about her relationship with her mother: "I love her more now than I ever have in my life. I think she also loves me. I understand even her jealousy. Why shouldn't she be jealous? Here's a woman who wanted a career for herself, but she was too frightened, too shy."

So when she saw her headstrong older daughter moving from Brooklyn to Manhattan at age seventeen, Diana was afraid for her. Then, when Barbra became successful, starring in *I Can Get It for You Wholesale* on Broadway two years later, Diana was stunned. Rather than risk giving Barbra a swelled head, Diana always minimized Barbra's achievements. This may have also been a way to protect her less successful daughter, Roslyn Kind. When Roz made her show business intentions known to her mother, Diana gave Roz her wholehearted support and encouragement instead of raining on her parade. Nine years younger than her half-sister, Roslyn chose to follow in Barbra's footsteps before she graduated from high school. But unlike Barbra, who had the acting bug by the time she was fourteen, Roz didn't pursue acting and singing by going out and getting

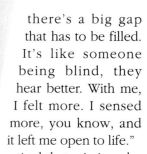

BARBRA AWAITS MILLION $ BABY

Barbra to Star as Mom.

some experience, by learning her craft. Barbra spent summers in stock theatres, painting scenery, sweeping stages, and doing bit parts. It was humbling, naturally, but for an aspiring Sarah Bernhardt, it was heaven. Roslyn had a different apprenticeship, if you could call it that. She attended dozens of performances of *Funny Girl* at the Winter Garden and became a perfect mimic of her sister.

Perhaps it was just the differences in the two personalities. Barbra had a dysfunctional childhood, one which definitely scarred her. As Barbra said in 1991, "If I had a normal childhood, I probably wouldn't be who I am today." Because of Manny Streisand's untimely death, Barbra was deprived of the fatherly love every little girl needs to nurture her. Barbra felt she was, in many ways, like a handicapped child: "When a kid grows up missing one parent,

there's a big gap that has to be filled. It's like someone being blind, they hear better. With me, I felt more. I sensed more, you know, and it left me open to life."

And that missing element was never replaced by a surrogate father. When Diana married Louis Kind in 1949, seven-year-old Barbra was a skinny, precocious little girl with a keen mind and an active imagination. She and Louis did not hit it off. Little Barbra perceived Louis as a threat to her relationship with her mother, a wedge to drive them apart. Since Diana was the only parent Barbra had, it was understandable that she was bratty to Mr. Kind and possessive of her mother. Rather than find a way to reach the child, Louis Kind was turned off by her antics and simply turned his back on her. "He disliked me," Barbra recalled in a 1968 *New York Post* interview. As Barbra would reveal when she was an adult, she could not recall a single conversation with her stepfather. It's entirely possible they didn't have one. "I had a terrible relationship with my stepfather. I was abused as well, not sexually, but emotionally. . . . I don't think this man asked me how I was in the seven years we lived together," Barbra recalled in 1987.

In 1951, Diana gave birth to Rosalind (changed to Roslyn when she was an adult), Louis's baby, and Barbra became even more of an outsider in her own family. Roz was the apple of her mother's eye—a fat, happy, blond, blue-eyed baby with a healthy appetite and a sweet disposition—and even though Barbra loved her baby sister, she had to feel envious of the attention Roz received. Louis would refer to

When Roz performed at a club in Hollywood, Barbra was there as the supportive big sister.

(*Top*) The New York *Daily News* was the first of many newspapers to dub Jason Barbra's Million Dollar Baby.

his daughter Rosalind as the beauty; Diana's other daughter, Barbra, was the beast. Out of this fray was Barbra's other sibling, her older brother Sheldon. Shelley was a teenager by the time Roz was born; he already had a foot out the door. There wasn't much Shelley could do for Barbra, even if he were aware that she was victimized by Louis Kind's emotional abuse. Brother and sister would become much closer when they were older, but that wasn't the case when Barbra was young: "We were never close because we're eight-and-a-half years apart. He was a grown-up when I was a little kid."

Louis Kind and Diana separated in 1953. Years later, when Barbra became a Broadway star in *Funny Girl*, gracing magazine covers and winning Grammys for her albums, Louis actually came to see her show. " . . . And that morning, I woke with a scratched cornea, so I almost couldn't go on," Barbra remembers. "But this was the day my stepfather was coming to see me, so I could go on. And he sent me the only thing he ever gave me, a basket of candies. And after all these years, I just [now] threw it out."

While Barbra was dazzling the world and fulfilling her childhood dreams of stardom, her little sister Roz was going through her own personal hell. "I had a serious weight problem as a child; at fourteen, I weighed 189 pounds. I was alone a lot when I was young. I was very self-conscious about my appearance, and I'd come home after school, watch television, eat, and go to bed. I was in a shell, with just a few close friends. My mother understood how I felt." At the opening night party for *Funny Girl* in 1964, Roz recalled that she looked so matronly that she was mistaken for Barbra's aunt!

Despite her weight, Roz was a natural performer. She

(Above) For a *Vogue* fashion layout, Barbra cuddled with Jason on the set of *Hello, Dolly!*

would sing and entertain at family gatherings—something Barbra had always been shy about doing. Like Barbra and Diana, Roslyn had a lovely voice, and by the time she was sixteen, she decided to become a singer. Interestingly, Diana was all for it; she didn't tell Roslyn to learn to type so she could get a job in the school system, as she did to Barbra, nor did she laugh at her belief that people would pay money to buy her records or see her in a nightclub. And she surely didn't tell Roz that she wouldn't make it because she was too fat to be a star. No, Diana was Roz's biggest fan. She saw no reason why her baby girl couldn't become a big, big star—perhaps as big as Barbra. Consequently, whenever she was interviewed about Barbra's success, Diana would take the opportunity to promote her undiscovered daughter, Roslyn.

But Roslyn never wanted Barbra's kind of stardom, and she never displayed the determination and desperation Barbra had to get it. "My sister had great incentive," Roslyn commented in a magazine article in 1969. "She wanted to make it and she was willing to do anything to get ahead. I'm different. I don't have that kind of chutzpah, and I can't push the way she did." Roz also saw up-close the trappings of her sister's success: the lack of privacy, the demands on your time, the constant pressure to maintain your status.

So while Roz and Barbra shared the same mother and grew up in the same home, their childhood experiences were vastly different. Roz didn't have the need to become a star; Barbra did. Once Roslyn set her goal to become a singer, she lost the weight (and kept it off) and was able to pursue her career without fear of rejection based on her looks. Barbra, on the other

hand,
has always needed to
express herself and to
receive the approbation
of the audience—about
her looks, her talent, her entire persona.

Roslyn Kind has yet to make her mark in the entertainment business. She made two RCA albums, *Give Me You* and *This Is Roslyn Kind*, as well as appearing on television shows like *Gimme a Break*, doing countless talk shows, and performing in nightclubs. She even made a low-budget feature film which was never released, *The Underachievers*. Her most successful project to date is a Broadway revue called *Three From Brooklyn*, which played in autumn 1991. It included a song set by Roz which began with her coming onstage singing "People," followed by an up-tempo "I've Got to Be Me." Barbra has been accused of not helping her sister to become a bigger star, but that's not entirely true. "There's a certain limit to what you can do. . . . I was able to get her a record contract, but I can't make them play the record," Barbra revealed in 1977. Still, Barbra has had the power to use her sister in any number of film or record projects, and she has never done it. When Roz appeared in *A Star Is Born* and *The Main Event*, it was strictly in the background as an extra.

In December 1993, Diana Kind celebrated her eighty-fifth birthday with a party given her by her daughters. Diana lives in a comfortable Beverly Hills condominium with Roslyn, not far from Barbra's Holmby Hills house. Despite rumors to the contrary, Diana's life is very comfortable and secure, and she is not estranged from Barbra. In fact, at Barbra's triumphant 1993 New Year's shows at the MGM-Grand, most of her family was in attendance, including Roslyn, Barbra's son Jason, and Diana Kind. In a moment of rare public intimacy, Barbra introduced her mother to the audience: "Without this woman, I would be nothing. Literally nothing"—a statement which is obvious but nonetheless very, very true.

In 1967, soon after giving birth to her only child, Jason Emanuel Gould, Barbra told *Look* magazine, "If I were a queen, they would never find fault. I produced an heir." Jason may bristle at the notion that he's inherited a throne, but if Barbra's ideals, beliefs, and philosophy are her most valuable assets, Jason is the embodiment of her legacy. And to Barbra Streisand, a lady who's done so many incredible things in her professional life, it is her son who is her greatest success. "He's incredible, an incredible little human being. A great joy. The only real contribution I will make to this world," she said in 1968.

Barbra Streisand has been called a mensch by many people. Mensch is a Yiddish word, and roughly

(Above) Jason was omnipresent on the *Hello, Dolly!* set.

translated, it means a good person, a quality human being, someone who does the right things. When Barbra appeared on *The Barbara Walters Special* in 1986, she was asked to describe what Jason was like now that he was a young man. "He's a mensch," Barbra said with pride, and her admittedly biased opinion of him has only increased as he's gotten older.

Jason Gould is the issue of Barbra Streisand and Elliott Gould's eight-year marriage. While Hollywood has left its stamp on some children, Jason seems to have emerged unscathed. "Look, I had advantages in certain ways, and there were a lot of disadvantages . . . people thinking they know you, having assumptions about you," Jason explained in a 1991 interview for *The Prince of Tides*. "In a way, I might have been too protective of him when he was younger," Barbra said in 1988. "And [because] I worked, I felt guilty. But I tried to explain to him always that work was also a part of my life." Although he must have wondered at times about the long hours his mother spent at the studio when he was young, on some level, Jason perceived that his mother would not have been the person she was if she didn't work that hard. And Barbra knew that Jason had an unusual childhood because of her stardom and celebrity: "It hasn't been easy [on him] being my son. We can't go out and do the things other mothers and children do together. My privacy is easily invaded, and his is, too, when he's with me."

As often happens with children, as an adult, Jason now emulates his mother in many ways. "Jason is very much like me," Barbra said in 1988. "He can't stand anything phony. He won't even ride in a limousine with me. He's also very tal-

ented and sensitive and kind. And he tells the truth. He doesn't understand people who don't. We're both fascinated by people who say things they don't mean. Honesty is a naive quality we both have." Jason is also very interested in music, acting, and filmmaking. In 1982, while Streisand was making *Yentl* in London, Jason worked with Barbra's personal assistant, Kim Skalecki, to create a special gift for his mother. For her fortieth birthday, he flew to England (along with Barbra's brother and his wife and daughter) and presented his mother with a specially-made videotape of her friends, her dogs, and her flowers and gardens. It was scored with one of Jason's original music compositions.

Aside from it being a beautiful, thoughtful gift, it represented the growth in their relationship. "Before, I felt guilty and hid things from him—all my fears, my flaws. I tried to play mother. But now I've stopped preaching, stopped judging. I tell him what I think or feel, and if he doesn't accept it, that's fine. Now the love is just there. It's unconditional, and it's very strong. It helps that Jason is an extraordinary person, very gifted at music and drawing. But I think the art he loves best is film," Barbra told *People* magazine in 1983.

As a child, Jason spent many hours on the sets of his mother's—and father's—movies. Barbra could never fathom the idea of not having her son nearby, and often Jason was in the care of a nanny in her dressing room. Behind-the-scene photos from *Funny Girl* and *Hello, Dolly!* reveal toddler Jason being held and kissed and otherwise bonding with his mother. Gene Kelly, who directed *Dolly!*, recalled in Clive Hirshhorn's biography that when he and Barbra would get together to rehearse on weekends,

(Above) While shooting *What's Up, Doc?* Barbra posed with Jason for the cover of *Show* magazine.

Jason had the opportunity to play on the carousel in Central Park while Barbra was filming *Up the Sandbox*.

Barbra would bring Jason, and Gene would bring his daughter, Bridget. While the adults figured out how to get the picture on track, Bridget and Jason played in the corner.

Jason first appeared onscreen in *Up the Sandbox*. "He was in the playground sequence. He pushed one of the rides and jumped on. It was beautiful. His hair goes flying," said Barbra when promoting the film in 1973. Three years later, he had a small, nonspeaking part in his father's film, *Harry and Walter Go to New York*. But those weren't real acting roles. He was playing, more than anything else. As Jason matured, grew, and developed, his artistic nature began to emerge. No one was more thrilled and proud than Barbra: "I'd never thought I'd ever have a child. I thought I was different from other people, as if it weren't meant to be," she commented in 1976. "I look at Jason now and remember that I carried him and gave birth to him, and now he sits at the piano composing music."

When Jason graduated from high school, he chose to attend college at the University of California at Berkeley and study filmmaking. He made an eighteen-minute student film in 1983 called *It's Up to You*. It starred Elliott, Diana and Roslyn Kind, and other family and friends. Barbra assisted behind the scenes and gave Jason advice on the editing. It was this experience, perhaps, which led Barbra to give Jason a unique opportunity: when *Yentl* had to be prepared for commercial-television broadcast, it needed to be shortened. Rather than have someone else arbitrarily cut out scenes and

sequences, Barbra asked Jason to reedit the film. As an adult, Jason seems to have come to a new understanding and appreciation of his mother's workaholic nature and all those long hours spent at the studio. "[My mother's] a perfectionist in everything she does. It seems ridiculous that you can get criticized for caring too much about your work."

In 1985, Jason was part of Steven Spielberg's production team for *The Color Purple*. Though he was only a production assistant, he was given a screen credit and had the privilege of working with one of America's premier filmmakers. But Jason's interests were not limited to being behind the camera. He had a bit of the acting bug, and he auditioned for film and television roles. Both Barbra and Elliott were supportive, but they knew how difficult a performing career might be for Jason. "It's not easy for a child to be the son of somebody famous. It gave him an extra hard road," Barbra reflected in 1991. Still, Jason showed some of his mother's determination. In 1988, he made his network television debut in the NBC drama *The Bronx Zoo*. His role, as Henry Dodd, was one among many, but it was an integral one. Dodd was a high-school kid who has overcome the stigma caused by his stuttering and gone on to become

Seven-year-old Jason on the set of *For Pete's Sake*.

When Jason began to make the rounds as an actor, his 8x10 showed he had inherited physical characteristics of both his parents. He has the Streisand nose. Bressler and Kelly (photo at left)

a fine student. When his scholarship for college is rescinded because of lack of funding, Henry loses his cool and destroys the chemistry lab. While this hardly was classic television, Jason's performance was excellent and indicative of things to come.

In 1989, Jason was seen in three features: *Say Anything, The Big Picture,* and *Listen to Me.* The roles in these films were small (and in *Listen to Me,* all his dialogue scenes were edited out), but both *Say Anything* and *The Big Picture* gave him a few precious moments onscreen in which to make a positive impression. Jason's roles in these two films, especially Cameron Crowe's excellent *Say Anything,* showed off his wry way with a line and his natural ability to handle comedy. *The Big Picture* also featured Jason in a clever scene, a true inside joke: at an awards ceremony honoring student films, Jason is one of the nominees, and when a clip of his movie is shown, the star of the film is Elliott Gould.

In 1992, Jason Gould got his most important film role to date: he was cast as Bernard Woodruff, Dr. Susan Lowenstein's son, in *The Prince of Tides.* Jason had read the script and wanted the part, but Barbra had reservations about casting her son to play her son. "My first instinct was that Jason was right [for Bernard]. I did have him read the part at the first reading of the script, and he was the best one there," she admitted to Gene Shalit on *The Today Show* in 1991. "He was extraordinary. He was the best one for the role, believe me. Very subtle, very understated. He was the guy." But could Barbra give her own kid the part? While she felt Jason was more than capable, she feared that they would both be victimized by the media. Pat Conroy, who wrote *The Prince of Tides,* convinced Streisand that Jason was perfect for Bernard. He saw a picture of Jason in Barbra's apartment when they were working on the screenplay. He told Barbra that he—the kid in the photograph—should play Bernard, completely unaware that "the kid" was Barbra's son. Barbra pointed out that Jason couldn't play football; and Conroy responded that Bernard couldn't either. Streisand reconsidered casting Jason in the film. She went to Jason and asked him if he would be able to withstand the potential criticism which was likely to be hurled their way. Jason said yes, and he proved to be up to the challenge both onscreen and off. "I was frightened to use my own son. What if they attack me for nepotism?" Streisand confessed after the film was completed. "But Pat said, `I'm telling you, this is the kid. How do you use an actor that doesn't look Jewish? He looks like you, he is you.' And then Jason, who is not very ambitious and has never asked for anything in his life, really wanted to play it. And I thought, `Screw all the possible negativity, I'm going to do what I think is ultimately right for the film.' "

Jason's performance in *The Prince of Tides* was solid and professional. He received excellent notices from the critics and not one journalist accused Streisand of giving her son a role he did not deserve. "I think it deepened our relationship on a personal level, the kind of trust you have to have between a director and an actor, and a mother and a son," Jason said in 1991. He also felt the experience had given mother and son a new appreciation of each other. "Absolutely. It was great for us on a personal level. We have a sophisticated relationship. You know, I didn't have a milk-and-cookies childhood. But in a sense, I'm glad because I have a much more adult, sophisticated, communicative relationship with her now."

When Barbra appeared on *Larry King Live* in 1992, the subject of *The Prince of Tides* and Jason was brought up. Streisand was effusive in her praise of her son: "Wasn't Jason good in [*The Prince of Tides*]? I'm so proud of him. I want him to work near me, by me, for the rest of my life. He made a brilliant film. He wrote it, directed it, edited it, and he's absolutely amazing. But I want to support him in anything he wants to do, so if he loves acting. . . . He likes to explore all different kinds of things. He's building a house now."

The relationship between mother and son is one of the true joys of Barbra Streisand's life. In 1992, she told interviewer Ryan Murphy, "[Jason's] a mature, wonderful human being. He's my friend. We're friends. I don't have to baby him. We're equals now. So talking back is no longer an issue. But I never talked down to him, even when he was a child. Now, he's the one I turn to for advice. He understands everything about me. I really think we have to let children be who they are—not extensions of

Jason bulked up to pull off the football scenes in *The Prince of Tides*. He also became proficient on the violin for scenes in which he was shown playing the instrument.

our own egos."

Jason Gould seems to be his own man. He could star in films in the future, or he could become a composer, or he could fade into obscurity. His plans are most decidedly his own. But there is little doubt he has benefited from the unconditional love and support of his family. When asked to reveal what he felt he had gotten from his parents, Jason said this: "My mother gave me a definite appreciation of art, of my creative side, because she's such a creative person. And my father, probably his humanity. He's a very down-to-earth guy."

In 1994, Jason attended both of his mother's concerts in Las Vegas at the MGM-Grand. With him was his father, and as they walked into the arena, the audience recognized them both and gave them a round of applause. Then when the spotlight was on Barbra, she openly acknowledged her son. She conceded that Jason is now a man and no longer in need of her as he had been as a child. But she promised that she would always be a part of his life, always be there for him, and in song ("Not While I'm Around"), she told Jason, "Nothing's gonna harm you, not while I'm around." It was a loving, moving tribute, one which epitomizes the depth of their relationship.

7

Seeing Stars

(Opposite top) On the set of *Nuts* Madonna—at the time shooting *Who's That Girl?* on the Warner lot — stopped by to visit with Richard Dreyfuss and Barbra.

(Opposite far left) While Barbra was starring on Broadway in *Funny Girl*, backstage visits by Hollywood stars like Natalie Wood were not unusual. The Michael Parenteau Collection

(Opposite left) One of the more simple and elegant moments in "Barbra Streisand . . . and Other Musical Instruments" was when Barbra sang a duet with Ray Charles. Steve Schapiro/ Columbia Records

(Above) Martial arts expert Chuck Norris gave Barbra some tips during a press conference where Jon Peters announced a Bruce Lee movie biography. The Peters project never came to pass.

(Above right) Barbra presented Kevin Costner the Oscar for Best Picture for *Dances With Wolves*.

Barbra stopped on the set of *WUSA*, a 1970 Joanne Woodward–Paul Newman movie. Maybe she's asking Joanne where she can find Paul? The Michel Parenteau Collection

(Top left) When Yul Brynner returned to Broadway in *The King and I* once again, Barbra visited him backstage.

(Middle left) What would a Marx Brothers party be without the real McCoy? Groucho was invited to *The Way We Were* shoot, where he and Barbra kibbitzed for a while.

(Bottom left) Barbra presented Steven Spielberg with the Scopus Award. Also pictured are Amy Irving, then Mrs. Spielberg, and the late singer-songwriter Peter Allen *(left)*.

(Below) Barbara Walters snared Barbra and Jon for her very first television special, in 1976.

(Center fold) Barbra, James Caan, Jimmy Stewart, and Lee Remick all had the opportunity to meet Queen Elizabeth when *Funny Lady* premiered in London.

(Above) Barbra came up with a curly blond wig for her first appearance at the Oscars. She presented Best Song in 1968 to Sammy Davis Jr. He was picking up the prize for Anthony Newley and Leslie Bricusse's song "If We Could Talk to the Animals" from *Doctor Dolittle*.

(Below) At an ASCAP Award dinner, Barbra, Stevie Wonder, and Lionel Ritchie all were honored for their songwriting.

8

Streisand Live: Something So Right

It was as a young girl growing up in Brooklyn that Barbra Streisand first fell in love with the movies. The beautiful Technicolor images which flashed across the screen of the Loew's King Theatre on Flatbush Avenue were the stuff of Barbara Joan's dreams, dreams which were brighter and more vibrant than the everyday life she saw all around her neighborhood. To get from where she was to where she wanted to be, however, would require a slow and steady climb. And along the way, most of the style and substance of Barbra Streisand—the performer—would be honed onstage. On Broadway, in *I Can Get It for You Wholesale* and *Funny Girl*, as well as in hundreds of club dates and concerts, Streisand became the consummate entertainer. She learned about timing, pacing, character, atmosphere, mood, dynamics, and audiences. She began as a gifted amateur but emerged in 1967's *A Happening in Central Park* with a Ph.D. in showmanship.

She has a great deal to give as an artist, and there are so many who want to see her live and in person . . . such is the conundrum for Streisand. She is the most in-demand entertainer in the world. She can receive exorbitant amounts of money to appear in concert, and yet she prefers to perform in the relative privacy and security of studio sets and recording booths. The thrilling adrenaline rush others feel when waves of grateful applause wash over them has little long-term effect on Streisand. She

likes and appreciates it, but it doesn't equal the satisfaction she gets from a finished album or, better still, a completed feature film. "I just don't enjoy performing live," she told columnist Larry King in 1991. "What can I tell you? I don't get off on it. It's nothing to do with singing, because I still like to sing. I like to make records. I love to make records. But I just don't enjoy performing live, that's all."

But there are reasons to venture out beyond the boundaries and overcome her anxieties. When Barbra has been motivated by political causes or worthy charities, she has stood before throngs of worshipful admirers and sung with heart and conviction. Those occasions, like the *One Voice* concert in September 1986, and the APLA Commitment to Life Awards concert in November 1992, were glorious. In January 1993, Barbra celebrated President Bill Clinton's inauguration with a memorable live appearance at the gala special. Her twenty-minute song set was the crowning performance in an all-star extravaganza.

Because Barbra gives live performances so infrequently, her appearances have become more and more special, and the expectations for them, therefore, are extremely high. Fortunately, Streisand has, thus far, lived up to audience expectations, which only generates more interest and desire for other people to see her live, to hear the voice. Ironically, her striving for perfection is what makes her not only uncomfortable in live performing but also a world-class entertainer.

For the past four decades, Barbra Streisand has been America's premier female pop vocalist, and that reputation has been fortified by her stellar, if only occasional, forays into live perfor-

(Left) The Streisand dilemma: "I just don't enjoy performing live, that's all."

(Inset left) Streisand's stage fright is so acute it has even warranted tabloid headlines.

mances. In every decade in which she's been active—the sixties, the seventies, the eighties, and the nineties—Streisand has brought her music to the concert stage, most often with masterful results. And in each decade, there are Barbra Streisand concerts which will stand the test of time for the brilliance of her singing and the magic of the moment.

The Sixties—A Happening Decade

From 1960 to 1969, Barbra Streisand performed in over fifty live singing engagements. She began in small nightclubs such as the Bon Soir in New York, the hungry in San Francisco, and the Caucus Club in Detroit, packing houses and establishing herself as an exciting young singer with an offbeat sense of humor, a powerful and distinctive voice, and a compelling stage presence. Her reputation as a dynamic live act was bolstered greatly by her enormously successful recording career and a few well-chosen television guest spots, like *The Judy Garland Show.* Contrary to the way things usually work in the music business, it was Barbra Streisand's albums which after the sixties helped sell her as a live

A moment from one of Barbra's over seven hundred performances of *Funny Girl* on Broadway. Yet, in the end she had developed more anxieties about performing live than when she began.

performer, more than her singing engagements helping to sell the albums. Traditionally, singers perform live in support of, and to promote, a record product. In her entire career, that is something Streisand has never done—nor has she ever had to do. What makes this such a remarkable feat is that from her very first solo album—*The Barbra Streisand Album*—through her most recent one—*Back to Broadway*—Streisand has enjoyed tremendous record sales.

Looking out at 70,000 screaming people, would you have stage fright?

It is unimaginable what kind of sales she may have generated had she ever toured or actively promoted (with singing appearances) a particular album.

By 1963, a scant three years after her first gig at The Lion in Greenwich Village, Streisand had graduated to much bigger performing venues such as the Hollywood Bowl, Soldier Field in Chicago, and JFK Stadium in Philadelphia. In 1966, she had planned a twenty-city concert tour (in stadiums) which was projected to earn her well over $1 million—a staggering sum for that time. However, in April 1966, Streisand announced that she was pregnant and would have to severely curtail her work schedule. The press dubbed the unborn child "Barbra's Million-Dollar Baby," a term she found offensive and crass. Nevertheless, the pregnant pause would turn out to be the only downtime Streisand would have for five years.

The proposed twenty-city tour was reduced to four—Philadelphia, Chicago, Atlanta, and Newport, Rhode Island. After having her son Jason, Barbra sang occasionally at charity functions, such as a 1968 antiwar rally called Broadway for Peace, a fund-raiser for Democratic presidential candidate Eugene McCarthy, and an Israeli Bond drive rally. Before the decade was over, Barbra would have only a few more major live singing engagements: concerts in New York's Central Park and the Hollywood Bowl in June 1967 and a three-week stint at the International Hotel in Las Vegas in July 1969. The concert in Central Park would turn out to be the crowning moment of her sixties live appearances. It is also the performance which best epitomizes the appeal and preeminence Streisand had attained in just six years. The massive turnout in Central Park was the most people ever gathered for a single performance—135,000—up to that time.

From the couple of dozen patrons at The Lion to the thousands in Central Park, Barbra was a spellbinder. She liked to sing Harold Arlen and Truman Capote's mysterious love song, "A Sleepin' Bee," in those days. Reportedly, Barbra could make audiences believe she really held the bee in the palm of her hand. In reality, what was firmly in the palm of her hand was the audience, mesmerized by the beauty of her voice.

A Happening in Central Park

The Time: June 17, 1967

The Place: Sheep Meadow, Central Park, New York City

The Hook: Hometown girl gives a songfest for free! Come one, come all . . .

The Expected: Barbra Streisand in concert

The Unexpected: 135,000 people attended, about 50,000 more than the estimate

The Highs: Killer rendition of "Cry Me a River," heavenly "Silent Night" (on a balmy summer night), "Second Hand Rose" sing-a-long with

In the early seventies Barbra fulfilled all of her live performance obligations by playing the Las Vegas Hilton (formerly the International) and the Riviera.

Because of her pregnancy, Barbra cut back her U.S. concert tour from twenty cities to only four.

the crowd, and beautiful new material: "Love Is Like a Newborn Child" and "Natural Sounds"

The Lows: Strained humor on "Marty the Martian"; the entire two-hour concert was recorded as an album and a television special, both of which were edited to less than one hour; substandard audio and video quality of the concert recording for television and LP were disappointing

The Program:

Act 1

"Any Place I Hang My Hat Is Home"
"My Honey's Lovin' Arms"
"I'll Tell the Man in the Street"
"Cry Me a River"
"Folk Monologue"/"Value"
"I Can See It"
"More Than You Know"
"All the Things You Are"
"Down With Love"
"Love Is Like a Newborn Child"
"What Now My Love"
"Free Again"
"When the Sun Comes Out"

Act 2

"Where Am I Going?"
"He Touched Me"
"Schloon Song"
"Stout-Hearted Men"
"I'm All Smiles"
"Marty the Martian"
"Love Is a Bore"
"I'm Always Chasing Rainbows"
"Natural Sounds"
"Second Hand Rose"
"People"
"Sleep in Heavenly Peace (Silent Night)"
"Happy Days Are Here Again"

The Seventies—Starting Here, Starting Over

In retrospect, the sixties were Barbra Streisand's most productive era as a live performer. By comparison, she would appear in a mere ten singing engagements in the seventies. For the most part, Streisand spent the decade making movies (eight of her total fifteen films were made during this era) and maintaining her stature as one of CBS Records' top stars. Barbra was contractually obligated to appear at two Las Vegas showrooms, the International Hotel (which became the Las Vegas Hilton in 1971) and the Riviera. Apparently, it was Streisand's intention to clear her slate of all obligations and to assume total control of her professional life. By 1972, Streisand had succeeded with regard to singing engagements. For the remainder of the decade, Barbra's only live appearances were one-night-only charity functions. In fact, it would be twenty-one *years* before she took another dime for standing in the spotlight and singing.

There were reasons why Streisand refrained from live performances, reasons which went beyond her desire to be free of contractual obligations. She had developed near-paralyzing stage fright, which she later would attribute to the death threats she received before the concert in Central Park. When doing her Las Vegas shows, Streisand posted a large calendar in her dressing room and marked off each day of her appearance with an X, much like a prisoner counting

Holding the note at the end of "He Touched Me"—one of the high points of *A Happening in Central Park*.

the days until her release. In the handful of performances Barbra gave in the seventies, she put on a brave face when she was required to sing live, but inside she was in utter agony.

Barbra gave two distinct mini-concert performances during these years, both tied in to movie projects. In 1975, as part of the world premiere festivities for *Funny Lady*, Barbra performed a few songs (plus a duet with costar James Caan) at the Kennedy Center in Washington, all to benefit the Special Olympics. The performance became the centerpiece of an ABC television special called *Funny Girl to Funny Lady*.

Exactly one year later, *A Star Is Born* was in production, shooting live concert sequences at Sun Devil Stadium in Tempe, Arizona. Approximately 60,000 people showed up to lend authenticity—creating a realistic backdrop to the film's rock milieu—and although she had not intended to perform, Barbra was the attraction most were expecting to see. According to reports, as the shoot dragged on and the crowd

grew increasingly restless, there were fears that the filming might be jeopardized. Streisand felt compelled to sing, and in a very short time, she had the audience eating out of her hand. She introduced two new numbers from *A Star Is Born*—"Evergreen" and "Woman in the Moon"— and sang two of her greatest hits, "The Way We Were" and "People."

This experience—which Barbra found extremely satisfying because of the audience's terrific response—coupled with the popular success of *A Star Is Born*, prompted Streisand to seriously consider a concert tour. She hadn't really thought about doing concerts since the abbreviated 1966 tour, mostly because she had been too preoccupied with her film work and her stage fright. But after *Star*, Barbra thought about it seriously enough to have Jon Peters make preliminary plans. Ultimately, another

With a more natural look, Streisand introduced *Stoney End* and *Barbra Joan* material in Vegas. By *Live Concert at the Forum*, she had a show quite different from *A Happening in Central Park*. The Michel Parenteau Collection

Streisand's voice was a bit shaky when she started singing "Evergreen" at the 1977 Oscars, but by the time she was done, her performance rated smiles all around.

newer albums like *Stoney End* and *Barbara Joan*—for example, "I Don't Know Where I Stand," "No Easy Way Down," and "Where You Lead"—as well as material from her recent films—"On a Clear Day," "My Man"—were interspersed with her sixties standards to create shows which were more eclectic and, at times, too scattershot. However, the experimentation in the recording studio and the diversity of material came together in 1972, when Streisand appeared at a benefit for Democratic presidential candidate George McGovern. As one of the "4 for McGovern"—the others being James Taylor, Carole King, and Quincy Jones—Barbra rose to the occasion to deliver her finest concert of the decade. It was recorded by Columbia and released as a live album, Barbra's second in four years.

film came up on Streisand's schedule, and she chose to do that rather than a concert tour. Considering that the movie—*The Main Event*—turned out to be a rather strident romantic comedy (although it was a box-office hit), she may have wished she had done a tour.

In 1978, a major charity event prompted Barbra to face a live audience once more. An all-star celebration was arranged in honor of the thirtieth anniversary of Israeli statehood. Barbra agreed to take part in the show and, backed by Zubin Mehta and the Los Angeles Philharmonic, sang four songs and spoke with the former prime minister of Israel, Golda Meir, via satellite hookup. The entire show was recorded as a television special called *Stars Salute Israel at 30*, and Barbra's performance was clearly the highlight. ABC television decided to televise the program as a special once Streisand agreed to participate, and as finally edited, Barbra had the lion's share of airtime, including the star spot: the closing. As she had in all her previous live appearances that decade, Streisand managed to cover her anxieties, never letting the audience see her sweat.

Streisand's singing engagements in the early seventies reflected the changes she was going through in her recording career. Her songs from

Once on stage at Sun Devil Stadium, Streisand won the crowd over with renditions of two new songs for *A Star Is Born*: "Woman in the Moon" and "Evergreen." The Dennis Pallante Collection

Live Concert at the Forum—4 for McGovern

The Time: April 15, 1972

The Place: The Forum, Los Angeles

The Hook: Show-biz liberals put on a show to raise money for the presidential hopeful

The Expected: James Taylor crooning "You've Got a Friend," Carole King's best from *Tapestry*, Quincy Jones's rocking band, Barbra Streisand in concert

The Unexpected: Streisand stealing the show; top box-office stars like Jack Nicholson, Gene Hackman, Shirley MacLaine, and Warren Beatty acting as ushers

The Highs: Barbra "getting down" in "Sweet Inspiration"/"Where You Lead," the heartbreaking "Didn't We," the audience choosing "Stoney End" instead of "Second Hand Rose," and Barbra reading the lyrics from the floor

The Lows: Dated comedy routine of Barbra smoking a joint

The Program:

"Sing"/"Make Your Own Kind of Music"
"Starting Here, Starting Now"
"Don't Rain on My Parade"
"On a Clear Day . . ."
"Sweet Inspiration"/"Where You Lead"
"Didn't We"
"My Man"
"Stoney End"
"Sing"/"Happy Days Are Here Again"
"People"

The Eighties—A Malibu Night to Remember

There would be a mere handful of live performances for Barbra Streisand in the eighties because of her paralyzing stage fright. On June 1, 1980, Barbra took part in an American Civil Liberties Union benefit evening in tribute to lyricists Alan and Marilyn Bergman at the Dorothy Chandler Pavillion in Los Angeles. Her desire to honor the Bergmans, two of her closest friends, was Streisand's motivation to sing live and face the fear she knew would grip her. On that occa-sion, Barbra's apprehensions were so great before the event that she resorted to consulting a yogi and even had him standing by in the wings during the show. Streisand looked wonderful and sang beautifully that night, including a surprise duet with Neil Dia-mond on "You Don't Bring Me Flowers," a repeat of the performance they did on the Grammy Awards telecast. The audience reaction to Streisand was overwhelmingly positive. Her singing was often interrupted by cries of "I love you" and shouts of her name from the crowd. The performance was not intended as an album—she did just six songs—but the rendition of "The Way We Weren't," a second unused version of the movie's title tune, did end up on *Just for the Record. . . .* Once again, Streisand overcame her phobia and rose above her fears. The memory of that fear, however, would keep her away from the concert stage for six more years.

It would take a major world event to prod Barbra to sing again. The disaster at the Soviet

To sing live onstage or not to sing live onstage, that is the question?

nuclear plant in Chernobyl was so cataclysmic and the effects so far-reaching that Streisand wanted to do something to prevent anything like that ever happening again. But as she herself said, what could one person do? What could she do? She was a world-famous celebrity, an actress, a singer, a producer, a writer, a director, and she was also a member of the Demo-cratic party. Streisand determined that she could use her voice to raise money to elect candidates who shared the beliefs she did. With the help of the Hollywood Women's Political Committee and the Bergmans, Streisand planned a one-night-only concert to raise money for six Democratic senatorial candidates. The show, which was called *One Voice*, was staged in Barbra's backyard in Malibu, and it was recorded and videotaped for an eventual album and television special. *One Voice* proved what one person could do—one person named Streisand, with that particular voice and a desire to make a difference. *One Voice* was a great achievement for Barbra and her most memorable live appearance from the decade.

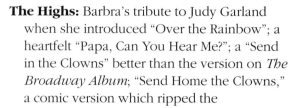

One Voice

The Time: September 6, 1986

The Place: Barbra's Ramirez Canyon estate, Malibu

The Hook: Barbra invites you to come to hear her sing. Tickets are only $2,500 each

The Expected: Barbra Streisand in concert

The Unexpected: Robin Williams doing a side-splitting comic opening, Barry Gibb's guest appearance to sing two songs from the *Guilty* album

(Above) In August 1979, *Ladies' Home Journal* speculated that Barbra might not ever perform on stage again.

The Highs: Barbra's tribute to Judy Garland when she introduced "Over the Rainbow"; a heartfelt "Papa, Can You Hear Me?"; a "Send in the Clowns" better than the version on *The Broadway Album*; "Send Home the Clowns," a comic version which ripped the Republicans; Streisand leading the all-star audience in "America, the Beautiful"

The Lows: Television special and album left out "Send Home the Clowns"; Barbra rushed through "The Way We Were"; Streisand's comments were occasionally preachy

The Program:

"Somewhere"
"Evergreen"
"Something's Comin' "
"People"
"Send in the Clowns"
"Send Home the Clowns"
"Over the Rainbow"
"Guilty" (with Barry Gibb)
"What Kind of Fool" (with Gibb)
"Papa, Can You Hear Me?"
"The Way We Were"
"It's a New World"
"Happy Days Are Here Again"
"America the Beautiful"

The Nineties—Happy New Year!

*If I could bring myself to tour—which, in theory, I'd like to do—I would break it in Las Vegas. When I first came there I was fascinated by the fact there were no clocks. Time stood still. . . .
     Someday I'll perform live, but it scares me.*
     —Barbra to Larry Grobel in *Newsday,* 1976

The nineties were a time of renewal for Barbra Streisand. According to Marilyn Bergman, Barbra was coming out of her cocoon—and she was coming out to sing. Age is a powerful liberator, because with it comes acceptance. That's what Streisand said in 1993 to explain why she was seriously considering a return to live performing. Coupled with that renewed outlook was a desire to give something back to the loyal fan following she has enjoyed throughout her entire professional life.

In October 1993, Streisand did something she had not done in twenty-one years: she agreed to return to the concert stage not as part of a charity benefit or a fund-raiser but as a paid performer. Promoter Kirk Kerkorian offered her a reported $20 million for two shows which would open his brand-new, $1 billion Las Vegas attraction, the MGM–Grand Hotel. In 1969, Kerkorian had enticed Streisand to open another of his Las Vegas attractions, the International Hotel, and she was a great draw. Twenty-five years later, Kerkorian wanted her to turn on the magic once again. His timing turned out to be perfect: Barbra Streisand was ready to face her fear, and a $20 million inducement didn't hurt.

In many ways, time did stand still on both December 31, 1993, and January 1, 1994. Barbra Streisand's return to the concert stage was *the* entertainment event of the season. There was a palpable, electric excitement in the air in Vegas, and Streisand's name was on the lips of every cab driver, waitress, and tourist in the glittery playground. Yes, Frank Sinatra was in town, as were Kenny Rogers and Kenny Loggins, and certainly Siegfried and Roy, but did any act pack the promise that Streisand's show did? Apparently not. Everybody who was anybody was heading to see Barbra Streisand. It was the place to be.

Was it because of the intensive hype? The annual New Year's merriment? Perhaps it was the celebrity-filled audience—including Mel Gibson, Michael Douglas, Steven Spielberg, Tom and Roseanne Arnold, Kim Basinger and Alec Baldwin, as well as Michael Jackson? No, it was much more than that. New Year's Eve, the media clamor, and the all-star wattage became mere footnotes once Barbra stepped into the spotlight. The applause which greeted her was deafening. The entire arena was on its feet— one of over a dozen standing ovations Streisand would warrant that night. Then she began to

Onstage with the Los Angeles Philharmonic for the *Stars Salute Israel at Thirty* television show. "Do I have time to introduce all the members of the band?" Barbra asked.

sing "As If We Never Said Goodbye," the *Sunset Boulevard* song which had been on her *Back to Broadway* album. In the MGM setting, the appropriateness of the lyrics offered a poignant and dramatic irony to her return. "I don't know why I'm frightened, I know my way around here," Barbra crooned softly, somewhat tentatively, and as she reached for the bannister on the staircase set, her hand seemed to be trembling. Was she as nervous as the lyrics suggested, or was the actress in song playing the role of the frightened singer returning to the stage for all it was worth?

Barbra's fear of live performing was well known, and despite weeks and weeks of rehearsals, she had apprehensions about living up to audience expectations. Could she overcome the anxiety, the nervousness, the butterflies in her belly? Was she worth the money— the ticket prices ranged from $50 to $1,000 (considerably more if you went through a ticket broker)? Was she deserving of all the hoopla? Certainly there was a segment of the media that hoped she wasn't. After all, it would make a great story. But Barbra Streisand has been an artist who rarely falters when the glare of the

For *One Voice*, Barbra set the terms for performing, including staging it at her Malibu ranch. The Dennis Pallante Collection

The Highs: Barbra's autobiographical first act, including a charming duet with the screen image of Marlon Brando from *Guys and Dolls*; Stephen Sondheim's new lyrics—all about Barbra—to "I'm Still Here"; riveting first act closer, "On a Clear Day"; Streisand sings Disney: "When You Wish Upon a Star" and "Someday My Prince Will Come"; inspiring new song, "Ordinary Miracles"; Streisand showing she's human when she muffed the opening line to "Evergreen" ("On my own song!"); wistful "For All We Know" to close the show

The Lows: Roughly blended medley of "I'm in the Mood for Love," "Speak Low," and "Guilty"; overly percussive arrangement of "What Is This Thing Called Love?"

The Program:

Act 1

"As If We Never Said Goodbye"

"I'm Still Here"

"Everybody Says Don't"/"Don't Rain on My Parade"

"Can't Help Lovin' Dat Man"

"I'll Know"

"People"

"Lover Man, Where Can You Be?"

"Will He Like Me?"

"He Touched Me"

"I'm in the Mood for Love"/"Speak Low"/ "Guilty"

"What Is This Thing Called Love?"

"The Man That Got Away"

"On a Clear Day"

Act 2

"The Way We Were"

"You Don't Bring Me Flowers"

"When You Wish Upon a Star"

"Someday My Prince Will Come"

"Not While I'm Around"

"Ordinary Miracles"

"Evergreen"

"Happy Days Are Here Again"

"My Man"

"For All We Know"

spotlight is upon her. She seems to rise to the occasion, to excel when the challenge is the greatest. These two shows would become part of her legend, yet another instance when her music, her presence, and her sense of the dramatic would create a magical moment. New Year's weekend 1994 at the MGM was a grand night of singing, and Streisand soared.

Barbra 1994-The Concert

The Time: December 31, 1993–January 1, 1994

The Place: MGM-Garden, Las Vegas

The Hook: Barbra's long-awaited return to live performance

The Expected: Barbra Streisand in concert

The Unexpected: Mike Myers's surprise appearance as "Linda Richman, *Coffee Talk*," his *Saturday Night Live* character; Streisand's opening up about her personal life by dedicating songs to her goddaughter Callie and her son Jason; the first act, which was more like her classic television specials—*My Name Is Barbra* and *Color Me Barbra*—than a typical concert

The World Tour

For the thousands who were fortunate enough to get tickets for Streisand's two Las Vegas concerts, Barbra's Las Vegas shows were like a dream come true. She could just as easily have sold out two dozen shows! When the results of Streisand's MGM engagement was calculated, the success was definitive and incontrovertible: the ticket sales alone grossed $12 million; the sales of licensed merchandise (a rarity for Streisand) brought in another million—twice the amount of any Super Bowl and three times what other musical acts sell; and the reviews were love letters. Not surprisingly, the requests from promoters and fans worldwide for Streisand to take her show on the road poured in. It was clear that now was the time for Barbra to face her fears and do what would be, perhaps, a once-in-a-lifetime world concert tour.

On February 14, 1994, Barbra Streisand had a Valentine's Day gift for her fans. It was announced that she would do a limited concert tour in the United States and Europe beginning in London on April 20. Streisand's two Wembley Arena shows sold out in three hours, prompting two additional concerts, including one to benefit the Prince's Trust. Like the crowds in Las Vegas, the British fans greeted Barbra—who appeared on stage in a long-sleeve, velvet version of the Donna Karan/Barbra Streisand design she wore in Vegas—with standing ovations the moment she stepped out on stage, before she even sang a note. And like New Year's, Streisand was ready, willing, and able to make music history: London was the first of twenty-four concerts which would set box office records, set critics off to find new words to describe Barbra's artistry, and set the world of Streisand fans into the stratosphere after having finally experienced Streisand's magic live.

Streisand, who would later call London her "out-of-town tryout," began the process of editing the concert. In much the same way a Broadway musical takes shape on the road, *The Concert* began to metamorphose. Barbra, who conceived and directed the concert, tightened the first act psychiatrist/patient comedy, incor-

porated more film clips, trimmed the length of some songs, such as "I'm Still Here," and added "Somewhere" as the new finale. She also heightened the poignant "Not While I'm Around," which she dedicated to her son, Jason Gould, by projecting photos of him through the years on the overhead screen. Barbra quite deliberately staged this song to shine the spotlight on her son, wanting the audience to concentrate entirely on the pictures of Jason and her uncompromising love for him as conveyed in Stephen Sondheim's gentle ballad. The revamped presentation was more sentimental, but it was also very effective and heartfelt, evoking tears from many concert-goers.

The biggest change in Streisand's show was a new second-act climax. In place of the Disney

During a dress rehearsal for *One Voice*. For the show, Barbra wore an all-white outfit instead. The Randy Emerian Collection

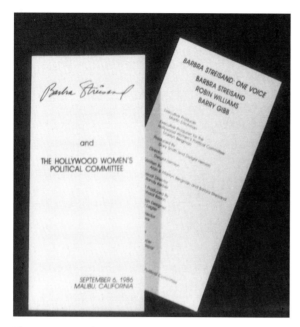

The invitation to the *One Voice* concert was a personalized audio cassette from Barbra . . . plus some information about the event.

her movements to match Yentl's, was masterly. Then, rather than sing the big, soaring last note of the song in unison with Yentl, Streisand sang counterpoint, in effect echoing and updating the meaning of the lyrics. The medley was brilliantly conceived, musically and visually, and it called upon Streisand to display her consummate skill as the world's premier actress in song. To her credit, she never failed to bring it off beautifully. The piece received a spontaneous standing ovation, with the audience on its feet before Streisand had even finished singing. After London, the *Yentl* medley was permanently added to the show as the penultimate moment in the second act.

The British audiences were overwhelmingly enthusiastic, and so were the reviews. "Last night Streisand looked well below her fifty-two years and her singing voice was still what lyricist Don Black described as 'liquid diamond,' " wrote David Lister in *The Independent.* In honor of Prince Charles's attendance on April 25, Streisand not only dedicated "Someday My Prince Will Come" to Charles, but she showed an archival news clip of her meeting him in Hollywood in 1975 while recording the *Funny Lady* soundtrack (although she mistakenly said it was 1972 and a *What's Up, Doc?* session). Barbra admitted that she had been so involved in her work that she wasn't as gracious to Charles as she might have been. "Imagine, if I had been a little friendlier, I might have become the first real Jewish princess! Can't you just see the headlines? *The Blintzes Princess Plays the Palace!* or *Babs Sinks Nails Into Prince of Wales!*"

Barbra's first live stage appearances in England in twenty-eight years touched off a media frenzy. The press analyzed her luggage when she landed at Heathrow (suggesting she brought her own personal disposal bucket: it was a hat box); followed Streisand everywhere; claimed that she had Wembley carpeted because she didn't like the floor (it was actually to improve the acoustics); and criticized her decision to use Teleprompters. Barbra defended her need for the Teleprompters. "I couldn't do this if I didn't have it as my security blanket.

medley (which she performed only on opening night in London), Streisand created a set piece derived from her most personal film, *Yentl.* The song suite began with the opening lines of "Where Is It Written?" prompting Barbra to briefly retell the story and explain what compelled her to do the film. A moving rendition of "Papa, Can You Hear Me?" led to more storytelling by Barbra: "It's a variation of the boy meets girl meets boy story . . . It's very nineties." The lovely "Will Someone Ever Look at Me That Way?" followed, accompanied by the clip from the movie, and as it came to an end, Barbra segued musically into the film's climactic finale, "A Piece of Sky." In a stunning turn, Streisand was joined by Yentl, her screen image, in a dramatic, dynamic duet. On screen, Streisand's soaring vocal reaches her epiphanic moment, while on stage, Streisand doubled the impact by not just singing along but adding new and different harmonies and musical interpolations. Streisand's staging of the sequence, placing herself in the precise spot where her screen image would appear, and then in the section where Yentl sings "Papa, I can see you, Papa, I can hear you, Papa, I can feel you," choreographing

Some people have worry beads; I have Teleprompters."

Streisand's concerts in England raised approximately $3 million for charity, and when she donated several mini-vans to the Variety Club charity, Barbra took the opportunity to tell the press exactly how to say her last name, amused and incredulous that after all these years, it's still mispronounced so often. "It's Streis-SAND. Listen, you've got to get this right. It's a soft 's,' Strei-SAND . . . like sand on the beach."

On May 10, Streisand had her American opening in Washington, D.C. The celebrity quota for her capital concerts was high: news media stars, Congressional members, and the First Family, the Clintons. As she did in London, Barbra paused in her rehearsal schedule for a public appearance, visiting a District of Columbia high school to present the music department with a $50,000 gift, one matched by Sony, Streisand's record company. Barbra made similar donations to area high schools on every tour stop, and in New York, the chosen school was her Brooklyn alma mater, Erasmus Hall High.

The Streisand Foundation, the organization Barbra created to dispense money to worthy charities, tried a new kind of philanthropy for the tour. The Foundation offered the charities a block of tickets which they could *buy* at face value—$350 each—and then resell for $1,000. The offer included a safety net: charities would get a full refund from the Foundation for any unsold tickets. While the press criticized Streisand and her Foundation, questioning why she didn't simply give the tickets away, the charities who benefited were grateful. In a *New York Times* letter to the editor on July 8, 1994, Addie Guttag of New York's Gay Men's Health Crisis, wrote: ". . . The Gay Men's Health Crisis would like to go on record as wholeheartedly grateful for her generosity. The singer's willingness to make 1,000 tickets available to our organization has enabled us to clear $650,000 without administrative or promotional costs. Ms. Streisand has made a tremendous difference in our ability to serve people affected by H.I.V.-

Stepping into the spotlight for a good cause: Barbra stages *One Voice*. The Dennis Pallante Collection

AIDS. For that, we are deeply appreciative."

The Washington concerts, which were held at the U.S. Air Arena in Landover, Maryland, were still undergoing change. Streisand sang "What Are You Doing the Rest of Your Life?" in place of the "I'm in the Mood for Love"/"Speak Low"/"Guilty" medley on one night, and she added "Lazy Afternoon" to act two. Once again, Streisand's reviews were excellent. "A dramatic peak was hit with a suite from the film *Yentl,* which the singer belted with a ferocious conviction. . . . Onstage, where retakes and retouching are impossible, the raw emotion runs free. Barbra in concert is Barbra at her best," wrote Stephen Holden in the *New York Times.*

On May 15, Streisand opened the first of three shows at the Palace in Auburn Hills outside Detroit, Michigan. Why Detroit? Streisand answered that question on stage: "It's kind of a sentimental journey because Detroit was my first club date outside New York in 1961. I remember all the friends I made here and how nice everyone was to me. And I remember my friends who came to every show and watched me and then took me into their homes and fed

For *One Voice*, Barbra sang "Over the Rainbow" as an homage to Judy Garland, referring to her as "a woman I had the privilege to work with." HBO

she had had to postpone four shows because of laryngitis. She made light of the rumors which suggested that the delay was caused by something *other* than illness by offering a *David Letterman Show*–inspired Top Ten list:

Barbra's Top Ten List of Reasons Why She Didn't Perform

10. I always wanted to spend four hot, muggy days in Anaheim in the middle of July.

9. I was trying to work out Dan Rostenkowski's plea bargain.

8. I didn't know it would take a whole week to dust all this furniture.

7. I was at home waiting for the cable guy.

6. I hurt my voice yelling "Yabba dabba doo!"

5. I wanted to get Barbra Streisand tongue depressors into the boutiques.

4. There was a shoe sale at Nordstrom's.

3. I thought my concert tour needed more publicity.

2. It took me three days to read Dan Quayle's new book—and four days to correct the spelling.

1. Every time I started to drive here, I got sidetracked and drove to Disneyland instead.

me, and I *never* forget people who feed me."

During the second show in Detroit, Barbra was running a fever of 102 degrees, and although she didn't know it at the time, she had come down with a severe case of viral laryngitis. She completed the last Detroit dates, then on May 26, Ken Sunshine, Streisand's tour publicist, announced that the first four dates at the Arrowhead Pond in Anaheim, California, would—unfortunately—have to be postponed. "She's been ordered not to talk at all. . . . Barbra feels terrible about this. People have flown in from all over the world." Despite the fact that the press releases clearly stated the shows would be rescheduled, rumors were rampant that Streisand was canceling the entire tour! The rumors ceased when the concerts (originally slated for May 25, 27, 29, 31) were rescheduled for July 18, 20, 22, 24.

On June 2, Barbra was back, standing center stage at the Arrowhead Pond, ready to perform again. Her voice actually sounded better when she sang than when she spoke, and at the very top of the show, Barbra addressed the fact that

During the June 4 show, Streisand was joined on stage by *Saturday Night Live* star Mike Myers. As he had in Barbra's two MGM shows, Myers appeared from the audience, dressed in drag as one of his comic creations, Linda Richman. Linda, a Long Island Jewish–American Princess who hosts a television show called *Coffee Talk*, adores Barbra. To Linda, Streisand is "just like butter!" Myers and Streisand reprised the Vegas comedy routine, one laced with Yiddishisms, i.e., when Linda becomes choked up—*verklempt*—about being so close to the one and only Barbra Joan Streisand. Throughout the tour, Streisand would use the *Coffee Talk* shtick in asides to the audience: when fans would inevitably shout out, "You're just like butter!" Barbra would smile and coo, "He says I'm just like butter. . . . Land of Lakes."

Myers appeared once more as Linda Richman for Streisand's last show in New York, on July 12.

Streisand's next stop was the San Jose Arena on June 7 and 9. By this time on the tour, Streisand's show was "a lock." She performed the same set of songs each show, and with the exception of some patter which was specific to the place where she was playing, most of the book stayed the same and continued to work very, very well. Although still suffering some post-laryngitis discomfort, Streisand's performances were getting better and better. She was loose and relaxed on stage, feeling more assured in the spotlight and pleased with the tour overall. She repeated her Anaheim Top Ten list in San Jose, adding three more reasons: "1. It took me a week to get seated at Denny's; 2. Someone used the helicopter that was to bring me to play golf; and 3. I kept driving around looking for a pond!"

The advertising promised a grand night of singing, and that's what it turned out to be.

On June 20, Barbra Streisand was home again in New York City, by her own admission the most important stop on her tour. New Yorkers had gone overboard trying to get Streisand tickets, with fans camping out in front of Madison Square Garden two days before tickets went on sale. Despite those efforts, Streisand tickets were completely sold out twenty minutes after they went on sale. Many fans were depicted in press reports as being brokenhearted when they were turned away empty-handed. Fortunately, most were eventually able to get tickets through other means, and many long-time fans were actually able to get tickets for more than one show.

Streisand's Madison Square Garden opening night was in many ways as electrifying as her *Funny Girl* opening night thirty years before. She stepped on stage in a gorgeous, shimmering, cream-colored, off-the-shoulder, empire waisted gown—one she wore that night only—and greeted her hometown fans with a high-voltage performance. In return, the superstar was embraced by New York as one of their own, with standing ovations after nearly every song. By this time, the lingering effects from the laryngitis were gone, and Streisand's singing appeared effortless and expert. She was sustaining notes with ease, discovering improvisations and harmonies in her vocals that had not been there before, and unleashing the most poised, polished and lovely music of her life. Her instrument was at peak performance level, and Barbra—a true *virtuosa*—was making the most it.

The New York critics were duly impressed. The *New York Times* heralded her triumphant performance with the understated headline, "Local Girl Makes Good, Sings." *Newsday* columnist Liz Smith wrote: "Barbra's event was beautifully staged, its emotional impact escalating in the second half. . . . As Barbara hit the final soul-searching notes of the evening's last song, 'Somewhere,' I thought the top of my head—and the roof of the Garden—would come off! All about her were hysterical, but Barbra was in total, brilliant control—the calm, glittering eye of her own self-created hurricane. . . . What a woman! What a talent! Barbra is a star for the ages."

For the first time in twenty-seven years, Barbra Streisand was back home to sing, and she gave the best shows of the entire tour in the Big Apple. She was greeted each and every night by ecstatic, enthusiastic fans, celebrities, and many, many old friends, such as Jimmy and Muriel Choy. Years before, when she was just a teenager, Barbra had worked as a cashier at

Choy's Orient in Brooklyn, the couple's Chinese restaurant. Liza Minnelli was in the audience for three shows, and on one occasion, after Barbra had sung the classic Judy Garland ballad, "The Man That Got Away," she smiled to Liza and said, "That was for your mom, Liza. She was the best."

On Friday, June 24, Streisand surprised everyone by adding an extra show to the New York engagement, on July 10. "This one is for the fans," said Streisand's publicist, adding, "[Barbra's] crazy about performing in New York, and she wanted to do more for the fans who had been shut out [when tickets sold out for the first five shows]." Once again, every seat was sold in minutes. The response was expected because one more date—July 12—was added, and it too sold out immediately. Streisand's seven Madison Square Garden concerts set new box-office records, grossing $16.6 million, surpassing the previous record of $13.7 million, which Streisand had set at the MGM–Grand on New Year's weekend.

The buzz in New York was all about Barbra, and thanks to the nightly mentions on *The Late Show With David Letterman,* the world knew that the most precious commodity around were Streisand tickets. On Tuesday, June 28, just as Letterman was complaining that even he couldn't get a ticket to see Streisand—the side door of the Ed Sullivan Theater opened and Barbra, nattily dressed in a black pin striped pantsuit, strolled over to Letterman's desk holding out two tickets for him. She gave the exclusive ducats to Dave and joked, "I just wanted to tell you to stop *kvetching* already!"

It seemed that there was no way to top the excitement and thrills Streisand was generating at the Garden, yet on July 12, Streisand found a way. She added a final grace note to her Manhattan engagement when it was announced that the last song of her last New York show

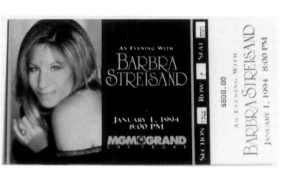
Now it's a collector's item: a ticket to Barbra's New Year's concert at the MGM–Grand in Las Vegas.

would be broadcast on the Sony Jumbotron screen in Times Square. "Barbra wanted to give a gift to her fans. She felt so good coming home, she wanted this to make one last gesture for the people," explained Sunshine. Thousands jammed the streets along Times Square as Steisand returned to Broadway, looming over the entire Great White Way, fifty feet high! "Hello, New York!" she cried from the stage of the Garden, reaching out to the fans in the streets. Before she sang "Somewhere," Streisand was like a cheerleader as she extolled her love of the city, saying, "Nowhere on this tour have I been so warmly welcomed as in the greatest city in the world, my hometown, New York City!"

Heading to Anaheim for the final four concerts of her 1994 tour, Streisand resisted the emotional letdown she might have experienced following her New York high by focusing on the task ahead: videotaping the July 22 and 24 concerts for an HBO special. The media had speculated that Streisand would do a pay-per-view broadcast of one of the Anaheim shows, but Streisand passed on that very lucrative option in favor of a taped broadcast. Television director Dwight Hemion—who has done most of Streisand's previous television shows—was in the control booth, capturing on tape—for posterity—Barbra's last two performances. *Barbra Streisand the Concert* aired on Sunday, August 21, 1994, becoming the highest rated original entertainment special in HBO history, with a Nielsen rating of 22.4 and a 31 share (11.4 million viewers).

That final concert on July 24 was in some ways the most memorable of the entire tour, and not only because of what happened during the show. With the houselights turned up for taping, Streisand was outgoing, playful, intimate, and yet in total command of the material, her voice, and the flow of the evening. During the performance, which was stopped eleven times for standing ovations, Barbra ad-libbed with the crowd, which included her eighty-six-year-old mother, Diana Kind. Streisand thanked her mom for being there and even asked her at one point, "Are you proud of your daughter?" Then, after the concert was over, Streisand returned to the stage, explaining that she needed to retape four songs for the television special and inviting the audience to stay and watch. Nearly everyone stayed, racing back to their seats, and as a thank-you, Streisand gave them a bonus: she sang "What Are You Doing the Rest of Your Life?" before calling it a night. That extra song was later used in the home video version of the special, part of a special promotion with the Blockbuster Video chain.

Barbra the Concert Tour came to a close that night in July, and despite astronomical financial offers to take the show to Japan and Australia, Barbra was through with the concert. She was moving on to new projects and new challenges, secure in the knowledge that she had accomplished the goal she had set for herself. She conquered her stage fright and faced singing live on stage once again. And more than that, she had created a spectacular muscial experience for millions of people who were able to attend—living up to the years of hype and anticipation about what she would do if she ever could overcome her fears. Musically, perhaps there was little doubt that she would excel—her track record was assurance of a top-notch production, a first-rate ensemble, and a body of work filled with well-loved, classic pop songs. But after so many years in the comfort and privacy of soundstages and recording studios, would Barbra Streisand still have the magic qualities which made her a star live and in person? The answer, it turned out, was an incontrovertible yes. Within two minutes of her entrance on stage, Barbra Streisand lived up to all the hype when she sang these new words to Andrew Lloyd Webber's "As If We Never Said Goodbye," and sent chills up the spine of every listener:

At the MGM–Grand, fans could get this overpowering Streisand T-shirt. It was one of many items that sold out instantly.

"I've been in the wings too long,
That's all in the past,
Now I'm standing center stage,
I've come home at last!"

Barbra Streisand the Concert was a once-in-a-lifetime event, the realization of a dream held by fans worldwide to see her on stage, to hear her singing live. If she had merely sat on a stool and sung her greatest hits, she would have thrilled most fans and come out a winner. But Streisand did far more than that by conceiving a program which was personal and polished and an embodiment of the best elements of her remarkable career. Her phenomonal success on tour in 1994 is the stuff of legends, more proof that, as we near the millenium, Barbra Streisand stands out as one of the twentieth century's greatest stars.

9

From the Cutting-Room Floor: Streisand's Lost Scenes, Missing Moments, and Unreleased Songs

As with many stars, Barbra Streisand has recorded countless songs, filmed hundreds of scenes, appeared in numerous production numbers, and committed to celluloid or tape a wide array of performances. The public has had the privilege of seeing or hearing Barbra Streisand's best, and she has been a stringent censor when it comes to judging what is good enough for the paying public. But what about the material which never made it into the final cut of a film, or a recording session which resulted in a few songs remaining on the shelf, or a song or scene from a film which Streisand felt wasn't up to her usual standards? Invariably, those items wind up edited out and shelved, presumably never to be seen or heard again.

Looking back, there are many moments which have failed to reach to the light of day . . . but they do exist. And as *Just for the Record . . .* revealed, the lost Streisand is often as fascinating as the songs and scenes which have etched her career. Hollywood films have notoriously cut entire musical numbers, crucial scenes, and a myriad of moments in the name of running time. In some instances, the reasoning is more complicated but the end result the same. Streisand—onscreen and in musical voice-over—has landed on the cutting-room floor in more than one instance in her career, beginning with her first film.

"A chicken or a duck is a mistake, when you do *Swan Lake*." Barbra in a tutu for *Funny Girl*.

The Movies

Funny Girl   Perhaps the most truncated Streisand musical number ever is the "The Swan," an elaborate parody of the classic *Swan Lake* ballet filmed for *Funny Girl*. The original number was twice as long as what appears on film, including Streisand's interaction with Tommy Rall as the Prince—a reportedly hilarious death scene in which the Prince shoots her with an arrow. Ironically, the cost of this one sequence was as much as "His Love Makes Me Beautiful"; three months of intensive rehearsal went into the number, and ten days were spent filming it. Still, because of the film's long running time, something had to be trimmed, and "The Swan" was the one extraneous number. It was an entertaining and showy piece for Streisand, but it did little to advance the plot; therefore, most of the number was excised. Ironically, when Streisand, producer Ray Stark, and choreographer-director Herbert Ross teamed up for the *Funny Girl* sequel *Funny Lady*, a minute or two from "The Swan" was used in the sequence detailing how Fanny was helping Billy Rose pull *Crazy Quilt* together while on the road. She tells him, "See, Billy, in a tutu, I can be funny," and the image shown is Fanny doing an exaggerated curtsy, like a ballerina, and landing on her duff. In January 1994, Herbert Ross was honored at New York's Lincoln Center for his creative use of the dance in films like *Pennies From Heaven, The Turning Point*, and *Funny Girl*. Many film clips were shown, and in honor of the occasion,

Three scenes from "The Swan," Fanny's comic ballet in *Funny Girl*.

Streisand sent a copy of "The Swan." It was the complete twenty-minute version, one which she had unearthed from her private film library.

"The Swan" wasn't the only victim of the editor's scissors. Before *Funny Girl* was released in 1968, Anne Francis, who played Georgia, accused Streisand of using her influence to have the actress cut out of the picture. The role of Georgia, Fanny's girlfriend in the *Follies,* was significantly trimmed, but Streisand claims to have had little to do with it . . . she didn't have the power (at least not then). Supporting Streisand's claim is the fact that onstage, it was Vera's role—similar to Georgia's—which was the first role to be curtailed. Still, Isobel Lennart's final shooting script included two good Georgia scenes: one where Georgia is reprimanded by Ziegfeld (played by Walter Pidgeon) and she explains to Fanny that she's probably in her last show because producers are always looking for younger, more beautiful girls, but that's something Fanny need never worry about because of her talent. The other scene had a drunken Georgia staggering into Fanny's Fifth Avenue apartment, venomously lacing into Fanny about how people around her—such as herself and Nick—feel pressured to live up to her high expectations. Fanny is cut to the quick, and it sets up Rosie (Kay Medford) telling her daughter that she must open her eyes to Nick's gambling problems and help him straighten himself out.

Barbra's costar, Omar Sharif, was a major movie name at the time, but he was not a singer. Still, there were two solos written for Nick, which Sharif recorded and filmed: "Temporary Arrangement" and "Pink Velvet Jail." The former came early in the film, before Nick even meets Fanny. It showed him as a ne'er-do-well gambler who moved from transient hotels to the elegant suites, depending on how the horses were running. "Pink Velvet Jail" detailed Nick's frustration in being married to Fanny: he loved her but felt he was suffocating in the trappings of her life.

On a Clear Day You Can See Forever
Director Vincente Minnelli's original cut for the film was 143 minutes long, which would not

This is a moment from one of Anne Francis's scenes that were trimmed from *Funny Girl.*

have been a problem had Paramount followed through with the original plan to release *Clear Day* as a road-show engagement. Instead, Paramount recut the film by nearly fifteen minutes and gave it a wide, general release. Lost in the editing were three musical numbers, which eventually turned up on an album called *Cut! Outtakes From Hollywood's Greatest Musicals.* They were: "Wait Till We're Sixty-Five," "She Isn't You," and "Who Is There Among Us Who Knows?" "Wait Till We're Sixty-Five" was a busy musical sequence featuring Streisand and costar Larry Blyden singing about the advantages of corporate retirement plans. As photographs from this scene reveal, there was a lot of choreographed business on Daisy's rooftop set, some dancing, and although it's hard to judge from only the vocal and the pictures, it seemed to be a very elaborate, old-fashioned musical number—one which may have looked jarringly out of place with the rest of the picture. "She Isn't You" was Dr. Chabot's (Yves Montand) musical counterpart to Melinda's (Barbra) "He Isn't

(Above) Jack Nicholson's singing debut in *Clear Day*, "Who Is There Among Us Who Knows?" only made it onto an album of Hollywood outtakes.

(Left) "Wait Till We're Sixty-Five" was a choreographed production number. It was excised from *Clear Day* when the film's distribution was changed from a road-show engagement to a wide release.

(Below) This may have been part of a planned futuristic musical number for *Clear Day* called "E.S.P." The Michel Parenteau Collection

You," and the two parts delineate the odd love affair between the present-day psychiatrist and Daisy's former incarnation. As it appears in the film, Melinda now sings her feelings to Chabot and he merely looks on without replying. Perhaps the most interesting of these three songs is "Who Is There Among Us Who Knows?" Jack Nicholson's musical debut. Nicholson is Daisy's soulmate and former stepbrother, Tad, and his vocal is sweet and the tone of the song ethereal. When Daisy complains about the problems of being clairvoyant,

Tad sings this song, suggesting she is more special than she realizes. Streisand is heard on the end of the recording, humming the melody. The subtext of the song is Tad's love for Daisy and his appreciation of her gifts. The song may seem innocuous now, but since the film ends with Daisy saying she was going back to her apartment to spend some time with Tad, this song would have helped to cement in the viewer's mind that Tad was ultimately the right man for Daisy . . . at least in this lifetime.

There were many trimmed scenes from *Clear Day*, including Robert and Melinda's marriage ceremony. That scene was actually part of the original lobby-card set, as was another showing Daisy and Warren in "Wait Till We're Sixty-Five." Photographs showing Streisand in a black and white, modernistic jumpsuit were from a sequence Minnelli filmed showing Daisy in a future incarnation. Although the music track has never surfaced, it is possible that this outfit was part of an elaborate musical number writer Alan Jay Lerner and Minnelli intended as the big finale, called "E. S. P."

The Owl and the Pussycat   There was one major sequence cut from this picture, but it was a highly significant one. As they are about to make love for the first time, Felix begins to undress Doris, but her outfit is so complicated she fears he'll tear it. Doris screeches for him to stop, and as Felix moves to the side, Doris undresses in front of him. The scene as described appears in the film, but once Doris is naked and lying on the bed, the shot blocks out all but Doris's head and shoulders. As filmed, this was Barbra Streisand's first—and only—nude scene. She took off her clothes, and the scene was filmed and printed, but once Stresiand saw the sequence intact, she had second thoughts. For the record, she said that in her opinion, the nude shot distracted from the comedy of the subsequent scene.

Since Streisand filmed it on the condition that it was her call as to whether it would be used, producer Ray Stark abided by her decision to cut it from the picture. The film was reportedly fogged so it could never come back to haunt Streisand. Of course, it did. In 1979, a sleazy

These two photos show more *Clear Day* scenes which may have been in Vincente Minnelli's original cut of the film.

magazine called *High Society* printed frames from the nude scene. Streisand threatened a $5 million lawsuit, and the magazine agreed to pull the pictures of a bare-breasted Barbra from the magazine and to delete the word "nude" from the cover shot, which showed Streisand in her Doris costume.

Streisand was quite determined that she would not be singing in *The Owl and the*

Barbra and company shlepped all the way to Africa to film sequences for *Up the Sandbox*, but scenes like this one with a tribal native never appeared in the final cut of the picture.

Pussycat. After three big-budget musicals, she felt the need to establish herself as an actress who could carry a film without using her solid-gold vocal cords. Therefore, even though Ray Stark kept telling reporters that Doris would be a "folk hooker"—a singing prostitute—his leading lady flatly refused. Composer Martin Charnin (*Annie*), nevertheless, wrote a song for Streisand to sing in the film called "The Best Thing You've Ever Done." It was to be used in the section of the movie when Doris and Felix are separated. Although Barbra was not interested in singing the song for *The Owl and the Pussycat*, she did like Charnin's song and recorded it. "The Best Thing You've Ever Done" wound up on Streisand's *The Way We Were* album.

Up the Sandbox *Sandbox* was filled with fantasy scenes, but none was more extravagant than the African tribal rites sequence. To film the elaborate fantasy, director Irvin Kershner

and Streisand ventured to Kenya. In the sequence occurring late in the movie, Margaret comes home from a party in honor of Dr. Beineke, an anthropologist who has just returned from the dark continent. After being knocked out by a mugger in the laundry room, she fantasizes that she's on safari with Beineke, trying to uncover the secret of painless childbirth. Of course, Margaret's own misgivings about her pregnancy is the triggering device. But the scene in the film was severely trimmed and rendered nearly inexplicable. The sequence, as written and filmed, was rather long. It entailed Beineke and Margaret being captured by native female warriors, and just as they are to be killed for daring to ask about their secret, Margaret tells them she is "with child." The warrior women embrace her as one of their own and invite her to watch a young woman who is about to give birth. In a dramatic turn, the painless childbirth goes awry, and she

The French lobby-card set for *The Way We Were* shows some of the forty-five minutes' worth of footage that landed on the cutting-room floor.

experiences pain. The baby is delivered, and instead of being black, it's white like Margaret. She is blamed for ruining things and immediately is stalked by the mob. Margaret awakens back in her bedroom.

One theme in much of the criticism of *Up the Sandbox* concerned the ambivalent ending: after Margaret follows Paul and the children to Central Park, she tells him she's pregnant, and he expresses optimism about their future . . . then Margaret drives away in a cab having been given a day to herself. Originally, this fade-out included a Streisand vocalization of the film's theme "If I Close My Eyes," by Billy Goldenberg and Marilyn and Alan Bergman. However, Streisand decided to not use her vocal over the end credits. While the song would not have explained exactly where the character was going or what she was thinking, the lyrics were insightful about Margaret's feelings and the positive value of her fantasies:

> . . . *Maybe dreams are dreamed*
> *so that we can see,*
> *just how real the dawn can be.*

The Way We Were According to director Sydney Pollack, there are forty-five minutes of unused footage from *The Way We Were*, enough material to be the basis for flashbacks if they ever get a sequel produced. The second half of the film is where the most substantive cutting occurred—scenes between Hubbell and Katie where he reveals to her that she has been named a Communist sympathiz-er by Frankie McVeigh (James Woods), an old acquaintance from college. If Katie refuses to testify—which she would—Hubbell would lose his job at the studio and his career would be destroyed. The choice for Katie was clear: agree to testify before the House Committee on Un-American Activities and name names, or she and Hubbell divorce so her refusing to testify will not affect his career. After these scenes were cut from the film, the breakup between Hubbell and Katie seems to be caused by her discovering he has cheated on her with socialite Carol Ann (Lois Chiles).

Other scenes that were cut from this same reel include Katie and Hubbell attending a conference on civil liberties where she is inspired by Brooks Carpenter's (Murray Hamilton) speech and Hubbell becomes aware that Katie is still as politically involved as she ever was. He walks out on the conference, and Katie finds him at the bar. Another cut scene was a confrontation between Katie and Rhea (Allyn Ann McLerie), Hubbell's agent, at the grocery store: Rhea has already been a friendly witness for the Committee, and she tries to justify her actions to Katie. Katie doesn't buy her excuses, and she tells Rhea off. Soon after this confrontation, another scene showed Katie driving by the University of Southern California (L. A.). She sees an intense young girl standing in the middle of a small gathering speaking out in defense of a professor who has been blackballed as a Communist. Sitting in her car, Katie watches and

Amazingly, this scene from *The Way We Were*, where Katie watches a student at U.S.C. give a speech, was included in the first broadcast on HBO.

tears fill her eyes as she obviously sees the girl she used to be in the proud, young student. Of all these scenes, the last somehow was reinserted in the film when it was broadcast on HBO in the late seventies. In subsequent cable viewings, the scene was deleted.

Photographs and alternate drafts of the script reveal some other scenes cut from the film, including Katie and Hubbell's wedding in New York, which introduces her father. Another quiet, revealing scene turned up on a 1990 television special called *Robert Redford and Sydney Pollack: The Men and Their Movies*. It was a snippet from the conversation between Katie and Hubbell during the college sequence, when he tells her he has just sold his first story. Katie looks at him and asks if he always smiles? Hubbell regales her with a story about when he was a little boy in school and was asked to take a note back and forth between all the teachers. When he realized it was always the same note, he read it for himself. It said, "Have you ever seen such a smile?" He then smiled at Katie. A minor moment, the scene was dropped from the film even though it gave Katie a glimpse of Hubbell's understanding of the power of his looks.

Finally, *The Way We Were* actually had more than one theme song. Lyricists Marilyn and Alan Bergman and composer Marvin Hamlisch had written one song called "The Way We Were" so quickly that they had enough time to write a second "The Way We Were" with different music and lyrics. Streisand recorded both versions, and a few years after the film's release, she appeared at a benefit in honor of the Bergmans and for the first time, introduced the unknown "The Way We Were." Streisand explained that they all called this lost song "The Way We Weren't," and it turned up on *Just for the Record*. . . . Both songs were very similar, with "The Way We Weren't" having equally nostalgic lyrics, although a touch more poetic:

> *In the places memories sleep,*
> *I keep the day we were,*
> *the way we were.*

Funny Lady   There were nearly as many music and scene cuts in *Funny Lady* as there were in *On a Clear Day*. A major reason for the cuts was the last minute reconstruction of the film. As written, *Funny Lady* began with Fanny sitting alone in the Cleveland train station following her breakup with Billy Rose. As she did in *Funny Girl* (where Fanny recalls her meteoric rise in the *Follies* and her love affair with Nick), in *Funny Lady* she would flash back to the events which brought Billy into her life and their unusual love story. In this cut, the film ended sadly, almost dejectedly, with Billy walking away from Fanny after he tells her he is in love with Eleanor Holm. This was a more realistic ending, but it wasn't what audiences were expecting from a film called *Funny Lady*—it lacked fun. Therefore, Streisand and Caan were brought in to shoot some additional footage which would still frame the film, but the flashbacks would begin from a later point in Fanny's life. An older, very content Fanny, living in Beverly Hills, welcomes a visit from her ex-husband Billy Rose. With Billy now a millionaire producer, he asks Fanny to consider working with him again. As they talk it over, they reminisce and trigger the flashback. This was the

Part of the elongated "Let's Hear It for Me" musical prologue from *Funny Lady* included Fanny stopping mid-song to place a call from the Beverly Hills Hotel. The Randy Emerian Collection

A musical *Uncle Tom's Cabin*? These shots are from the abbreviated "So Long, Honey Lamb" number from *Funny Lady*.

version which became the final release, and though it's more upbeat than the other, it still gave *Funny Lady* an awkward structure.

Invariably, all this editing and reediting resulted in scenes and musical numbers being dropped or recut, often in bizarre ways. "Am I Blue," "So Long, Honey Lamb," and "Let's Hear It for Me" all had longer versions than the ones in the final cut. "Am I Blue" is heard as a ballad for the most part on the soundtrack, and that was how it was filmed—with Fanny alone onstage singing the torch song in homage to Nick. Then, in an abrupt mood change, she ends the number comically. In the film, all that appeared was the comedy. In the case of "So Long, Honey Lamb," a musical send-up of *Uncle Tom's Cabin*, again the soundtrack contains more of the song than the film. Photos from the number suggest an overly produced sketch starring Streisand and Ben Vereen, which culminates with Barbra flying across the set like an angel in heaven. Onscreen, all that remains of "So Long, Honey Lamb" is a thirty-second snippet which does not look funny. This may have

been one number which deserved to be left on the cutting-room floor. "Let's Hear It for Me," *Funny Lady's* song à la "Don't Rain on My Parade," originally included a long middle section, set in the lobby of the Beverly Hills Hotel as Fanny is calling Cleveland, looking for Billy.

Fanny explains to her daughter Fran why she has just married Billy Rose, in this lost scene from *Funny Lady*.

While waiting on the phone, Fanny sings a recitative which delineates the differences between Nick and Billy and why she is now ready to choose Billy:

> *Billy's an alley cat, that's for*
> *   sure,*
> *Nick's from a horsier class.*
> *But I'd rather be with a genuine*
> *   alley cat,*
> *Than a genuine, thoroughbred-*
> *   horse's ass!*

The extra sequence was interesting, but the song became more like an aria than a musical number, and as the lyrics indicate, it was terribly redundant.

There were other scenes from *Funny Lady* which never made it into the final cut, such as the one showing Billy composing "Does Your Chewing Gum Lose Its Flavor (on the Bedpost Overnight)?" on the typewriter. Another was an intimate scene between Fanny and her daughter Fran which came on Fanny's wedding day to Billy. Eight-year-old Fran locks herself in the bathroom to protest the marriage. She lets Fanny in, and her mother tries to explain why she has just married Billy Rose. "I fell in like

with him," she says, assuring her daughter that Nick, Fran's father, would always be her one true love, but that she doesn't want to be alone anymore. The scene ends with Fran and Fanny joining the reception in the living room. Other scenes feature Streisand and Roddy McDowall coming into Fanny's home and Fanny explaining her auctioning her furniture to raise money. Finally, Streisand's imitation of Baby Snooks, Fanny Brice's most famous character, was filmed to show how successful Fanny had been on the radio. The Baby Snooks scenes, alas, were cut to less than one minute of film time.

A Star Is Born   When director Frank Pierson wrapped production on *A Star Is Born*, he had six weeks to deliver his director's cut. He did, and then Streisand put together her version, the final cut, of *A Star Is Born*. As executive producer, it was her version which was released. The one scene which was most problematic turned out to be the last one: Esther's concert. Multiple cameras captured the musical number from a variety of angles, including full shots of the crowd exulting in her perfomance. When Streisand edited her version, she discovered the coverage of the finale was spotty, and she didn't have the shot selection to put the piece together as she envisioned it. Her solution to the problem was to take a radical approach. Instead of multiple angles, the musical sequence would be shown in one, uninterrupted medium close-up. All the emotional turmoil of the scene would play in Streisand's eyes, her movements, and her music. When the documentary based on *A Star is Born* (*With One More Look at You*) was shown on syndicated television, alternate shots from the finale were revealed. Producer Jon Peters showed two other cut scenes on a 1977 television special called *Hollywood Outtakes*. One had Streisand as Esther playing the guitar and singing "Evergreen" to John Norman Howard, who is reclining on her couch. She is shy and turns her back to him to sing, and when she's finished, Esther asks him what he thought. He doesn't answer, and she turns to see he has fallen asleep. The other scene Peters introduced on this show was a comical bit with Esther trying to cook. Streisand is making bread, covered with flour, and talking to her rising dough like Julia Child. A pair of steaks in the oven then catch fire, and she screams for Johnny to come quickly. He then pulls the fiery steaks from the broiler and rushes them outside the house where he beats them until the flames die.

When *A Star Is Born* was first broadcast on ABC, an extra scene suddenly appeared which had never been in any other version. During the recording sessions John was producing for Esther, he calls a break, and Chinese food is brought into the studio. Esther is petulant and upset, and when John tries to find out why, she tells him the song she's been recording (with which he is satisfied) isn't the way she wants it. He assures her they will play the song exactly as she wants to do it—it's her song. That scene then cuts to Esther singing "Evergreen" into the studio mike with John providing backup. The cut scene was sweet and charming, and perhaps the only reason it was dropped in the release print was the fact that it contained a continuity error: the outfit Esther is wearing in the Chinese food scene is different from the one she is wearing to sing the song a few minutes later.

A sign of how broke Hillary had become, she had to fill up the Rolls-Royce at the self-serve island. This scene never made it into *The Main Event*.

For this scene in *A Star Is Born*, Streisand learned to play guitar so she could accompany herself. The scene was cut from the film, nullifying her effort as well as simple, lovely rendition of "Evergreen."

Musically, two songs which were intended for *A Star Is Born*, "Answer Me" and "Lullaby for Myself," turned up on Streisand's follow-up album to the soundtrack, *Streisand Superman*. "Answer Me" was replaced by "Lost Inside of You"; "Lullaby for Myself" was replaced by "Everything."

The Main Event While they were filming *The Main Event*, screenwriters Gail Parent and Andrew Smith continued reworking the script. Subsequently, there were two endings for the film: the one which was released, and another which was in the final shooting script. The latter had Hillary discovering that Leo Gough (James Gregory) had double-crossed them: all the Kid's fights had been fixed, and in the big rematch bout with Hector Mantilla (Richard Lawson), he was going to be massacred. In the dressing room before the big fight, Hillary tells him the truth about the fights and also admits she loves him. They run off to South America, and in the last shot, Kid is running a driving school out of a new building (shaped like a boxing glove), while a very pregnant and contented Hillary is mixing perfumes in her home lab. Like *A Star Is Born*, there was a syndicated television special made to promote the film, called *Getting in Shape for "The Main Event,"* and in it are clips from Hillary and the Kid's locker-room scene. It was decided that while this ending was funny, it lacked the punch necessary for the film. The

Yentl contemplates another date with the matchmaker, a scene dropped from the 1983 release.

final fight sequence was choreographed, and the movie ended in a highly compromised fashion when Hillary threw in the towel to call off the fight.

Once the picture was in the can, Howard Zieff delivered the director's cut to Barwood Films. It was then Streisand's prerogative to recut the film: she again (as with *A Star Is Born*) retained the right to final cut. After putting the picture together, she thought a crucial moment was missing: a morning-after scene for Kid and Hillary. What was the aftermath of their sleeping together? What had changed? Streisand and Ryan O'Neal shot a new scene, which she directed, to carry the dramatic thread of their transformed relationship through to the finish.

To add a powerful plus to the conclusion, Streisand recorded "Fight"/"The Main Event," a disco number concocted by Paul Jabara, Bruce Roberts, and Bob Esty. It was a big hit, landing on the top of the radio charts. But there was another theme for *The Main Event*, a musical composition by Streisand which was a romantic ballad. Streisand's melody was eventually married to lyrics by Richard Baskin for the *Emotion*

album; the song was called "Here We Are at Last."

Yentl   Barbra Streisand had planned the filming of her first directorial effort so meticulously it is not surprising that there are very few (known) cut scenes. Photographs and the final shooting script reveal a sequence from the first part of the picture where Yentl is coerced into meeting a prospective groom to please her father and the matchmaker. However, when the young man is asked to show off his brilliance by interpreting a story from the Talmud, Yentl cannot be silent. She horrifies the potential fiancé and his family by correcting him and interpreting the passage in question. Yentl successfully sabotages the efforts of the matchmaker, much to her father's displeasure.

Musically, some additional chanting and two songs have emerged which were intended for *Yentl*: "The Moon and I" and "Several Sins a Day." The former was replaced in the film by "No Matter What Happens," a song which is much more obvious about Yentl's desire to set things right with Hadass and return to her life as a woman by revealing herself to Avigdor. "The Moon and I" turned up on *Just for the Record. . . .* On the other hand, "Several Sins a Day" was only unearthed on a bootleg Streisand album called *Lost in Time*. The song deals with the contradiction of Yentl's devoutly studying the Torah and the Talmud while she is in effect sinning daily by masquerading as a boy to do so. The lyrics, by the Bergmans, are wonderfully macabre as Yentl reveals her fears about divine retribution:

> *It's worth the price if I can get*
> *the learning that I crave,*
> *Even though I know my father's*
> *spinning in his grave,*
> *It wouldn't hurt if I was also*
> *learning to be brave,*
> *For the time when I'll pay for*
> *my several sins a day!*

One criticism Streisand endured from some corners was her decision to be the lone musical voice in *Yentl*. Streisand never intended for

Yentl to be a traditional musical, with all the characters expressing their emotions and desires through song. Rather, Yentl's songs were the only way the audience was aware of their protagonist's intentions. The songs were intended to be similar to Shakespeare's soliloquies. When Mandy Patinkin was cast as Avigdor, Streisand and company were aware of his magnificent singing voice. For a time, they considered how to rework the film to get him some songs. In the end, Streisand decided it was not possible to get Patinkin into the film musically, but some tapes have emerged indicating how she tried to give his voice a chance to shine. His voice was recorded singing two folk songs which were heard in the background as Yentl rode in a wagon with the other yeshiva boys to Bechev. Patinkin sang the ditties in both his chest voice and his distinctive falsetto. In another recording, his voice is one among many, chanting prayers in synagogue.

Nuts There is only one significant scene from *Nuts* which landed on the cutting-room floor: a flashback showing Claudia and her college boyfriend, Peter Draper. Dancing together at a party, Peter asks Claudia to marry him, but she's not interested in becoming anyone's wife. She suggests he marry some other girl so that Claudia could be the other woman in his life. Finally, as the scene ends, she agrees to be his wife. As the photograph from this scene reveals, Streisand wore a long-haired wig for the scene, and neither she nor the actor playing Peter look like college students from the seventies. There was also additional footage shot showing Claudia's emancipation at the end of the picture.

The Prince of Tides There were a few extra scenes which were no doubt cut for length, including one where Tom taught Lowenstein how to bake bread (to send to Bernard in school). This also echoes the cut bread-baking scene from *A Star Is Born*. There are two other scenes which delineate more of Lowenstein and Tom's deepening affair: the two making love in Savannah's bedroom, and Tom and Lowenstein walking across the Brooklyn Bridge where he is telling her about growing up in the south. Ironically, although it was cut from

In a flashback, Claudia recalls Peter Draper asking her to marry him. The scene was edited out of *Nuts*, perhaps because Barbra was having a bad wig day?

the final print, the latter scene was used in the trailer and print advertising. There was, interestingly, some significant lost dialogue in the scene featuring Savannah and Tom walking near the river. There were also references to sequences in Conroy's novel: as teens, Tom, Luke, and Savannah rescuing a white porpoise, named Carolina Snow, from an aquarium; and as children, Luke and Tom putting a dead sea turtle into Reese Newbury's bed. Since these two long and complicated flashbacks could not be fit into the film, these references may have prompted the complaints of some critics who felt Streisand hadn't put enough of Conroy's original novel into the movie.

Finally, Streisand recorded a beautiful, romantic ballad called "The Places That Belong to You," which was the love theme from *The Prince of Tides*. Originally, the Marilyn and Alan Bergman–James Newton Howard song was going to be heard over the end credits. However, Barbra Streisand, the director, felt the film should not end with Barbra Streisand, the singer (or Lowenstein, if you will), distracting viewers from the denouement. The song was released as a single and appears on the soundtrack album, as does an extra Streisand vocal of

THE PRINCE OF TIDES

"For
All We Know,"
which is strictly an instrumental in
the Rainbow Room scene in the film. Streisand
did have a video created incorporating *The
Prince of Tides* footage with shots of her singing
the song in a recording studio, but because
"The Places That Belong to You" was not sung
in the movie (or over the credits), it was not eligible for an Academy Award nomination as Best
Song. Her decision not to use the song recalls
her pulling "If I Close My Eyes" from *Up the
Sandbox.*

Other Long-Lost Treasures

In Barbra Streisand's career, there have been
some projects that have just not worked out.
Fortunately for her fans, there have not been
too many, but the few have been significant
nonetheless.

Streisand's Viva Las Vegas *Es Muerte*
On July 2, 1969, Barbra Streisand opened the
new International Hotel in Las Vegas and for a
cool million bucks played the showroom for
four weeks. It was a staggering amount of
money—for that time—and both her salary and
her performance received enormous publicity.
Cognizant of her agreement with CBS, Streisand

(Above) This romantic image of Tom and Lowenstein on the
Brooklyn Bridge promenade appeared in the trailer as well as
advertising for *The Prince of Tides*, but it was cut from the film.

had the two evening performances from July 28
videotaped as a possible special. The shows
were also recorded as a potential soundtrack
from the special. However, Streisand ultimately decided not to use the Vegas shows. Not
long after this appearance, Barbra began working with Richard Perry on *Stoney End*, and her
more contemporary image did not jibe with the
glamour-queen musical diva on display in
Vegas. Some of the footage did appear on *The
Ed Sullivan Show* on September 28, 1969:
Streisand's *Hello, Dolly!* medley—"Hello,
Dolly!"/"Before the Parade Passes By"/"So Long,
Dearie!" And nearly a year later, when Sullivan's
show hosted the American Guild of Variety
Artists' (AGVA) Georgie Awards, Streisand
allowed a video clip from the Vegas show—her
singing "On a Clear Day"—to set up her appearance onstage to receive the award (presented
by New York City Mayor John V. Lindsay).

Frost Show Is Frozen in Time
In 1970,
David Frost was hosting a syndicated talk show
which was renowned for its one-on-one, in-
depth interviews. Frost convinced Streisand to
share an hour with him and she sang two
songs—"Didn't We" and "I Don't Know Where I
Stand"—as well. The hour was taped and
hyped, but at the last minute, CBS complained
that Streisand was in breach of her contract with
them. Frost's show was on the Metromedia network. CBS prevailed, and the Streisand hour
was never aired.

Between Yesterday and Never
Long
before Streisand, Legrand, and Alan and Marilyn
Bergman collaborated on *Yentl*, they conceived
a theme album called *Between Yesterday and
Tomorrow*. It became known as *Life Cycle of a
Woman*, because essentially that is what it was
to be. Through song, Streisand would portray
the life of a woman—as a child, a young
woman awakening to adulthood, the first feelings of love, motherhood, lost love, et al. It was
an ambitious and potentially blockbuster project. A few of the songs were recorded in April,
1973, including "Between Yesterday and
Tomorrow," "Can You Tell The Moment?" and
"Mother and Child." This one session, however,
was all that was ever done for the album.

Streisand was circumspect about her reasons in the liner notes for *Just for the Record . . .* , where two of these cuts surfaced, but Michel Legrand suggested in an interview that Barbra felt too close to the project. He seemed to think the songs stirred up emotions too close to the bone for her. Whatever the reasons, it's a shame to realize that material of this caliber—tailor-made for Streisand—is lost forever.

The Director's Special Edition, Not!   In the past few years, it has become quite the vogue for the director of a successful film to provide detailed background and lost scenes as part of a specially created laser disc or video-tape release. Danny DeVito did it with *War of the Roses*; Ridley Scott did it with *Blade Runner*. Streisand was approached by Criterion Laser Discs to create a special edition of *The Prince of Tides*, followed by a new version of *Yentl*. Streisand was enthusiastic and put many hours and much effort into the *Tides* disc, providing commentary, costume and rehearsal tapes, behind-the-scenes footage, and cut scenes. However, problems arose with Criterion when it came to signing off on the project. Streisand demanded final approval, and Criterion promised to give her just that. But Criterion jumped the gun on Streisand. They believed they had made her final changes, unaware that Barbra wanted to proof those changes before the disc went into production. Without getting that final check-off, the company pressed 10,000 copies of the disc.

From Streisand's point of view, the disc was unacceptable. From Criterion's point of view, the 10,000 discs were ready to be shipped. Barbra would not allow the discs to be released, and Criterion refused to dump the 10,000 discs and press a new set. Ultimately, the Criterion special edition of *The Prince of Tides* was shelved indefinitely. Hopefully, Streisand and Criterion will come to some compromise agreement, and the disc will be redone or released . . . paving the way for Streisand to do a director's special edition of *Yentl*, and any other future projects.

On Broadway, On Video   In 1988, Streisand and composer-arranger Rupert Holmes worked on music for the sequel to *The Broadway Album, Back to Broadway*. Recorded at MGM-Lorimar in a huge studio to accommodate the one-hundred-piece orchestra, Holmes found it nearly impossible to see Streisand in her recording booth and to be seen by the orchestra at the same time. He suggested setting up one video camera on Barbra and one on himself, with monitors for each of them to be able to see the other. The video could also, if necessary, be used in a behind-the-scenes documentary about the album, à la *Putting It Together: The Making of "The Broadway Album."* The session produced only two songs with which Streisand was totally happy—"You'll Never Know" and "Warm All Over." Both were used on *Just for the Record . . .* , and a few clips of "Warm All Over" were

Streisand took a musical swipe at the Republicans with a version of "Send in the Clowns" called "Send Home the Clowns." It was edited from the HBO broadcast and home video of *One Voice.*

Barbra's concert in Central Park ran more than two hours. The television special and album were about half as long.

cert—all two hours' worth—was recorded and filmed. Those lost songs include: "Any Place I Hang My Hat Is Home," "My Honey's Lovin' Arms," "I'll Tell the Man in the Street," "Where Am I Going?," "More Than You Know," "All the Things You Are," "I Wish You Love," "What Now My Love?" "Free Again," "When the Sun Comes Out," "I'm Always Chasing Rainbows," "Stout-Hearted Men," and "I'm All Smiles."

One More Moment From One Voice Streisand's 1986 Malibu fund-raiser for six Democratic senatorial candidates, *One Voice*, was recorded as an album, a television special for HBO, and a home video release. The program was complete, save one number. Lyricists Alan and Marilyn Bergman wrote special, derisive lyrics to Stephen Sondheim's classic ballad, "Send in the Clowns." The parody was called "Send Home the Clowns," and it took nasty swipes at the Reagan-Bush administration. Since the album–television special–video were essentially apolitical, this song was cut and Streisand's performance lost forever.

Closed Circuit Only . . . The Clinton Fund-Raiser: Voices for Change '92 On October 16, 1992, Streisand was the star of a Beverly Hills concert to raise money for another Democrat, Bill Clinton. In order to enlist donations from other parts of the country, the performance was telecast via satellite to locations around the country . . . including the Tribeca Grill Restaurant in New York City. Streisand sang "On a Clear Day," "Come Rain or Come Shine," "Children Will Listen," "Happy Days Are Here Again," and "God Bless America." Like "Send Home the Clowns" in *One Voice*, Streisand also sang a specialty number for Clinton called "It Has to Be You." Again the Bergmans provided the perfectly wry, wickedly critical lyrics about why Clinton had to win the election:

> *George Bush and Dan Quayle,*
> *they golf and they sail.*
> *One doesn't look well,*
> *the other can't spell.*

used to publicize the boxed set. The rest of the Holmes *Back to Broadway* sessions were shelved by Barbra, including video and audio of her singing "How Are Things in Glocca Moora"/"Heather on the Hill" from *Finian's Rainbow* and *Brigadoon*, respectively; "Make Our Garden Grow" from *Candide*; "A Funny Thing Happened on My Way to Love" from *I Can Get It for You Wholesale*; "Moonfall" from *The Mystery of Edwin Drood*; and "On My Own" from *Les Misérables*.

U. K. Only . . . The Making of The Prince of Tides A behind-the-scenes documentary about *The Prince of Tides* was a special promotional tape sold with copies of the movie when the video was released . . . but only in England.

An American in London While Streisand was in England doing *Funny Girl* in spring 1966, she was asked to take part in a show at the U. S. Embassy. The Festival of American Arts, held on June 12, 1966, celebrated the American musical theatre. Streisand sang a medley from *Porgy and Bess*, "Where Am I Going?" and "People." The show was broadcast on the BBC, and home recordings of the program have circulated among fans.

Twice As Much Happening in Central Park Streisand's fourth television special was a one-hour, edited version of her concert in Central Park on June 17, 1967. The entire con-

Streisand's Unreleased Music Videos

"My Heart Belongs to Me" Way back in 1977, Barbra Streisand appeared in her first music video: "My Heart Belongs to Me" from *Streisand Superman*. Crudely created with hand-held footage of Streisand as she appeared on the album cover, Barbra mouthed the song as the music track played. The whole thing seems like a joke, and Streisand clowns a bit, pretending to cough because of the manufactured mist wafting around her. This film was never meant to be a music video, rather it was made for a Columbia Records convention in anticipation of Streisand's new album. Although it was never released to home video or broadcast, fuzzy video copies of it have surfaced among fans. By 1981, MTV was booming, and music videos were becoming very popular.

"Woman in Love" The international success of *Guilty* warranted music videos to accompany the hit singles; however, Streisand was wrapped up in preproduction on *Yentl* and simply didn't have the time or inclination to do music videos. In England, Columbia Records created a video comprised of still shots of Streisand and Barry Gibb from the album jacket and film clips of Barbra from *A Star Is Born* and *What's Up, Doc?* It was only aired in Europe, but fans in America have obtained copies of it.

"For All We Know" A montage sequence from *The Prince of Tides* to "The Places That Belong to You" was released, but the other Streisand vocal, "For All We Know" was also put together as a video. However, it was never broadcast in full. Snippets of it appeared in the introduction to Streisand's *60 Minutes* interview in November 1991.

Recording Sessions

There have been hundreds of songs recorded by Barbra Streisand. Most end up on albums or singles, and some were unearthed for the *Just for the Record . . .* retrospective boxed set. However, there are many songs which remain locked in Streisand's personal music library, as well as the Columbia Records vault. Here's a list of the songs you've never heard but that Barbra has sung.

1955   "Zing, Went the Strings of My Heart"
1962   "Napoleon"
1963   "Who Would Have Dreamed"
1967   "Willow Weep for Me"
1968   "Lost in Wonderland"
1969   "Tomorrow I Will Bring You a Rose"
1970   "I Think It's Gonna Rain Today," "Living Without You," "He's a Runner," "Because," "Your Loves Return"
1971   "Talk About Your Troubles"
1973   "The Way We Weren't" (rehearsed only), "Once You've Been in Love," "Mother and Child," "The Smile I Never Smiled," "La Revision," "And Sylvia," "Better," "Do Me Wrong, But Do Me," "Make the Man Love Me" (different than the one on *Simply Streisand*)
1974   "You Light Up My Life" (by Carole King, not Joseph Brooks), "Type Thang," "Everything Must Change," "On Broadway" (rehearsed only)
1977   "Shadow in the City," "Try to Win a Friend," "I Love Making Love to You," "Music Man," "Till I Get It Right," "Nightmoves"
1978   "Lookin' Out for Number One"
1979   "I Am Alone Tonight," "Understand Your Man," "Something's Missing From My Life," "Rainbow Connection," "Tracks of My Tears"
1982   "The Moon and I," "Several Sins a Day"
1984   "When the Lovin' Goes Out of Love," "How Do You Keep the Music Playing?"
1985   "Being Good Isn't Good Enough," "Home," "An Unusual Way," "Show Me," "Shall We Dance"/"Hello, Young Lovers"
1988   "How Are Things in Glocca Morra"/"Heather on the Hill," "Make Our Garden Grow," "A Funny Thing Happened on My Way to Love," "Moonfall," "On My Own," "Keeper of the Flame," "Give Me Tonight"
1989   "Halfway Through the Night"

(Above) Bill Moore and Chris Nickens are two of the gifted artists who have created beautiful pencil sketches and lithographs of Barbra. Christopher Nickens (right), Moore Legends (left)

(Left) This international poster for the film of *Funny Girl* emphasized the romance.

(Lower left) This idea for a *Hello, Dolly!* poster was rejected. *Barbra Quarterly*

(Lower right) Another foreign *Funny Girl* poster offered ten different images from the movie. *Barbra Quarterly*

10

Through the Artists' Eyes

*I*n *The Barbra Streisand Album*, composer Harold Arlen described Barbra Streisand by evoking the image of a painting by Modigliani. In movie posters, on magazine covers, and on canvases in art galleries, Barbra Streisand's face and figure have been the inspiration for many interpretations.

Because of her exotic features, especially her famous nose, artists have tried to capture the unusual quality that is Barbra Streisand. Through some eyes, she's been depicted as a great beauty; through others, a bizarre alien. Here are some of the more interesting artists' renditions of Barbra.

(Above left) The British poster for *Hello, Dolly!* was busy and inviting.

(Above right) The American poster for *On a Clear Day You Can See Forever* was rather unattractive.

(Left) The British version of the poster was probably the most interesting and arresting image. *Barbra Quarterly*

FIDA

EDMONDO AMATI presenta

Barbra Streisand
in
Voglio la Libertà

BARBRA
STREISAND
ROBERT
REDFORD

por primera vez juntos!

dos seres sin nada en común en pos de un amor imposible
en

TAL COMO ERAMO
(THE WAY WE W

con
Bradford Dillman · Viveca Lindfors · Herb Edelman
Murray Hamilton · Patrick O'neal

DIRECTOR: SYDNEY POLLACK   Panavisión   Color

COLUMBIA FILMS Y RASTAR PRODUCTIONS

(Top left) In one foreign poster for *Up the Sandbox*, the Castro
character seemed more important to the film than Barbra!
Barbra Quarterly

(Bottom left) Fan Ron Hardcastle came up with this artful
photo for an invitation to a party in honor of Barbra's birthday.
Christopher Nickens

(Top right) This was the Spanish poster for *The Way We Were*.
Aye, carumba! *Barbra Quarterly*

(Bottom right) One of the rejected posters for *The Way We
Were. Barbra Quarterly*

STREISAND & REDFORD

THE WAY
WE WERE

Katie Morosky

& Hubbell Gardiner.

Flatbush Ave.

& Sutton Place.

Maybe it'll work!

(Top left) Scavullo's photograph for the poster of *A Star Is Born* became instantly recognizable.

(Above) Richard Amsel drew this lovely image of Barbra for a proposed *TV Guide* cover. The Dennis Palante Collection

(Top right) The *Mad* magazine spoof of Barbra's first three movies prompted this infamous cover art.

(Right) Other magazines have found Barbra's image the inspiration for artful interpretation.

11

The Ones That Got Away: Streisand Projects That Might Have Been

In every star's career, his or her name is often attached to proposed films. Often it's merely gossip or conjecture or wishful thinking to say such and such an actor is going to do this or that film. The Hollywood buzz is filled with films which never come together in the way the gossips suggested. With Streisand's immediate success in movies, her name was great copy, and she was reported to be talking film projects with every Tom, Dick, and Harry. Looking back over the past twenty-five years, the lost Streisand—the film projects which never came together—make for a fascinating and illuminating exercise in speculation.

The Films Most Likely to Be Produced

These are legitimate films in development. The only question is, when will they ever reach the screen . . . and will Barbra Streisand still be involved when they do?

The Mirror Has Two Faces Screenwriter Richard LaGravanese (*The Fisher King*) has adapted this modern fairy tale for Barwood Films. Barbra will direct and star, possibly with Harrison Ford as her leading man, with Elizabeth Taylor cast as her mother. Streisand would play Rose, a plain, single professor of English literature, who has never believed she was pretty enough for any man to love, thanks to a damaged self-image, courtesy of her mother, Hannah, a great beauty (described in the screenplay as "an Elizabeth Taylor type"). Ford would play Gregory, a mathematics professor, who was so hurt by his first love that he has sworn off romance. He proposes a mathematical formula for marriage and picks Rose as the perfect partner. Once they're married, unex-pected love blossoms, and when she wants their relationship to become more intimate, he's scared to death. She believes his rejection is because of her looks. Her mother wants to help her—realizing the wrong she did Rose as a child. With makeup and clothes and attitude, Rose is transformed into a beauty. Meanwhile, Greg goes off the deep end, unable to deal with love. Finally, he comes to realize that his fear of losing Rose is greater than his fear of loving her. The gentle romantic comedy ends with the lovers reunited, transformed by love. This is probably one of the top Streisand film projects which could get made in 1995.

The Normal Heart Larry Kramer worked on the screenplay for his powerful play about the beginnings of the AIDS epidemic within the gay community, and the uncooperative, disbelieving authorities in New York and the country who refuse to face the reality of the disease for Barwood in the mid-eighties. A falling-out with Streisand resulted in his shopping the project elsewhere. He ultimately brought *The Normal Heart* back to Barbra, and she is now very actively working on the film, which she will direct and appear in (in a small role). Dustin Hoffman is rumored to be her first choice for the starring role of Ned Weeks. On April 18, 1993, she attended a reading of the play to benefit AIDS research at the Broadhurst Theatre in New York. If *The Mirror Has Two Faces* doesn't get made in 1994, *The Normal Heart* probably will.

The Margaret Bourke-White Story Producer Linda Yellen and Barwood president Cis Corman were developing a film biography of Bourke-White detailing the famed *Life* magazine photographer's life, marriage to author Erskine Caldwell, and world-wide travels in the

If *The Way We Changed* is ever made, it will include forty-five minutes of flashbacks from *The Way We Were*. Perhaps even this scene will see the light of day.

thirties and forties (which resulted in well-known photographs of such international leaders as FDR and Gandhi). However, in 1989, director Lawrence Schiller filmed a television movie, *The Margaret Bourke-White Story*, with Farrah Fawcett in the title role, and the Yellen project went onto the back burner, where it presumably remains to this day.

The Jackson Pollock Story Robert De Niro and Barbra are developing this film biography about the famed modern artist and his wife, Lee Krasner. The project was first announced in 1993; no word yet on whether Streisand or De Niro will direct, or if someone else, possibly Martin Scorsese or Sydney Pollack, will be brought in.

Third Time Lucky A romantic drama about a mentally disturbed woman and the younger man who enters her life, which Streisand has had in development for over ten years.

The Story of a Town Streisand purchased the rights to Joyce Maynard's 1986 *New York Times Sunday Magazine* story about a group of citizens fighting the dumping of nuclear waste in their New Hampshire village. This could become a television movie.

The Way We Changed The long-talked-about sequel to *The Way We Were*, with Streisand, Robert Redford, and Sydney Pollack reteaming. According to Pollack, the story would pick up Hubbell and Katie's separate lives in the turbulent sixties. Their daughter, Rachel, is a student at Berkeley, becoming very involved in the antiwar movement. When she gets into trouble, Katie turns to Hubbell for help with Rachel. Katie and Hubbell reunite, older and wiser and still in love. Pollack would use nearly forty-five minutes of footage from the original film as flashbacks. The last time this project was discussed, in 1986, the salaries for Streisand and Redford were $10 million each.

Broadway Barbra

Having begun her musical comedy career on Broadway, Barbra Streisand was at one time considered its savior. Therefore, it's not surprising that she has been suggested to star in film versions of these Broadway musicals:

Seesaw 1973 musical version of William Gibson's play *Two for the Seesaw* with a score by Cy Coleman and Dorothy Fields. Story of a self-deprecating, Jewish New York girl, Gittel Mosca, and her ill-fated love affair with Jerry Ryan, a WASP lawyer from the Midwest. Broadway cast: Michele Lee and Ken Howard. Proposed Hollywood casting: Barbra and Ken Howard.

They're Playing Our Song 1979 Marvin Hamlisch–Carole Bayer Sager musical, with a book by Neil Simon. Successful bachelor songwriter finds an unlikely romance with a free-spirited lyricist. Broadway cast: Lucie Arnaz and

Barbra and Elliott Gould were divorced in 1971, but their names were still linked for a film version of the Broadway musical *They're Playing Our Song.*

Robert Klein. Proposed Hollywood cast: Barbra and Elliott Gould.

Chicago Musical adaptation of the story of Roxy Hart. Set in Chicago in the Roaring Twenties, the 1975 show, with a score by Fred Ebb and John Kander, was directed and choreographed by Bob Fosse. Broadway cast: Gwen Verdon and Chita Rivera. Proposed Hollywood cast: Barbra and Goldie Hawn.

Ballroom Original television musical *The Queen of the Stardust Ballroom*, adapted for Broadway by director-choreographer Michael Bennett. Score by Billy Goldenberg and Marilyn and Alan Bergman. Original television cast: Maureen Stapleton. Proposed Hollywood cast: Barbra.

Evita Andrew Lloyd Webber and Tim Rice smash pop-opera based on the life and legend of Eva Peron, the wife of Argentinian dictator Juan Peron. Cuban rebel Che Guevera comments on the action. Broadway cast: Patti LuPone and Mandy Patinkin. Proposed Hollywood cast: Barbra and Mandy. Despite her name being attached to it for years, Barbra has said she never wanted to do the role and would not appear in any film version of *Evita.*

Follies 1971 Stephen Sondheim musical

about the reunion of former showgirls. Set in the remains of a soon-to-be demolished theatre, the four main characters—Sally and Phyllis and their husbands Buddy and Ben—are haunted by their memories and images of their younger selves. Broadway cast: Dorothy Collins, Alexis Smith, Gene Nelson, and John McMartin. Proposed Hollywood cast: Barbra and Liza Minnelli.

Legends   Carol Channing and Mary Martin toured in this version of James Kirkwood's comedy *Diary of a Mad Playwright*, about two famous actresses who are working together for the first time and the problems which arise. Proposed Hollywood cast: Barbra and Bette Midler . . . and a musical score.

Those Lost Oscars

As the top female box-office star in the seventies, Barbra Streisand was approached with many screenplays. Here are some of the more noteworthy projects she's passed on. Ironically, in each case, the actress who played the role Barbra turned down went on to be nominated and, in many cases, actually received the Oscar for Best Actress.

Diary of a Mad Housewife   In 1970, Carrie Snodgress costarred with Richard Benjamin as a put-upon young wife and mother, emotionally abused by her cruel husband. Streisand chose to do *Up the Sandbox*, covering similar territory, instead. Snodgress was nominated as Best Actress.

They Shoot Horses, Don't They?   This 1969 Sydney Pollack drama, examining desperate characters participating in a dance marathon during the Depression, was probably offered to Barbra while she was in the midst of *Hello, Dolly!*, with *On a Clear Day* scheduled to follow. Ultimately, Jane Fonda and Michael Sarrazin starred in the movie. Fonda was nominated for an Oscar. "The other part appealed to me more, the Susannah York part, the blond, crazy girl," Streisand told Larry Grobel in 1977. "Also, I remember thinking I couldn't dance that long."

Klute   1971 detective thriller about the rela-

Barbra has always found working with Marilyn and Alan Bergman *(standing left)* stimulating and satisfying. Will she star in a film version of their musical *Ballroom* some time in the future?

tionship between an out-of-town cop and a hard-boiled, New York call girl. Directed by Alan J. Pakula, it starred Jane Fonda and Donald Sutherland. Fonda won her first Oscar for the role of Bree Daniels. According to Barbra, when she read an early version of the screenplay, "[It] was a silly script, plus there was no director attached to it. If I had known it was Alan J. Pakula, I would have done it."

Cabaret   Liza Minnelli seemed born to play Sally Bowles, but Barbra was approached soon after the show opened on Broadway. The 1972 film musical by Bob Fosse was a major success, winning eight Academy Awards, including Liza's for Best Actress.

The Exorcist   Big-screen adaptation of William Peter Blatty's novel about a young girl being possessed by the devil. The 1973 William Friedkin film starred Linda Blair as the possessed child and Ellen Burstyn as her mother. Can we see Streisand cleaning up Linda's spewing green pea soup? Still, Burstyn was nominated as Best Actress.

Julia   Lillian Hellman's recollections of her

friend Julia, from the book *Pentimento*. Fred Zinnemann directed this 1977 adaptation, with Jane Fonda as Lillian and Vanessa Redgrave as Julia. Both actresses were nominated for Oscars; Redgrave won in the supporting category.

Alice Doesn't Live Here Anymore   A 1975 drama, directed by Martin Scorsese, starred Ellen Burstyn as Alice, a young widow and mother who aspires to be a singer but ends up slinging hash in a diner. "I should have been older to have a twelve-year-old son. Also, the script wasn't as good [as it was eventually]. . . . And Martin Scorsese wasn't involved with it. I didn't feel people would really believe me playing the part. You believe Ellen Burstyn, she was wonderful—and sang just right. I would have botched up the screenplay if I played it," Streisand said in 1977. Streisand wasn't the only one who thought Burstyn was wonderful; she won the Oscar as Best Actress. Streisand's reasons are all good, but in 1974, her film was *For Pete's Sake*. In retrospect, *Alice* would have been a worthier effort.

Sophie's Choice   Grim, tragic story of a Polish-Catholic woman who is living in Brooklyn after World War II, trying to deal with her horri-ble memories of the Holocaust, including the death of her baby. The 1982 Alan J. Pakula film was a tour de force for Meryl Streep, who won an Oscar—her second—for the title role.

Shadowlands   The successful Broadway play, based on the real-life, unlikely love story between the British writer C. S. Lewis and American divorcee Joy Gresham, was originally discussed as a project for Sean Connery and Barbra Streisand. In 1993, the film was made with Anthony Hopkins and Debra Winger in the lead roles, and Winger was nominated for the Oscar as Best Actress.

Playing for Time   In 1980, the idea of Barbra appearing in a television movie must have seemed ludicrous: she was the top female movie star in the world (according to the box office). Therefore, she (or her representatives) passed on this Arthur Miller teleplay based on the real story of Fania Fenelon, who survived life in Auschwitz by performing in a makeshift orchestra of prisoners. It was a first-rate script and an important story, but, reportedly, Barbra wanted too much money to do the television film. The role was eventually played by Vanessa Redgrave. She won an Emmy for her performance, and the show was honored as Outstanding Drama of the Year.

Good Idea . . . But What's the Story?

Some film projects are pipe dreams, ideas without any substantive chance of coming to the screen. But the titles make great copy anyway.

You Don't Bring Me Flowers   A romantic drama about a failing marriage. It was conceived as a film for Barbra and Neil Diamond, since they sang the number-one hit duet.

Napoleon and Josephine   Anthony Newley conceived this tale about the lives of French dictator Napoleon Bonaparte and his lover Josephine as a starring vehicle for himself and Barbra, with a musical score by Newley and lyricist Leslie Bricusse.

The Divine Sarah   A film biography of French actress Sarah Bernhardt for MGM/UA, reportedly part of the deal which brought *Yentl* to the studio.

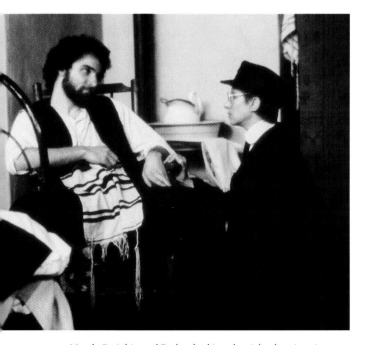

Mandy Patinkin and Barbra had just the right chemistry in *Yentl*. Could they have succeeded in a film version of his stage hit *Evita*?

Wait Til the Sun Shines   A musical to be produced by Ray Stark for Columbia Pictures.

My Way   A film based on Frank Sinatra's signature song.

Ringside at the Copa   A romantic drama set in a nightclub, the Copacabana, during the fifties.

La Vera Storia   Film version of the modern Italian opera *The True Story*.

Novel Reading

The Prince of Tides, Up the Sandbox, and *The Way We Were* were novels before they were feature films. There have been quite a few works of fiction which have been optioned for Hollywood movies, some with Barbra in mind.

Where or When   Novelist Anne Shreve's romance set in New England.

The White Hotel   D. M. Thomas's complex novel about an emotionally troubled opera singer who is treated by Sigmund Freud.

The Second Lady   Irving Wallace wrote this story about the wife of an American president who is replaced by a Russian secret agent.

The Triangle Factory Fire   Jane Fonda and Barbra were to team up in a film adaptation of Leon Stein's novel, set in the early days of the American labor movement, about the tragic New York City fire which killed 146 female garment workers in a lower East Side sweatshop. Fonda was to play the labor organizer, Streisand the leader of the workers. (A television-movie was made of the incident in 1979.)

Hot Flashes   Barbra Raskin novel about a group of women over forty.

Absence of Pain   Streisand optioned Barbara Victor's novel, the story of Maggie Sommers, a television journalist who covers the Middle East and falls in love with an officer in the Israeli army. He's married and committed to his country; she's forced to choose between her career and the man she loves.

If It Worked Once . . .

Once upon a time, Hollywood was prone to reworking stories over and over, doing remakes of scripts which worked one time and might be successful again. Although *What's Up, Doc?* borrows liberally, some would argue, from Howard Hawks's *Bringing Up Baby* (it does), and *Hello, Dolly!* is a musical version of Thorton Wilder's *The Matchmaker* (it is), Barbra Streisand has starred in only one true remake, *A Star Is Born.* Still, she has been considered for updated, reworked, or otherwise doctored versions of many other films. Here's a sampling:

Sabrina   A remake of the 1954 Audrey Hepburn–Humphrey Bogart film, directed by Billy Wilder and based on Samuel Taylor's play *Sabrina Fair.* This is a Cinderella tale about a chauffeur's daughter who is transformed from a gangly girl to a beautiful young woman, and her romantic adventures with the two rich but very different sons of her father's employer. The proposed updated Streisand version was discussed in 1971 and would be remade as a musical. In 1993, producer Scott Rudin acquired the rights and planned on doing a remake, presumably not as a musical, and definitely not with fifty-one-year-old Barbra.

Funny Face   Another remake of an Audrey Hepburn film, this one the 1957 Stanley Donen musical which costarred Fred Astaire. Audrey played a student, working in a Greenwich Village bookstore, who is discovered by Fred, a world-famous photographer. He likes her unusual looks and transforms her into a high-fashion model. While shooting magazine layouts in Paris, they fall in love. The film featured a beautiful score culled from the George and Ira Gershwin catalog. Streisand's remake would include the score and the same basic story.

Camille   If it was good enough for Garbo, why not Streisand? In 1971, independent producer Samuel Z. Arkoff tried to entice Barbra into starring in a remake of the classic Dumas tragedy about the wanton French courtesan who falls for a young, upper-class lover, Armand, and must die to prove her love.

Annie Get Your Gun   First Artists acquired

Barbra joyfully presented a special Grammy to Mrs. Ira Gershwin in 1986, but when it came to remaking George and Ira Gershwin's *Funny Face*, Barbra hesitated.

Barbra and Stephen Sondheim have shared terrific collaborations on *The Broadway Album* and *Back to Broadway*. Will Barbra and Steve team up in the future for the film version of *Follies*? Columbia Records

the rights to Irving Berlin's musical about the real-life sharpshooter, Annie Oakley, in 1977. MGM's 1950 musical starred Betty Hutton (a last-minute replacement for the ailing Judy Garland) and Howard Keel. The score includes: "There's No Business Like Show Business," "Anything You Can Do," "They Say That Falling in Love Is Wonderful," and "Doin' What Comes Naturally." Jon Peters was going to produce, and the scuttlebutt at the time suggested Robert Redford as her leading man, Frank Butler. For Streisand, not to mention Redford, the musical would have been quite a change of pace.

Random Harvest Ray Stark proposed an updated, musical version of this poignant 1942 Greer Garson and Ronald Colman love story. Colman was a war vet with amnesia, who wandered away from his army hospital and into the life of a local cabaret singer. Despite his lack of identity, they fall in love and soon after get married; but on a day trip to Liverpool, he is hit by a car and regains his memory. He has no recollection of the girl and their life. Eventually, she finds him and tries to work her way back into his world. Stark envisioned Streisand in the Garson role.

The Merry Widow Erich Von Stroheim, Ernst Lubitsch, and Curtis Bernhardt filmed versions of this classic Franz Lehar operetta about a rich American widow being courted by a foreign prince. Ingmar Bergman discussed producing a remake, to be shot in Stockholm, in 1978 with Barbra in the title role. Talks broke down and the project floundered. Director Franco Zeffirelli resurrected it in the early eighties, possibly teaming Barbra with Placido Domingo.

Much Ado About Nothing Zeffirelli first approached Barbra in 1970 about starring in a film version of the Shakespeare comedy. Barbra moved on to other projects when Zeffirelli couldn't get financial backing. (Kenneth Branagh and Emma Thompson finally remade it in 1993.)

And Now My Love A 1975 French film by Claude Lelouch, which starred Marthe Keller, about an unconventional romance.

History Is Made at Night Frank Borzage directed this highly regarded 1937 drama, which starred Jean Arthur and Charles Boyer, about a woman fleeing her jealous husband and falling in love with a Parisian maitre d'.

The Captain's Paradise 1953 British comedy with Alec Guinness as a ship's captain with wives in different ports. The update, discussed in 1984, would have cast Streisand as an airline pilot with a husband on the East Coast and another on the West. Barra Grant was assigned to write the screenplay.

Caesar and Cleopatra The George Bernard Shaw comedy about the unusual romance between Cleopatra, Queen of the Nile, and Julius Caesar, the Roman emperor. It was filmed in 1946 with Claude Rains and Vivien Leigh. Proposed Hollywood remake: Barbra and Marlon Brando.

The Women   An all-star update of Claire Booth's all-female play was proposed in the early eighties, with Barbra playing the role Rosalind Russell had in the definitive 1939 version directed by George Cukor. More contemporary casting suggested Jane Fonda (in Norma Shearer's role) and Faye Dunaway (in Joan Crawford's role). Julia Roberts and Meg Ryan signed for the remake in April 1994.

We Got It Made

There have been pictures which have had Streisand's name attached but finally reached the screen without her . . . like these:

Little Shop of Horrors   Ellen Greene, rather than Barbra, costarred with Rick Moranis in this 1986 version of the Howard Ashman–Alan Menken Off-Broadway musical about a man-eating plant named Audrey.

Casino Royale   It seemed as though every star in Hollywood (and out of Hollywood) had a cameo or bit in this wildly overproduced takeoff on James Bond. It was actually based on an Ian Fleming story, but the 1967 tongue-in-cheek version was unlike any of the Bond adventures with Sean Connery, Roger Moore, or Timothy Dalton. It was a disaster. Streisand was invited to do a walk-on, but she wasn't interested. One reason was that by the time they were filming, she was pregnant with her son Jason.

Oliver!   The film of Lionel Bart's successful Broadway musical version of Dickens's *Oliver Twist* was once suggested with Barbra as Nancy and Peter Sellers as Fagin. In 1968, Shani Wallis and Ron Moody were cast in the roles, and the film went on to win the Oscar for Best Picture.

Freaky Friday   Originally, this mother-daughter role-reversal comedy, based on Mary Rodgers's children's book, was earmarked for Barbra as early as 1970. In 1977, Barbara Harris starred in a Disney version with Jodie Foster as her daughter.

Every Time We Say Goodbye   A love story based on the Cole Porter song. Filmed in 1986, it was the story of an American pilot who falls in love with a Sephardic Jew in Israel, with Tom Hanks as the flyer.

The Good Mother   Diane Keaton starred in this 1988 adaptation of Sue Miller's novel. It is the story of a divorced mother of a young girl who finds sexual fulfillment with a new man, only to have her ex-husband sue for custody of the daughter.

The Devils   A 1971 drama directed by Ken Russell, starring Oliver Reed and Vanessa Redgrave, and set in the seventeenth century. It dealt with the Church, witchcraft, and politics. Russell envisioned Streisand in the Redgrave role, that of a rebellious nun.

Big Business   Bette Midler and Lily Tomlin starred in this 1988 comedy as sets of twins who were mixed up at birth. It was originally conceived as a vehicle for Barbra and Goldie Hawn.

Superman   When the big-screen version of the comic-book adventure was released in 1978, the casting of Christopher Reeve and Margot Kidder was hailed as a triumph. But before the picture was shot, there were big-name stars being considered for the roles of Clark Kent and Lois Lane. With box office in mind, Streisand's name was mentioned for Lois, with Burt Reynolds, James Caan, Nick Nolte, or Robert Redford as Clark/Superman.

Frankie and Johnny   The role of the sad, frumpy waitress Frankie was played onstage by Kathy Bates. In 1992, the film was made with Al Pacino cast as Johnny. To create some high-voltage Hollywood chemistry, the young, beautiful Michelle Pfeiffer was chosen to play Frankie, and she downplayed her looks to get into the role. Streisand wanted to play Frankie and has said that if director Garry Marshall had approached her, she would have done the picture.

Gypsy   Arthur Laurents, who wrote *The Way We Were*, also wrote the book for the musical *Gypsy*. Composer Jule Styne wrote the music for *Gypsy*, as well as *Funny Girl*. Laurents was the first to propose Streisand as the perfect woman to play Mama Rose, the role Ethel

Merman made famous in the original Broadway production. Laurents envisioned Rose as a younger woman than Merman was when she played it. Styne concurred, adding that Streisand could sing the score like no one else. The 1962 film version with Rosalind Russell and Natalie Wood is considered a pedestrian Hollywood adaptation, and both Laurents and Styne hoped to someday see *Gypsy* get treated with the respect it deserves in a top-flight film version. Streisand's *Gypsy* never materialized, but in 1993, Bette Midler starred in a television movie adaptation of the Styne-Sondheim musical which garnered rave reviews and scored high in the ratings.

Born Yesterday Garson Kanin's comedy was filmed in 1950 with Judy Holliday as Billie Dawn, William Holden as her teacher-lover Paul, and Broderick Crawford as Harry Brock, the self-made millionaire who thinks he "owns" her. In 1970, a musical version was conceived for Barbra and Frank Sinatra (as Harry). It never came together. In 1992, Disney filmed a remake with Melanie Griffith, Don Johnson, and John Goodman.

So Many Titles, So Few Films

Has anyone ever seen one of these pictures? At one time or another, the titles were bandied about as future films for Barbra, developed by Barwood Films or First Artists productions.

Spoils of War In 1990, Kate Nelligan starred in Michael Weller's psychologically complex drama about an independent divorcee and mother. Barbra was mentioned for the film version, but Nelligan made a television movie of it in 1993.

Two Dolls From the Bronx Scenarist Byron Grinnin concocted this comedy about two rival actresses in a Broadway show who try to destroy each other every night onstage. Barbra and Whoopi Goldberg were supposedly earmarked for the film.

The Diane Arbus Story Another biography based on the life of photographer Diane Arbus, from the book by Patricia Bosworth.

Bent Jane In 1971, director Lee Katzin was preparing this story about a compulsive murderess, proposing Streisand as the killer.

Loveland The story of a woman's determination to become a lawyer, set in the sixties. Jon Peters was developing this film as a follow-up to *A Star Is Born* for Barbra.

Jazz Baby Liza Minnelli, Diana Ross, and Barbra as singers in Paris in the twenties.

Dry Hustle A drama based on Sarah Kernochan's novel about a prostitute who turns the tables on prospective johns by robbing them before sex. It was hotly discussed as a possible Barbra vehicle in 1977. When Streisand's version didn't materialize, Glenda Jackson was in line for the role, then Deborah Raffin, and, finally, Bette Midler.

The Gift Shoppe A feminist comedy similar in tone to *The Main Event.*

Dead: A Love Story A thriller based on the twenties Ruth Snyder murder case, with Barbra as the killer.

Lovesounds A drama from First Artists productions.

Fancy Hardware A love story set in the forties about a plain-Jane New Englander who falls in love with a pilot. It was once proposed as a project for Streisand and John Travolta.

Neil Diamond and Barbra's beautiful duet "You Don't Bring Me Flowers" inevitably made people wonder if they would make a film together based on the song. It wasn't meant to be.

12

Streisand on Streisand
. . . and Other Subjects

Singing

● "Whether an album sells or not is not of consequence. The reward for me is in the process. If it sells . . . then that's a bonus."—1988

● "I've always had a good voice, never trained it and never thought about it. I sing as an actress. What I look for are songs with a beginning, a middle meaning, and an end."—1964

● "You'd find every take I do is different. I believe in the moment. I like to experiment and make changes. . . . [When I began singing] I was showing off too much [by holding long notes]. Now I don't have to show off. . . . Sometimes I feel almost immodest if I hold it too long."—1983

● "I never intellectualize my musical sound. I've always heard orchestrations in my head and other melodies when I sing. 'Evergreen' began with me learning some basic guitar chords and building a melody from that. I get such a kick out of it when I hear other people sing it now because here I was just fooling around with this instrument for a movie, and now other people actually sing it at weddings! Winning the Oscar for Best Song was more thrilling than getting it for Best Actress. And writing the score for *Nuts* was challenging. Since I don't read music, I hummed the lines to an orchestrator. I've written the music to six songs so far and the lyrics to one, and I'd like the time to write more."—1988

● "Judy Garland, Ethel Merman, if you're talking about powerful and athletic, I think they had more powerful voices than I do. I think I had a higher voice, maybe a purer voice, but not necessarily a stronger voice. Garland had a fabulous voice, but she had more of a vibrato than I do. I think she was a great, great singer."—1983

● "Performing, to me, is very, very special. It's a very intimate experience, very private, very personal. I just can't get up and sing in somebody's living room. I'd be scared to death. I'm so shy, really. I freeze. I get up in front of an audience and get tongue-tied."—1976

● "I don't enjoy performing before a bunch of strangers. Some performers get a thrill out of winning over a cold audience. I talked to Elvis about it last night; he does—I don't. It turns me off."—1969

● "I'd never seen a live performance [singing act] until I performed on stage myself. But nervousness is great. It shows you are alive. It makes your adrenalin flow and your sensitivity higher. It even makes your voice higher—when you're frightened, your voice can soar. It's just a matter of using the fear. It would be unnatural not to have it."—1975

● "What can I say? When I sing, people shut up."—1963

"My life is better now than it has ever been. I appreciate things more and feel more grateful for what I have. One thing I've never done is pay attention to my voice. I've never pampered it or thought about it. It just served me. Now, I realize I'm at an age where it's not automatically going to serve me for much longer."—1985

The Work

● "It's just wild, but all I have ever really

"I'm simply complex."

223

"There are people who tell me I'm beautiful this way. Well, they're wrong. Beautiful I'm not, and never will be."

learned from experience is what I don't like. The positive things I've learned from instincts. I inject something different—right or wrong, good or bad, and then I see if it feels natural for me. I've done that in my performing, in the way I dress, in the way I decorate my homes. Whatever come naturally for a person, I think that is the right thing. I never force an issue."—1965

● "I never had power before. If I did, some of my movies would have been better. When I record an album, I have complete artistic freedom. But when I've made movies in the past, I haven't had the same freedom. The director would say one thing and although I might disagree, I always gave in. And, of course, I had no say in the editing or anything like that. In this movie [*A Star Is Born*], I'm in control."—1977

● "I'm under pressure because I excel in all things. I design my own album covers. I insist on the artistic control of everything I do. On my TV show, I am not only the producer, but I oversee the lighting, the sound, and everything else. CBS doesn't have any idea of what my show's going to be until I produce it. Who do you think writes my show? Do you think I just mouth someone else's words? I write it. I don't want anything I do to be ordinary. It has to be very special."—1966

● "*The Broadway Album* has kept me away from directing for eight months. I have to get back to making movies. It's a question of how many battles you can gear up for every year. The record business has changed so much."—1985

● "I have a terrible memory when it comes to personal things, but I can always remember everything that concerns my work. I can remember something that was said about one of my songs four years ago. But at home, I have to keep lists all over the house and every morning I go around gathering up all the lists and then I still forget something."—1969

People Who Need People

● "No one who is a bitch to the people she or he works with gets to the top. There's too much cooperative effort, too many people involved in that kind of success. And even if someone like that did make it, he wouldn't last very long. Because no one would work with him/her. The unfortunate thing is that millions of people who don't know the industry read and listen to that nonsense and believe it."—1971

● "I don't want people to think I am a terrible human being. I'm not. If I were, it would show through on the screen. But when you are a star, you are an open target—and the bigger the star, the bigger the target. You can't win. If you're bitchy and pompous, they don't like you. If you're normal and unassuming, they say you're uninteresting. If you ride in a chauffeur-driven limousine, they think you're acting hotsy-totsy, showing off. If you drive the limousine yourself, they don't like that either. Maybe you'd better just walk to work."—1968

Temperamental or a Perfectionist?

• "Anyone who knows his craft or is worth his salt and his sensitivity and intelligence, doesn't throw tantrums. To have temperament, to be able to get angry and to cry, to be vulnerable to emotion, is a terrific thing. But negative temperament is childish nonsense."—1968

• "They say I'm controlling and I'm difficult. Well, I guess I am. I pay attention to detail. I like detail. I love detail. So if that's called difficult, then I'm difficult. Control means artistic responsibility. Yes, I do want that. I'm responsible for the product that I give the people."—1983

• "My grandmother couldn't handle me. She called me *fabrent* [on fire, in Yiddish]. If I was sick with the chicken pox and I wanted to go out and play, I put on my clothes, climbed out the window, and went out to play."—1983

The Nose

• "Why should I get it straightened and ruin my career?"—1968

• "I didn't have the money, first of all. But if I did think about having my nose done, and I did think about it, I didn't trust the doctors to do it right."—1986

• "I've told everyone I never had my nose done because I preferred it this way, but that's not all true. I really didn't have it done because of the pain. I'm afraid of the pain. Then there are people who tell me I'm beautiful this way. Well, they're wrong. Beautiful I'm not, and never will be."—1964

• "They [critics] weren't reviewing the film [*A Star Is Born*], they were reviewing me. I'm criticized for my looks, my nose. It's awfully late in

the game for that. Why can't I be judged for the quality of my work, and not the way I look?"—1977

• "I grew into my nose. I grew into my face. I was this absolute misfit. I wanted to express my feelings and have people feel they could identify with me."—1991

• "My face? I never worried about it. Funny thing about my face, it has always photographed well—always. Besides, most of the stars who made it have unusual faces—Claudette Colbert, Marlon Brando, Humphrey Bogart."—1966

"When I go to a movie, the screaming and the photographers frighten me." At the premiere of *Hello, Dolly!* in New York in 1969, Barbra was nearly trampled by the crowds of fans and press.

• "I have two very different sides of my face. My left side is more feminine. My right side is more masculine. In the movie [*Yentl*], I had myself photographed from the right to show a side of me that had hardly ever been seen."—1983

• "In my earlier periods, when I would have liked to look like Catherine Deneuve, I considered having my nose fixed. If I could do it myself with a mirror, I would straighten my nose and take off that little piece of cartilage from the tip. . . . See, I wouldn't do it conventionally. . . . I think Silvana Mangano, the Italian actress, has the most beautiful nose there is. An incredible nose, Roman, bumpy, like from an old piece of sculpture. That's what I consider beautiful. I certainly don't like pug noses or little tiny noses."—1977

Personal Philosophies

• "I'm really a conglomerate of contradictions. But how can you appreciate the summer if you never have the winter?"—1968

• "I'm an adolescent who is very mature; I'm lazy and ambitious; I love fancy food, beautifully served, yet enjoy it when it's simple, reheated, and eaten out of the pot; I love rice pudding from a diner on Tenth Avenue and the chocolate souffle from '21'; in the movies I care about how I look, but would rather sleep the extra half hour than put on false eyelashes; I would like my figure to look great, but wouldn't dream of refusing that extra piece of pizza; I have been on the best dressed list and at the same time on the worst-dressed list; I have been called crude and I have been called elegant; I have been called ugly and I have been called beautiful."—1970

• "I wouldn't trade my life for anyone else's. But it's a drag being public. People want so much from you . . . it's not enough to give your work. I always feel, 'Why isn't it enough?' "—1976

• "Some of the things I've done I'm not proud of. I've done movies at times for the wrong reasons. I want to return to the dreams I never fulfilled. I mean, I really want to do Shakespeare

"Performing for me is very, very special . . ."

and Chekhov and Ibsen, parts that I've always wanted to play and said I would play. I'm tired of saying, 'I could have done this.' I want to do it. Because life is growing short. Maybe because my father was so young when he died, I seem to have a drive to get it all in. I want to take chances now."—1982

• "I'm blunt. I say what I mean. I don't court popularity, but I am sensitive. And I insist on retaining most of myself for myself. Is that asking too much?"—1982

• "To me being rich means being born to money: you can travel around Europe for five years and know all your bills will be paid."—1966

• "Success is having a baked potato come out of the oven just right. Not raw and not overdone. Success to me is having ten honeydew melons and eating only the top half of each one."—1962

• "I feel that self-doubt is both my biggest virtue and my worst fault. Self-doubt is a virtue because it never lets me assume anything. I feel it's better to be open and vulnerable to hurt in doing one's work. But self-doubt can be a fault also. In everyday life, people can take advantage of it and wound you."—1968

• "I was on Nixon's enemies list because I supported Gene McCarthy in 1968 and raised funds for Daniel Ellsberg in the Pentagon Papers trial. Then I did a concert for George McGovern. I campaigned for Bella Abzug from the back of a truck when she was elected to Congress. I was operating off my instincts, doing what I felt was right as a citizen. I'm not a full-time activist. I've always been pro-choice, for the equality of women, for the protection of the environment. That's why I have a foundation to fortify my beliefs. That's how I give back. That's how I raise my voice. And whether the right-wing conservatives like it or not, I will keep on raising it."—1993

Dealing With the Press

• "When I go to a movie, the screaming and the photographers frighten me. People demand your autograph and if you don't give them one, they yell at you. These are not the people who really enjoy your work or appreciate it. They're not the ones who write me sensible letters. I love people who take the time to express their feelings intelligently. I save those letters."—1968

• "Just the nature of being interviewed disturbs me, and therefore what I say comes out hostile or defensive. When I try to put things into words, the whole meaning of what I feel is altered."—1983

• "Let me tell you another reason why I don't like interviews—because you're here, I'm not having lunch with the director, the producer. I'm not discussing the shots and angles we'll be working on for the next seven or eight hours. Yet what goes into those hours is forever, for posterity! That's my show [*Barbra Streisand . . . and Other Musical Instruments*] and a part of

"To me being really famous is being a movie star." At the 1992 Oscar nominee luncheon, Barbra stopped the presses simply by showing up.

my life. The next hours are going to be crucial to me for a very long time. But what am I going to get out of an interview? It doesn't help the work to do an interview."—1974

• "I'm both a singer and an actress. But I really prefer to be known as Barbra Streisand."—1966

• "My downfall may be that I care what people think about me. I want people I like and respect to feel the same way towards me. I wonder what they think."—1966

Moviemaking

• "I never really wanted to be a movie star in terms of signing autographs and being recognized and all that. I really wanted to be the character in the movie. I wanted to be . . . not myself. I wanted to be Scarlett O'Hara—not Vivien Leigh."—1969

• "I absolutely love the experience of filmmaking. It reminds me of being eighteen years old and doing everything people said I couldn't do."—1976

"It's wild, but all I have ever really learned from experience is what I don't like."

● "But in Hollywood, generally, they are still not used to women. All along the line, it is still more difficult for women to be in a position of authority in this industry. . . . And for me, from the beginning, it was, 'Who is this girl? What does she know about movies?' Well, you either have imagination, see things in terms of composition and color, or you don't."—1976

● "It's the hardest work I've ever known. They gave me a chair with my name on it. So when do I get to use it?"—1967

● "When I look at a film, my own work, I'm very objective. I see it from the photographer's point of view. I'm interested in photography, in composition, I'm interested in the total concept of something. I'm not just interested in my lines, and my part, that would be terribly boring. On the other hand, I wouldn't want to have to tell people what to do. That would be too frustrating. That requires tact and stuff like that I don't have time for. But I do see things."—1969

● "I don't have to direct every one of my movies. I'd love to work with a lot of foreign directors. . . . I can't wait to be directed by somebody else who is good; I can have a home life during the making of the picture. But as I learned on my last few films, if I can't get somebody good to direct a film I'm going to be in, then I should do it myself. Otherwise I'll have more trouble than it's worth, dealing with a middle man."—1984

"Just the nature of being interviewed disturbs me . . ." Facing hordes of journalists at the *Star Is Born* press junket in Tempe, Arizona.

Starstruck

• "When I find people who are talented and gifted, it is inspirational to me. When I see somebody like Meryl Streep in a wonderful piece of work, it just inspires me. I don't dislike her or wish her ill. It just makes me want to do better work. So I don't understand that part of people's nature that just wants to put down something."—1988

• "I would love to work with Robert Redford again. . . . [He was] always interesting, always fascinating. A good guy. I think he's a wonderful actor. I'd love to work with [director] Sydney Pollack again. We have to have meetings again and talk about [a sequel to *The Way We Were*] because it's hard to do sequels when the first film was so successful. But I do think there's a sequel there."—1992

• "I will never forgive my fellow actor Ronald Reagan for the genocidal denial of the illness's existence, for his refusal to even utter the word AIDS for seven years, and for blocking adequate funding for research and education which could have saved hundreds of thousands of lives."—1992

• "Marlon Brando happens to be the greatest actor who ever lived, in my opinion. I would work with him in a second. I don't care what the rumors or the stories are [about him]."—1991

• "The only autograph that I asked for was President Kennedy, for my mother. . . . He signed a card for me and I said, 'You're a doll.' I remember saying that in Brooklyn to people, some real Brooklyn expression. I really didn't mean to say it, it just came out. . . . He laughed and asked me how long I was singing and I said as long as he was president, because it was true. I mean, we sort of started at the same time, you know, in the public eye."—1963

• "I'm not comfortable with my success. I don't like to be recognized. I don't feel like a famous person or star; I feel like a workaholic. Sometimes when I was around people like Sophia Loren or Elizabeth Taylor, they were like stars to me. They acted in a certain kind of way. They're very comfortable with the press, with

"Judy Garland, Ethel Merman, if you're talking about powerful and athletic, they had more powerful voices than I do." Merman and Streisand backstage during Barbra's Broadway run of *Funny Girl*. The Michel Parenteau Collection

photographers. You see pictures in the paper of Jackie Onassis or Elizabeth Taylor, they're always smiling like ladies. You see pictures of me, it's like, you know, leave me alone, get outta here."—1982

Specifics

• "Even in *The Way We Were* I was playing a girl who is a political activist because she feels she doesn't look like someone who could be Robert Redford's girlfriend. People think I'm really like my movies, that my roles are somehow an extension of myself. Totally false."—1975

"I like awards . . . it gives me something tangible."

Fame, Stardom, and Hollywood

● "The pressures of this business can destroy you, like they did Judy Garland. You have to be very strong to avoid it. The thing that keeps me sane is living here [in Malibu]. It's away from it all. I don't hear any traffic sounds. I don't answer the phone much on weekends. I garden or walk or ride my bike."—1976

● "I always thought that having French furniture and art was Gentile. Now I realize I'm glad I'm Jewish. And I don't want the art. I'll go and look at it in a museum. I don't want any more for my own. It was a need for status."—1973

● "I was never the figment of anyone's imagination. I wasn't created. Whatever motivated me when I was twelve motivates me now . . . I was a peculiar kid. I had things on my mind. . . . My ambitions to be an actress."—1968

● "Some people look at me and say, 'Success has gone to her head,' but that's not true. I've always been this way. I'm no good at dealing with people or being tactful. I say whatever is on my mine. I go by instinct. I don't worry about experience: I want to do things my way. I was like that when I was twelve."—1975

● "I loved doing *The Broadway Album*—really loved that. These were songs that I just loved and that had stories attached to them, really intelligent lyrics, gorgeous melodies. And it was really fun to have an artistic success when I didn't plan on it at all. It was a total labor of love, you know, and when it was a commercial hit, that was like icing on the cake. That was fabulous."—1992

● "[I made] *For Pete's Sake* . . . because I didn't want to be in L. A. any longer and figured I'd go to New York and escape. When I made *All Night Long*, I was writing *Yentl*, and I was so lonely in this room writing, I needed to act. So I just took this job because it was for six weeks. Those are bad decisions to have made."—1991

● "I think my album called *ButterFly* . . . I thought that was pretty lousy. I think that's the only one, actually, that I didn't love. I just don't remember the songs. I can't remember what was on it. I don't remember doing it."—1992

"I absolutely love the experience of filmmaking."

• "I want to be famous. I don't care whether it's by singing or acting or what, I want everybody to know my name. Even the cowboys."—1962

• "I never said I didn't like being born in Brooklyn. I'm happy about the way I was brought up, on the streets. It has to do with the way I am, the way I sing, my talent."—1963

• "I like getting awards—I can see in black and white I was voted top female vocalist or my album is a bestseller. It gives me something tangible."—1966

• "This is a terribly bitter profession. Everyone will 'honey' and 'yes' you, but are out to cut your throat at every turn. If I hadn't made it [by] now, I might have given it all up. This is a ridiculously painful business and I couldn't have stood becoming as bitter as some chorus people twice my age."—1966

• "I remember a long time ago when I was a kid, I thought, 'I don't want to be just a movie star like Greta Garbo.' . . . I decided I didn't want to be the best of one thing. I would be the best singer, best actress, best Broadway star, and best movie star. That was my challenge."—1966

• "They told me to change Streisand, so I changed Barbara to spite them. I dropped the 'a' out."—1963

• "Life has never really changed for me. At sixteen, I knew I would be famous. I never really pushed."—1964

• "The most thrilling time was when I was eighteen. I knew then I'd be famous, but no one else did. It was my secret and I always had something to look forward to. Excitement came in the proving. Once you are accepted, it takes away the thrill. All that is left is work, work and more work."—1966

• "It changed a lot for me, becoming famous. I thought I handled it quite well on the whole. It didn't really go to my head. It didn't change me

"I would love to work with Robert Redford again . . ."

as a person. But it did make me more frightened about the expectations of the audience. It's funny, I don't know which is worse, the fear of failure or the fear of success."—1983

• "To me being really famous is being a movie star."—1966

• "What do I want? Everything! I'd like to win the Tony, the Emmy, the Oscar, the Grammy, the works. Maybe someday I will."—1963

13

The Top Ten Myths About Barbra Streisand

Myth 1—
Barbra Streisand has had a nose job

At the age of fifty-two, Barbra Streisand, in the opinion of many people, looks better than she did when she was twenty-one. Why? Is it the fact that she's very conscious of her diet and has lost the baby fat she once carried in her cheeks? Is it because her age has given her face a longer, more aquiline look? Is it perhaps the way she does her makeup, opting for a more natural facade? What about cosmetic surgery? Sounds strange, but one of the reasons most strongly perpetuated is that Streisand has had a nose job—a slight one—to make herself more beautiful. It has also been suggested that she had the tip of her nose—the piece which connects the nose to the upper lip—lifted. Theorists go on to suggest she had this surgery before *Yentl* in 1982—when she was forty.

There is no support for this theory, and when you compare photos of Streisand's profile from the early sixties to the nineties, you can see her nose is unchanged. Barbra Streisand has commented on the idea of having her nose fixed since she first gained notice in *I Can Get It for You Wholesale*. She has always claimed to be afraid of the pain she would have to endure to have her world-famous nose trimmed to a more traditional size. But in her in-depth *Playboy* interview in 1977, Streisand revealed an even more important consideration in her decision to

(Opposite) In *The Owl and the Pussycat*, Doris appears in a porno flick called *Cycle Sluts*. These publicity photos are as close to porn as Streisand has ever gotten.

(Inset) Barbra took it off for *Playboy*—her socks and sneakers! She told Larry Grobel about the myth of her skin flick.

never get a nose job: she had been advised by doctors that changing her nose could change the sound of her voice. For that reason alone, Barbra Streisand will never get a nose job . . . no matter what the tabloids write.

Myth 2—
Barbra Streisand appeared in a pornographic film

It's not unusual for stars to try and hide potentially embarrassing chapters from the early days of their career before they become famous. For Streisand, the early days were marked by casting directors rejecting her because of lack of experience and her looks. With her thrift-shop clothes, dramatic makeup—Cleopatra eyes and pale, white pancake—and very prominent nose, Streisand had a hard time getting people to take her seriously as an actress. In order to get attention, Streisand turned to singing. After winning a talent contest at The Lion, a gay nightclub in Greenwich Village in 1961, nineteen-year-old Barbra Streisand finally began to win jobs in musicals, as an actress who sings.

Still, in the seventies, a rumor emerged that Barbra Streisand appeared in a pornographic movie when she was sixteen. That would have been 1958, and Barbra was still a student at Erasmus Hall High School. Streisand commented about this myth in *Playboy*: "Take that porno film I'm supposed to be in. When I first heard the rumor, I thought it was a put-on. But these people [who] you never can seem to find were selling the film and claiming it was me. I couldn't resist the temptation to see what the actress looked like, so we got a copy. The film, naturally, is very blurred. The girl has long hair, like I did back in the sixties, although she was chubby, while I was very skinny. But the dead giveaway came when the camera zoomed in on her hands around the guy's you-know-what. There they were: short, stubby fingers. Definitely not mine."

This myth resurfaced in 1992, only in this new retelling, the porno movie was supposedly done in the early sixties. The girl in the film has long brown hair and, when dressed, is wearing a miniskirt. The first miniskirts were popular in 1966: that was the year Barbra Streisand did *Color Me Barbra*, had a mini-concert tour in America, and gave birth to Jason in December.

Myth 3—
Streisand is a born-again Jew

In 1980, Jason Gould was bar mitzvahed at the Pacific Jewish Center in Venice, California. Coinciding with Jason's religious rite of passage, Streisand was immersed in preproduction for her first film as a director, *Yentl*. Streisand was raised in the Jewish tradition, but she had never seriously practiced her religion or studied it. In order to prepare for *Yentl*, Streisand became a student and sought out rabbis, teachers, writers, anyone and everyone who could help her learn as much about Jewish law and scripture—as quickly as possible. Streisand was like a sponge, sopping up age-old wisdom and new age interpretations as she looked for ways to bring authenticity and detail to her film.

But her fervor wasn't merely for the movie. Jason had a major impact on her beginning to look at Judaism more seriously. He agreed to be bar mitzvahed, but he questioned the importance of the ritual since neither his mother

nor his father were educated in their religion. Barbra decided to take the same classes as Jason, to learn everything he had to to be bar mitzvahed. In addition, she and Elliott attended Sabbath services in anticipation of Jason's ceremony.

It was because of this intense, obsessive journey that Streisand was dubbed a born-again Jew. In a national woman's magazine, an article about "born again" stars roped Streisand in with other celebrities who legitimately labeled themselves as such. Streisand was offended that her interest in her faith should be so misconstrued. "I was doing research for my film, [and] studying the Talmud is a fascinating, enriching experience. I came out of it being proud I was a Jew, but I don't go to synagogue regularly. Calling me a born-again Jew is ridiculous," Barbra said in *Ladies Home Journal* in December 1983. Barbra Streisand had never been estranged from her religion and has always taken pride in her heritage. In reality, Streisand was generally regarded as perhaps the world's foremost Jewish entertainer. She still is.

Myth 4—
Streisand did not write "Evergreen"

In September 1985, Shaun Considine wrote an unauthorized biography called *Barbra Streisand: The Woman, the Myth, and the Music*. One of Considine's most bizarre notions in the book was the claim that the music for "Evergreen, the Love Theme From *A Star Is Born*" was not written by Barbra Streisand. Considine contended that Rupert Holmes had cowritten the song with her but never

(Above) On magazine covers nearly thirty years apart, the profile hasn't changed.

Streisand rarely likes to accentuate her right profile because it makes her nose look longer. But in these shots from *The Way We Were* and *Yentl*, the nose looks almost regal.

took a credit for it. And when the song went on to an Oscar and a Grammy, it was Streisand (and lyricist Paul Williams) who won the awards, not Holmes.

Considine's source was an unnamed Columbia Records employee. There was no confirmation by Holmes or anyone else con-

nected with *A Star Is Born*. When he was contacted after the book was released, Rupert Holmes vehemently denied any authorship of "Evergreen." "Ridiculous. If I had [written it], I'd have taken credit both for the money involved and the industry recognition," Holmes told columnist Liz Smith. Yes, he had worked on *A Star Is Born*, but Holmes was adamant about who wrote "Evergreen"—Barbra Streisand.

Myth 5—
Barbra Streisand will run for a New York Senate seat

Barbra Streisand has been politically active for most of her adult life. She sang for President John F. Kennedy in 1963, entertained for LBJ at the 1964 inaugural gala, and campaigned for Senator Eugene McCarthy in the 1968 Democratic presidential race. In 1972, she joined Carole King, James Taylor, and Quincy Jones in a major concert benefiting candidate George McGovern. And perhaps in her most partisan political effort of all, she staged *One Voice*, a fund-raising concert in her Malibu backyard which raised millions for six Democratic senatorial candidates. Recently, the rumor spread that Barbra was interested running for office, making politics her new career.

Because of Streisand's prominent role in fund-raising for Bill Clinton in his 1992 presidential campaign, and then her stellar performance at Clinton's inaugural gala—which was televised as a CBS special—speculation began that Streisand was plotting either a campaign to run for office or perhaps contemplating a position in the Clinton administration. The latter notion was certainly possible; after all, actor John Gavin (*Psycho, Thoroughly Modern Millie*) was appointed U. S. ambassador to Mexico by Ronald Reagan. And Shirley Temple was U. S. ambassador to Ghana under Nixon and to Czechoslovakia under Bush.

Streisand inadvertently added fuel to the fire with her public appearances in late 1992. It was the star's electrifying speech at the AIDS Project Los Angeles Commitment to Life awards which really had people talking. In accepting the acco-

Streisand's interest in Judaism intensified when she prepared
for and filmed *Yentl*, but she was never a born-again Jew.

for dinner with Attorney General Janet Reno, and
appearing at the White House Correspondents'
Dinner where she was photographed with the
former head of the Joint Chiefs of Staff, Colin
Powell. Within a week, Streisand was on the
cover of the *New York Post* with the headline
"Senator Yentl." According to the tabloid,
Streisand was planning to run in New York
against Senator Daniel Moynihan when he came
up for reelection in 1994. Streisand denied the
story and expressed no interest in ever going into
politics: "Political passion should not be con-
fused with political ambition."

Myth 6—
Barbra really directed Funny Girl and Hello, Dolly!

With both *Funny Girl* and *Hello, Dolly!*, Barbra
Streisand was not only characterized as a temperamental actress, she was also accused of

lade, Streisand gave a politically charged
address, one decidedly liberal. In reference to
an antigay ordinance which recently had been
passed in the state of Colorado, she said, "If we
are asked to, we should refuse to play where
they discriminate." Her words were taken as a
call to boycott, and she brought national attention to an issue which had yet to journey
beyond the gay community.

In subsequent weeks, Streisand was under
pressure from influential Hollywood friends,
who coincidentally had winter homes in Aspen,
to rescind or amend her statement. Some press,
including the *New York Times*, inferred that the
peer pressure had silenced Barbra. Streisand
then appeared at a benefit for the American Civil
Liberties Union of Southern California, and in
her speech, she reasserted her position on the
Colorado ordinance: "The last time I spoke, a
few weeks ago, I made some serious comments
that seemed obvious to me but which some in
the media had difficulty grasping. . . . I did not
back off, back down or back away from my
original statement, as some of the press reported." Her intensity rallied the audience, and again
people wondered if Barbra was thinking about a
making politics her new métier.

In May 1993, Streisand visited Washington. She
was spotted attending Senate hearings, meeting

Barbra not only wrote the music for "Evergreen (Love Theme
From *A Star Is Born*)," she even learned to play the guitar.

directing her directors. In *Funny Girl*, Barbra was being guided by film veteran William Wyler, whose credits included *The Letter* with Bette Davis, *Detective Story* with Kirk Douglas, *Roman Holiday* with Audrey Hepburn, *Ben Hur* with Charlton Heston, among others. True, *Funny Girl* was Wyler's only musical, but the Oscar-winning director was a brilliant craftsman, and he had a firm grasp on what he was doing with *Funny Girl*. The notion that Barbra was telling Wyler what to do arose because of Streisand's tendency to express her ideas about a scene to the director in vivid detail. She also had the experience of all those performances of *Funny Girl* onstage: she knew what worked with audiences and what didn't. She felt compelled to make suggestions. Wyler never resented Streisand's comments, or did he ask her to keep them to herself. If anything, Willie saw in Barbra the ability to someday step behind the camera and become a director herself, as she did in 1983 with *Yentl*. Still, the gossips preferred to write that the upstart Streisand was mouthing off to Wyler, bullying the older man.

When Streisand moved on to begin *Hello, Dolly!* the rumors followed her, only this time she was telling Gene Kelly how to direct. Again, there was nothing to substantiate the conjec-

Contrary to popular rumor, Barbra Streisand did not tell Oscar-winner William Wyler how to direct her in *Funny Girl*.

ture. Nothing except Barbra's style of work: to offer ideas to her director and her costars, to do whatever she could to make the film better. The media was fascinated by the notion that veteran talent like Gene Kelly and Walter Matthau were putting the superstar in her place. Or perhaps it just made good gossip. The principals involved spent nearly as much time denying the rumors as they did making the picture.

"She is amazing," commented Gene Kelly in 1969. "She has great show business sense and she has it intuitively, which make her a great performer. She is interested in the difference between playing a scene on the stage and before the camera. She wants to know why this camera, that light is here or there. She's a worker and an indefatigable trouper." Producer Ernest Lehman also had to deal with the gossip. In 1968, he responded to questions about the rumors in an interview in the *New York Times*: "No, it's not true that Barbra Streisand told Gene Kelly to drop dead, and that he said to her, 'I've been in the business long before you were and I'll be in it long after you're gone.' How inaccurate can gossip be? Barbra's determined, but who isn't? Gene and I both feel that none of us has ever worked with anyone who is that dedicated to trying to make things better. Thank God for that kind of difficulty."

The difficult Streisand is a label which she

Who's giving direction in this shot from *Hello, Dolly!* Barbra or Gene Kelly?

has yet to shake. However, the rumor of Streisand directing her directors, which dogged her for years, finally disappeared in 1983. That was when she directed her first movie, *Yentl*.

Myth 7—
Steven Spielberg helped direct Yentl

When Barbra made the decision to not only star in *Yentl* but direct, cowrite, and produce it as well, she elicited the advice and opinions of her friends, family, coworkers, peers, and colleagues. One of those friends was Steven Spielberg. While Streisand was editing *Yentl* in London, Spielberg was working on *Indiana Jones and the Temple of Doom*. "I know he knows what works," Barbra told *Harper's Bazaar* in 1983. "I showed him an early print of *Yentl*, and I thought he'd look at it and say, 'Well, it's much too long or you should cut this or cut that.' " He was enthusiastic about her direction, calling it the best film debut since *Citizen Kane*. "Barbra really pulled this one off," he concluded. And he told her not to change a frame.

Streisand was so pleased about his reaction that when she began doing interviews to promote *Yentl's* release, she told reporters what Steven had said about the movie. The *Los Angeles Times* printed what Streisand said, but did so in such a way as to make it seem as though Spielberg helped her by directing sequences in the film. In 1991, Streisand was still railing about the misconception. "People took that and ran with it. They began to infer that I couldn't have done this all by myself, that not only did I need the help of a man, but the biggest Hollywood director in the world," Barbra told Joey Berlin in *Empire* magazine.

Myth 8—
Barbra tried to have Omar Sharif fired because he was an Arab

In order to pump up interest in *Funny Girl*, pro-

Shooting *Yentl* in Czechoslovakia, the only director on the set was Barbra Streisand. Steven Spielberg was nowhere in sight.

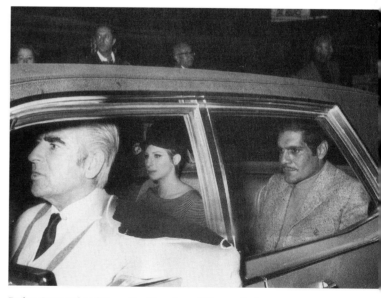

Barbra Streisand and Omar Sharif are from different ethnic backgrounds. She's a Jew, he's an Arab, but that was no reason for them not to work together in *Funny Girl*. They reteamed for scenes in *Funny Lady*, too. Christopher Nickens Collection

ducer Ray Stark had the Columbia press department working overtime to keep the film and its stars in the public's mind. Amid the cover stories, the puff pieces, the promotional tie-ins and the constant press releases were the rumors, the innuendo, and the gossip. Perhaps one of the strangest rumors was one which happened very

(Opposite) If Streisand ran for the New York Senate seat, would she still be able to perform in concert, make records, direct movies, build a new house, and have time to spend with her friends and her family? I don't think so.

early in the production. *Funny Girl* began pre-production in May, 1967. The Six-Day War between Egypt and Israel started on June 6, 1967. Remarkably, in only six days, the Israeli army attacked the Egyptian forces in occupied territories and drove them back to their original boundaries. Barbra was a strong supporter of Israel, having sung in fund-raisers for Israel and contributed money out of her own pocket.

Streisand's leading man in *Funny Girl* was Omar Sharif, who was born in Egypt. As filming was about to commence, a rumor spread in Hollywood that Barbra wanted Omar replaced because she didn't want to work with an Arab. The idea not only was racist, it was ridiculous. The rumor died down once shooting started, and by then a new rumor—one diametrically opposed to the first one—had taken its place: Omar and Barbra were having an affair. In this instance, amazingly enough, the rumor had some truth to it. In his memoirs years later, Omar Sharif claimed he and Barbra were lovers for a time while they were making *Funny Girl*.

Myth 9—
Jon Peters was Barbra's Svengali

When Barbra Streisand and Jon Peters went public with their love affair in 1974, it was in part to deny the notion that Jon had mesmerized Barbra to the point where she was under his spell—that she was Trilby to his Svengali. Barbra was perceived as the most powerful woman in Hollywood at the time, being the most bankable female star of the seventies and the only one beginning to produce her own projects. As soon as Jon entered her life, Barbra began including him in her work. It was nothing new for her: she had involved ex-husband Elliott Gould in the production of her television specials and had asked him to take on more responsibilities in their company, Ellbar Productions (Gould declined because he wanted to pursue his acting career instead).

Jon Peters is a dynamic personality, and at that time, Hollywood had little idea of who he was . . . except that he had a string of successful beauty salons. Jon's business acumen—he sold

Streisand had pondered for years how she would direct *Yentl*. The vision was entirely her own.

the salons for millions of dollars—led to his taking an active role in the management of Barbra's career. His first step was getting involved with Columbia Records, and he produced her album *ButterFly*. Soon after, he read a screenplay called *Rainbow Road*, a new version of *A Star Is Born*, and convinced Barbra to make the film and let him produce it. It was a bold move for Peters, and because Barbra supported him and believed in his abilities, she was seen as "a woman under the influence." Had she lost her mind? Was she being led astray by a

Barbra and Jon Peters were many things to one another, but was she Trilby to his Svengali? Apparently not. Maybe it was just the beard?

Svengali? "Who's to say I'm not his Svengali?" Barbra shot back in answer to that very question.

Lesley Ann Warren, Jon's ex-wife, offered her assessment of Jon and Barbra's relationship: "Barbra is a woman with a reputation for never letting anyone have control, from William Wyler on down. Jon's resented because he's dealing with studio heads and he hasn't paid one [obscenity] due. But he's always been a successful businessman." And he was destined to become a successful producer. Time revealed that Streisand was hardly being duped. Yes, she was a woman in love, but she was not wrong to trust Peters's instincts about her career. Jon had a lot of *chutzpah* and he influenced Barbra tremendously, but Peters backed up his bravado with box-office hits. Today, he's one of the richest independent producers in Hollywood, has run a film studio, and, although they are no longer romantically involved, he continues to be a strong presence in Barbra Streisand's life, and a trusted advisor.

Myth 10—
Barbra Streisand cannot sing anymore

On September 6, 1986, Barbra staged the *One Voice* concert in Malibu. News reports of the event included a brief clip of Streisand onstage singing "Something's Comin'," and unlike the version of the song on *The Broadway Album*, the live clip included a clinker, a slightly sour note. When HBO aired the *One Voice* concert three months later, "Something's Comin' " was all cleaned up; it no longer included the sour note. In the time between the concert and the broadcast, Streisand had redone a few notes here and there to improve her overall performance. Being a perfectionist, Barbra was dissatisfied with the totally live experience. Since this special (and subsequent home video and album) were going to be a permanent document of *One Voice*, she decided to make it a little better than it was originally: not an unusual practice for live albums.

Because of this *One Voice* situation, a rumor

Streisand in the recording studio in 1982. Singing live in Las Vegas at the MGM-Grand, Barbra proved that she still has the muscle to knock out audiences with the power of her voice.

grew that Barbra could no longer sing the way she had in the past; that she had lost her voice. The notion was that she would record dozens of takes on any given song for an album, then cut and paste a finished product with the help of sophisticated sound equipment. Adding fuel to the fire was her continued reluctance to sing live in concert: her reported stage fright was a cover for her inability to sing as she once had. All of this speculation was complete and utter nonsense. Unlike Milli Vanilli, Barbra Streisand is in no way a fraudulent talent. The people who had attended *One Voice* heard the pure, unaltered Streisand in song and it was clear she could still sing.

A few years later, when *Just for the Record . . .* came out, new recordings of "You'll Never Know" and "Warm All Over" were included. Videotape of those recording sessions were made, and are proof positive of the still-intense power of Barbra's singing voice. More live singing appearances—the APLA concert in 1992, the Clinton Inaugural, and, finally, her incredibly successful world tour in 1994, where she conquered her stage fright—confirm that fact.

14

A Director Is Born

Perhaps the greatest professional leap Barbra Streisand ever made was when she went from being an award-winning actress and singer to a film director. Other stars had taken the leap—Woody Allen, Warren Beatty, Robert Redford, Paul Newman—but Streisand was the first major female star to give it a try. Her attempt, *Yentl*, was not a small-budget, low-profile project. No, Streisand went for the brass ring on her very first film: a $14 million, unconventional musical, shot on location in Europe, based on a short story by a Pulitzer Prize–winning author.

The chances for failure were very, very high, and to add to the risk, Streisand chose to cowrite, coproduce, direct, and star in the film. That was a feat only accomplished in motion-picture history by Orson Welles, Woody Allen, and Warren Beatty. Hollywood and the world were duly impressed. As Sydney Pollack, Barbra's friend and the director of *The Way We Were*, noted: "It's a terrific *twentieth* movie by a director, never mind a *first* movie. It is the work of a mature artist."

Streisand's abilities as a director encompass a variety of skills, many of which are evident in other creative outlets she has pursued. For starters, Barbra's eye for detail has been very evident in her well-documented collecting of fine art and furnishings, as well as the decorating and design of her homes and properties. She has even drawn an analogy between decorating a room to dressing a film set. The cos-

tumes, props, sets, and locations in a Streisand film reflect that same kind of attention to detail. Amy Irving commented that, in *Yentl*, Barbra tried to match the color of Amy's lipstick to the fruit on the table, so meticulous was her eye, so exacting her sense of coordination. To convey her idea for the look of the film to director of photography David Watkin, Barbra asked him to try and match the quality of browns and golds found in Rembrandt's paintings. She even went to the Netherlands to study the Dutch master's work up close, so that she would know the exact look of the golden sepia-tone when Watkin captured it.

The attention to pace and rhythm and dynamics seem to stem from her unique qualities as a musician. Streisand has always had ideas of how a song should sound—how the orchestration should complement it, whether it should be sung slowly or quickly—what she has called a "total *vision* of the finished song." In filmmaking, a director must have a vision of the final product and be able to apply the principles of pace, rhythm, and dynamics to the cutting of a scene,

(Opposite) In years to come, will Barbra Streisand's legacy be as a great film director? Nothing's impossible.

(Right) One of the most important cover stories Streisand ever received was this one as the auteur of *Yentl*.

the use of sound and lighting, the beat from shot to shot, scene to scene. A masterful example of these skills is found in the editing of Tom Wingo's confession in *The Prince of Tides*. Streisand skillfully arranges sounds and silences, shots in Susan Lowenstein's Manhattan office with fragmented memories of Tom's South Carolina home on a rainy night, blending the contrasting dramatic elements to create a scene both suspenseful and heartbreaking. This sequence has all the elements found in the performance of a great Streisand ballad: a slow, tentative beginning, rising to a soaring climax, followed by a cathartic denouement.

Streisand's understanding of theatricality and drama seem directly linked to her stage experience as a singer, in particular the analysis she applies to a lyric to make a song into a three-act play. This same skill applies to the mood and ambience of a film. The way she can break down a song, finding the essence of the emotion, then setting a scene and a style, is not unlike her ability to synthesize a script and make the most effective connection to the audience. In *Yentl*, Barbra made the conscious choice to let the audience share Yentl's secret

Barbra, shown here on the set of *On a Clear Day*, learned about cameras and lighting from cinematographers like Harry Stradling. The knowledge would prove invaluable in years to come.

On *Hello, Dolly!* she was shooting Super 8 movies. A few years later, she was shooting home video in Europe to try out ideas for *Yentl*.

feelings through the use of songs, songs which also serve to comment on the people and situations in which she finds herself. This approach lent the piece an artistry and air of fantasy which it otherwise may not have had. It was theatrical and akin to her Broadway background.

Finally, as an actress who has always loved the process of acting, Streisand behind the camera is a very giving and supportive director. In the two films she has made, the actors who have worked in them have commented that Barbra is exceptionally attuned to their needs. That is an asset which cannot be assumed with all actors-turned-directors, but it is one she possesses. Directing Amy Irving, who played Hadass, in a scene from *Yentl*, Streisand employed a technique she had first seen Swedish auteur Ingmar Bergman use while directing Elliott Gould in *The Touch*: to elicit a particular response from Amy, Barbra knelt down out of camera range and manipulated a "Hadass" doll, giving Amy all the off-camera encouragement and inspiration she needed to come up with just the right reaction.

It was in 1970 that Barbra saw Bergman at work. She probably was not studying his methods with the idea that someday she'd be a direc-

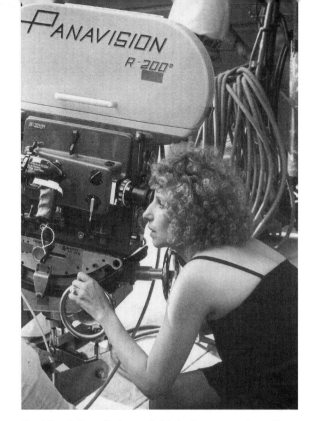

On *A Star Is Born*, Barbra probably had more experience lining up shots than Frank Pierson did.

tor herself, but somewhere in the back of her mind, she stored away that bit of motion-picture ingenuity. Bergman wasn't the only director who influenced her. Working with a handful of top directors in her motion-picture career, Barbra learned things from all of them as well. She had a unique film education, and there is evidence of their influence in some of the work she's directed. Vincente Minnelli, who directed *On a Clear Day You Can See Forever*, was a master of *mise en scène*: his films are noted for their dramatic use of color, a vigorous attention to detail, and a lavish, sumptuous visual style. All these elements are emphasized in *Yentl* and *The Prince of Tides* (and before those projects, in her television specials).

In *The Way We Were*, Barbra clicked with director Sydney Pollack, a former actor who has excelled as a film director. Pollack rarely fails to bring out the best in his actors, and he spends as much time nurturing their performances as he does conceiving a series of shots to create a scene. In many ways, Streisand emulates Pollack's way with actors. The superb performances in both Streisand-directed films—resulting in Oscar nominations for Nick Nolte, Kate Nelligan, and Amy Irving—are evidence of that.

At the time Peter Bogdanovich made *What's*

Up, Doc? he was hailed as one of Hollywood's brightest young directors. Somewhere along the way, Bogdanovich lost the touch he had in *Doc, The Last Picture Show*, and *Paper Moon*. What made those films so strong and successful was the sense of a single, total vision behind the picture. In *Doc*, Bogdanovich had a framework so precise he was able to accept improvisation by the actors within those boundaries and still deliver the screwball comedy he had conceived, one which was an homage to classic films like *Bringing Up Baby*. Barbra has had that same kind of single vision in both *Yentl* and *The Prince of Tides*, knowing exactly what she had in mind for the overall picture yet being flexible enough to accept an idea from an actor or member of the crew without sacrificing her concept.

Irvin Kershner, Streisand's director in *Up the Sandbox*, succeeded in his films when observing everyday human behavior with all its feats and foibles. He realizes that actors speak with more than words, and in *Sandbox*, Kershner captured in Barbra's performance a myriad of emotions with the mere cast of her eyes, as when she watches her husband with another woman. Streisand's direction of Nick Nolte in

Was Barbra looking over Howard Zieff's shoulder on *The Main Event*, or was he looking over hers?

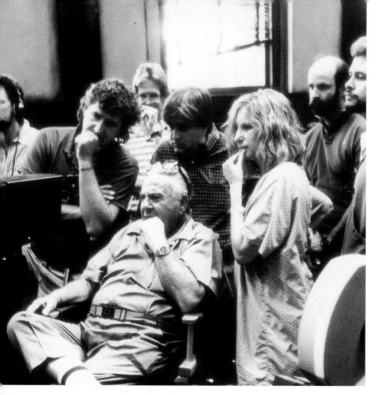

Although Martin Ritt was a seasoned pro, *Nuts* was a Barwood Film. Streisand had final cut, not Ritt.

The Prince of Tides, especially the scene when Tom relates what happened the night three intruders attacked the Wingo family, draws dramatic resonance from Nolte's body language as well as his dialogue. In another *Tides* moment, there are volumes of emotion from Lowenstein and Tom when they share a look at each other from across a street. He stands there, slouch-shouldered, finishing a cigarette. She spots him and smiles. But as Lowenstein reads his expression, she knows he has bad news for her. She takes a deep breath, bites her lower lip, and the smile fades from her face as she walks toward him. It's a powerful scene and, in its dramatic simplicity, the essence of film acting.

Director Herbert Ross began his career as a choreographer on Broadway. His contribution to *Funny Girl*, the direction of the musical numbers, practically warranted a codirecting credit with William Wyler. Ross went on to direct Barbra in *The Owl and the Pussycat* and *Funny Lady*, but it was Ross's choreography in *Funny Girl* which stands out. Capturing a musical number with the movement of the actor, as well as the camera, in a sequence which drives to the beat of the music and reflects the tempo, was never more perfectly executed than it was in the "Don't Rain on My Parade" number from *Funny Girl*. In *Yentl*, that kind of tempo and

pace enliven Yentl's musical soliloquies. By having the camera's movements choreographed as well as the performers', the sequences were fluid and visually musical. When shots were static, as in "No Wonder," the editing created the illusion of movement and complemented the music's rhythm and tempo.

William Wyler was a master filmmaker, perhaps the finest of all the directors with whom Streisand has worked. However, it is very difficult to define Wyler's genius. The man himself was not particularly articulate about his work. It is easier to admire the body of work, the legacy he left behind. Perhaps the one thing Streisand learned from Wyler was to not just get the job done, but to get the job done *right*. Wyler couldn't always communicate exactly what quality he was looking for in a scene, but he knew it when he saw it. His commitment to excellence and the determination to stick with it until it was right were principles Streisand had prior to filming *Funny Girl*. But by experiencing intimately Wyler's perfectionism, that principle was reinforced for Barbra. When she filmed *Yentl*, Barbra remembered Wyler often, thinking to herself, "What would Willie do?"

There is one other director with whom Barbra has worked who had a profound effect upon her: Frank Pierson. Relatively inexperienced when given the opportunity to direct the 1976 musical remake of *A Star Is Born*, Pierson impressed Streisand with his ideas and interest. However, once the filming commenced, Pierson seemingly gave up on the film, surrendering all responsibility to the executive producer, i. e., Barbra. When Kris Kristofferson and Barbra looked to Pierson for direction, they were, more often than not, given none. With her name and money (her company was responsible for any expenses over the budget of $6 million) on the line, Barbra stepped in and took control. It made for a tension-filled set, but in her estimation, she had no choice.

After the shoot, Kristofferson recalled what it was like on *Star*. "Barbra was even ordering [the] lenses. I thought I was doing good just getting to work on time, and she's out practically building sets. Barbra even wrote a couple of songs that are in the film. She never let up. I'll bet she'll turn out to be a terrific director in her own right one of these days." Kristofferson was correct in his prediction, and *A Star Is Born* was the film which gave her the first taste of the power of directing and its incredible creative opportunity. In the weeks she spent editing the movie, Barbra learned a lot about the technical side of filmmaking, like shot selection, coverage, cutaways, and alternate takes. All in all, Pierson's influence on Streisand's film education was essentially a negative one—she learned by trying to clean up his mess. Without the experience of *A Star Is Born*, Streisand would not have taken on the challenge of directing *Yentl*.

Sydney Pollack commented about *Yentl* in 1983, recognizing how far she had come in so short a time: "Usually with novice directors, you can see the wheels turning, see the ideas at work. But Barbra's film is so seamless, so fluid. I don't know whether she would have made this movie this well thirteen years ago. She has grown so much, as a person and as an actress. To have all that responsibility, to have so many people—and other actors—depending on you takes a maturity that I'm not sure Barbra had before the last couple of years."

Streisand's accomplishment was impressive with *Yentl*, and had that been her only directing effort, it would be a great one. *Yentl*, however, was simply her debut. She backed up the promise of *Yentl* with *The Prince of Tides*, again coproducing and starring; as time passed, it became apparent that handling more than one job at a time seems to suit her well. With *Tides*, Barbra again had a difficult project to adapt: Pat Conroy's voluminous novel about a dysfunctional Southern family. Her success was noted in both box-office receipts and critical bouquets. The movie was nominated for seven Oscars, including Best Picture, and Barbra received a nomination as Best Director from the Directors Guild of America—only the third woman ever nominated for that honor.

One of America's most accomplished contemporary filmmakers, Steven Spielberg, holds Streisand in high regard as a director and as a fellow artist. He is effusive in his praise of her work: "I have a feeling that all this comes from her experience . . . as a musician and a vocalist. She's had final cut over her songs since she was a little girl. If you listen to her songs, they're impeccable, on every level. That's really Barbra directing herself." Peter Bogdanovich recognized in her the skills of a director in 1972: "I'm not surprised that Barbra has become a director. . . . She's got great instincts, and she's

Barbra Streisand—actress, singer, producer, writer, composer—and with *Yentl* and *The Prince of Tides*, director.

fascinated by every little detail. I think one of the reasons she's so popular is that she's a strong, liberated woman in a time when women want to be that way. . . . I respect her and I enjoyed working with her. I'd love to work with her again."

The future for Streisand is most assuredly going to be as a director. As an actress, she will find it more and more difficult to develop projects in which to star simply because of her age. Musically, her voice continues to be spellbinding, but there will come a time, inevitably, when it will not sound as it did when she was in her prime. But behind the camera, Barbra Streisand will flourish with time. It is very possible that the best of Barbra is still to come.

15

First and Foremost: The Awards, Honors, and Records

*I*n a career marked by a wide variety of both artistic and commercial accomplishments, in nearly all aspects of entertainment, Barbra Streisand has been recognized and honored with every major award. She has also been a record-setter and become the "one and only" at some things. She is perhaps the most honored woman in show business.

Just for the Record Book

• She was one of the two artists to have been honored with an Oscar, Tony, Emmy, Grammy, and Golden Globe awards. Liza Minnelli was the other.

• The first to be honored with the grand slam of awards—Oscar, Tony, Emmy, and Grammy by 1970.

• First actress to produce, star in, and compose the score for a major film, *Nuts*.

• First actress to write, produce, direct, and star in a major film, *Yentl*.

• Streisand won the Grammy for her first album . . . the Emmy for her first TV special . . . the Oscar for her first film.

• *One Voice* raised $1.5 million for the Hollywood Women's Political Committee, the largest amount ever raised by a one-night live performance in the history of California, which went to support the election campaigns of six Democratic candidates for U. S. Senate.

• Streisand has ten Golden Globe Awards, more than any other star; won in five different categories: World Film Favorite; Best Actress–Musical; Best Song; Best Director; Best Picture.

(Opposite) First time out, Streisand won the Oscar for her performance in *Funny Girl*.

• Barbra has the most Grammy nominations (eight) in different categories: Album of the Year; Record of the Year; Best Female Vocalist; Traditional Pop Vocalist; Pop Duet; Classical Vocal Solo; Original Score; Best Performance–Music Video

• *Back to Broadway* debuted in the number-one spot on the Billboard Top 200 chart; it was the first time she had ever entered the chart at number one.

• Overall, twenty-two of Streisand's fifty albums have landed in the top ten on the *Billboard* Top 200 chart.

• In the sixties, nine of sixteen Streisand albums landed in the Top Ten on *Billboard's* album chart. One reached number one on the chart—*People*.

• In the seventies, six of twenty Streisand albums landed in the Top Ten on *Billboard's*

Barbra also won the Emmy for her first television special, *My Name Is Barbra*.

album chart. Three reached number one on the charts—*The Way We Were, A Star Is Born, Barbra Streisand's Greatest Hits, Volume 2.*

● In the eighties, six of Streisand's eight solo albums landed in the Top Ten on *Billboard's* album chart. Two reached number one on the *Billboard* chart—*Guilty* and *The Broadway Album.*

● In the nineties, one of Streisand's two solo albums (or boxed sets) landed in the Top Ten on *Billboard's* album chart. One reached number one on the *Billboard* chart—*Back to Broadway.*

● Streisand music has appeared on thirteen different *Billboard* charts: Albums; Hot 100; Easy Listening/Adult Contemporary; Christmas Albums; R & B; Country; Classical; CD; Music Video; Video Rental; Video Sales; Disco/Dance; and Disco/Action.

● Barbra has recorded songs in seven different languages: English, French, German, Spanish, Italian, Hebrew, and Latin.

● Streisand is tied with Journey, Van Halen,

Grammy number eight was for *The Broadway Album*, 1986.

and Billy Joel for most multiplatinum albums (sales of more than one million units)—11.

● Streisand has the second most platinum albums—21.

● She is second to Elvis Presley in gold albums—36.

● She has the longest time frame of number-one albums—twenty-nine years. Her first was in 1964 for *People*; her most recent was *Back to Broadway* in 1993. In between, she reached number one in 1974 with *The Way We Were*; 1976, *A Star Is Born*; 1978, *Barbra Streisand's Greatest Hits, Volume 2*; 1981, *Guilty*; and 1985, *The Broadway Album.*

● Streisand was the first guest star ever to be nominated for an Emmy in the category Outstanding Performance in a Variety or Musical Program or Series, in 1963, for her appearance on *The Judy Garland Show.*

● Barbra was the youngest performer (twenty-three) as of 1965 to win an Emmy for a nationally broadcast program—*My Name Is Barbra.*

● Barbra's Tony Award is honorary, but it was the first "On-Stage Hall of Fame Award" from the National Academy of the Living Theater Foundation. She was saluted as "Star of the Decade."

Streisand never looked happier than when she won two Golden Globes for *Yentl*, one for Best Director, the other for Best Picture—Comedy or Musical.

• Streisand's seven shows at Madison Square Garden in June and July 1994 grossed over $16 million, becoming the single largest grossing engagement in American music history; this tops her previous record of $12 million in two shows at the MGM Grand in Las Vegas, December 31, 1993, and January 1, 1994.

• Sales of on-site merchandise for the MGM-Grand concerts reached more than $1 million; this averages $40 per person. It was a new record, more than triple the amount for other pop superstars, and more than double the take from any NFL Superbowl.

• In 1994, her HBO special, *Barbra, The Concert,* became the highest rated original program in HBO history, garnering a 22.4/31 share.

Entertainment Awards and Honors

• Two Oscars (Academy of Motion Picture Arts and Sciences): Best Actress—*Funny Girl,* 1968; Best Song (with Paul Williams)—"Love Theme From *A Star Is Born* (Evergreen)," 1976; four nominations overall.

• Two Emmys (National Academy of Television Arts and Sciences): Outstanding [Individual] Achievement in Entertainment—*My Name Is Barbra,* 1965; Outstanding Program Achievement in Entertainment—*My Name Is Barbra,* 1965; six nominations overall.

• Eight Grammys (National Academy of Recording Arts and Sciences): Album of the Year—*The Barbra Streisand Album,* 1963; Best Female Vocal Performance—*The Barbra Streisand Album,* 1963; Best Female Vocal Performance—"People," 1964; Best Female Vocal Performance—*My Name Is Barbra,* 1965; Song of the Year (with Paul Williams)—"Love Theme From *A Star Is Born* (Evergreen)," 1977; Best Pop Vocal Performance by a Duo, Group, or Chorus—"Guilty" (with Barry Gibb), 1981; Best Pop Female Vocal Performance—*The Broadway Album,* 1986; thirty-two nominations overall. In addition, she has been given the Grammy Living Legend Award, 1991.

• Ten Golden Globes (Hollywood Foreign Press Association): Best Actress in a Comedy or

In 1969, Barbra and Clint Eastwood were awarded special Golden Globes as World Film Favorites. Twenty-four years later, Barbra presented the Best Director Oscar to Clint for *Unforgiven.*

Musical—*Funny Girl,* 1968; World Film Favorite—Female, 1969; World Film Favorite—Female, 1970; World Film Favorite—Female, 1974; Best Film Comedy or Musical—*A Star Is Born,* 1976; Best Actress Comedy or Musical—*A Star Is Born,* 1976; Best Song (with Paul Williams)—"Love Theme From *A Star Is Born* (Evergreen)," 1976; World Film Favorite—Female, 1977; Best Director—*Yentl,* 1983; Best Film Comedy or Musical—*Yentl,* 1983; nineteen nominations overall.

• Tony (Antoinette Perry) Award: Star of the Decade, 1970; two nominations overall.

• Five People's Choice Awards: Favorite Female Vocalist, 1975; Favorite Motion Picture Actress, 1977; Favorite Motion Picture Actress, 1978; Favorite All-Around Female Entertainer, 1985; Favorite All-Time Musical Star, 1988; twenty-one nominations overall.

• Four Georgie (American Guild of Variety Artists) Awards: 1970, 1972, 1977, 1980.

The National Association of Record Merchants (NARM) gave Streisand the President's Award in 1988.

• National Association of Record Merchandisers (NARM) President's Award, 1988

• Seven *Billboard* "No. 1 in the Nation" Awards: Female Vocalist, 1964; Top Pop Single—"The Way Were Were," 1974; Top Pop Single—"Love Theme From *A Star Is Born* (Evergreen)," 1977; Top Female Pop Singles Artist, 1977; Top Easy Listening Artist, 1977; Top Soundtrack—*A Star Is Born*, 1977; "Love Theme From *A Star Is Born* (Evergreen)," 1977.

• ASCAP Pied Piper Award, 1969.

• ASCAP Songwriter's Award: To the Writers of "Love Theme From *A Star Is Born* (Evergreen)" (1976–1985) (For composing one of the most performed pop standards of the previous decade.)

• ASCAP Film and Television Award, 1988: To the writers of "Love Theme From *A Star Is Born* (Evergreen)." (For composing one of the top five most performed standards from a feature film, 1978–1989.)

• ASCAP Harry Chapin Humanitarian Award, 1994.

• New York Drama Critics: Best Supporting Actress in a Musical—*I Can Get It for You Wholesale*, 1962.

• London Variety Poll: Best Foreign Actress—*Funny Girl*, 1966.

• George Foster Peabody Broadcasting Pioneers Award: Distinguished Achievement in Television—*My Name Is Barbra*, 1966.

• American Music Award: Favorite Female Vocalist Pop/Rock, 1980; six nominations overall.

• Eight National Association of Record Merchandisers (NARM) Awards: Best Selling Female Vocalist, 1963, 1964, 1965, 1966, 1976; Best Selling Soundtrack—*A Star Is Born*, 1977; Best Selling LP by a Female Vocalist—*Barbra Streisand's Greatest Hits, Volume 2*, 1978; Best Selling LP by a Female Vocalist—*Guilty*, 1981.

Winning the Scopus Laureate from the American Friends of Hebrew University in 1984, Streisand said, "I feel like this is my bat mitzvah." Also pictured, Shirley MacLaine, Neil Diamond, and then-Warners chief, Steve Ross. The Randy Emerian Collection

Winning Oscar number two in 1977, this one for composing "Evergreen."

- Six Quigley Poll Honors: Top Female Box-Office Star, 1970, 1972, 1973, 1974, 1975, 1977.
- National Association of Theatre Owners (NATO): Star of the Year, 1968.
- National Association of Theatre Owners (NATO): Star of the Decade, 1980.
- ShoWest: Star of the Decade, 1991.
- Women in Film Crystal Award, 1984.
- Women in Film Dorothy Arzner Special Recognition, 1992.
- *People* Magazine Readers Poll: Favorite Female Vocalist, 1981, 1982, 1983, 1986, 1989, 1990; Favorite Motion Picture Actress, 1979.
- *Playboy* Music Poll: Leading Female Vocalist, 1965; Leading Female Vocalist (Jazz), 1979.
- *US* Magazine Readers Poll: Favorite Pop Singer, 1982.
- Two *Cue* Magazine Entertainer of the Year Awards: 1963, 1970.

- Crystal Globe (CBS Records International) (for over $5 million in album sales outside U. S.).
- *Video Review* Award: Best Pop Music Home Video—*My Name Is Barbra/Color Me Barbra,* 1987.

Additional Honors

- *Mademoiselle* magazine: Distinguished Merit Award, 1964.
- *Encyclopaedia Britannica*: Fashion Trendsetter of 1964.
- International Best Dressed List, 1965.
- Golden Apple (Hollywood Women's Press Club), 1968.
- Most Imaginative Woman in Fashion List, 1968.
- Freedom Medal of the State of Israel, 1968.
- Friars Club: Entertainer of the Year, 1969.
- United Nations Peace Medal, 1973.
- *Seventeen* magazine: Most Admired Woman, 1975.
- Crystal Apple (City of New York), 1976.
- Star on Hollywood Walk of Fame, 1976.
- Anti-Defamation League (ADL): Woman of Achievement in the Arts, 1977.
- United Jewish Appeal (UJA) Music Division: Woman of the Year, 1983.
- American Friends of Hebrew University: Scopus Laureate, 1984.
- National Organization of Women (NOW): Woman of Courage Award, 1984.
- La Croix D'Officier Des Arts Et Lettres (France), 1984.
- Weizman Institute of Science (Israel): Award in Science and Humanity, 1988.
- Borough of Brooklyn, New York: Hall of Fame, 1989.
- Women, Men and the Media: Breakthrough Award, 1991.
- AIDS Project Los Angeles (APLA): Commitment to Life Award, 1992.
- American Civil Liberties Union of Southern California: Bill of Rights Award, 1992.

16

The Barbra Streisand Trivia Quiz

1. Which Streisand leading men have costarred with Barbra not once but twice?
2. At the beginning of *The Way We Were*, Katie is working in a radio station for which government agency?
3. Who is Laura Caswell? In which Streisand film does her name come up?
4. What is the dedication at the end of *Yentl*?
5. What is the only Barbra Streisand album in which the first word of the first song is the same as the last word of the last song?
6. In which Streisand film(s) does her sister, Rosyln Kind, appear as an extra?
7. What is Doris's real last name in *The Owl and the Pussycat*?
8. What was Jon Peters's first credit on a Barbra Streisand film?
9. Name the Streisand film in which the following landmark locations are used:
   a. Plaza Hotel
   b. Royal Pavillion in Brighton
   c. Borough Hall
   d. Charles Bridge
   e. Rainbow Room
   f. Chinatown
10. Which Streisand album is dedicted to Gladyce Begelman?
11. In *The Way We Were*, what is the name of Hubbell Gardiner's first novel?
12. What is the title of Doris's porno flick in *The Owl and the Pussycat*?
13. At age twelve, Streisand saw her first Broadway show, and it inspired her to became an actress. What was the play?

14. In Streisand films, what do characters played by Kay Medford, Jane Hoffman, Liam Dunn, and Nehemiah Persoff have in common?
15. What is Miss Marmelstein's full name in *I Can Get It for You Wholesale*?
16. In *All Night Long*, what does Cheryl suggest George call the new mirror he's invented?
17. In whose office does Fanny Brice meet Billy Rose in *Funny Lady*?
18. Who wrote the liner notes for *Simply Streisand*?
19. In what film is Barbra's character given the code name Tiger 7?
20. Which Streisand films are set completely outside of New York City?
21. True or false: Streisand wrote the lyrics for the song "Step in the Right Direction" on the *Emotion* album?
22. What are the names of Margaret's children in *Up the Sandbox*?
23. In which Streisand film are the following characters: Bill Verso, J. J. Jones, Paula Reisner, and Pony Dunbar?
24. Which of the following names has Barbra used as an alias?
   a. Angelina Scarangella
   b. Joan Rosen
   c. Barbara Goldstein
   d. Katie Morosky
   e. All of the above
25. To whom does Barbra sing "Look at That Face" in the television special *Color Me Barbra*?
26. Name the Streisand albums (including soundtracks) which have one-word titles. (Hint: There are nine.)

(Opposite) Dressed to the nines as Melinda in *On a Clear Day*, Barbra and company shot these sumptuous scenes on location at a famous British landmark.

27. In *Funny Girl,* in what city do Fanny and Nick have their first romantic tryst?

28. On *A Christmas Album,* Streisand does a number called "The Best Gift." What exactly is she singing about?

29. Believe it or not, Barbra munches on carrots in five different films. Name them.

30. Okay, in what film does Streisand pass on the carrots?

31. What was the date of the *One Voice* concert?

32. Which Streisand films have scenes set in New York's Central Park?

33. Who is Claudia Faith Draper?

34. Who are the only two directors who have helmed not one but two Barbra Streisand films?

35. What is unusual about Nick Arnstein's tuxe-

Margaret and Paul have two kids in *Up the Sandbox,* and one on the way.

do when Fanny meets him for the first time in *Funny Girl*?

36. Streisand is shown driving a Rolls-Royce in two different films. Name them.

37. Who wrote the liner notes for *The Broadway Album*?

38. To whom did Streisand dedicate the *Back to Broadway* album?

39. In *The Way We Were,* what is the name of the synopsis Katie's describing to Hubbell just before she tells him she's pregnant?

40. When Barbra and Barry Gibb presented a Grammy in 1981 at Radio City Music Hall, who did they announce had won for Best Male Vocal—Rock?

41. What was the name of the brand new Las Vegas hotel Barbra opened in 1969?

In *I Can Get It for You Wholesale,* Miss Marmelstein didn't sing hearts and flowers. She had a name fixation.

ANSWERS

1. Omar Sharif: *Funny Girl* and *Funny Lady*;
   Ryan O'Neal: *What's Up, Doc?* and *The Main Event*
2. OWI (Office of War Information)
3. She is the character Streisand will become in a future incarnation, revealed at the end of *On a Clear Day You Can See Forever*
4. "For my father, and for all our fathers . . ."
5. *Wet*
6. *A Star Is Born* and *The Main Event*
7. Wilgus
8. Miss Streisand's hairstyles designed by Jon Peters
9. a. *The Way We Were*
   b. *On a Clear Day . . .*
   c. *For Pete's Sake*
   d. *Yentl*
   e. *The Prince of Tides*
   f. *What's Up, Doc?*
10. *One Voice*
11. *A Country Made of Ice Cream*
12. *Cycle Sluts*
13. *The Diary of Anne Frank*

42. In which films has Barbra been pregnant?
43. In which films is Barbra shown in a bath-tub?
44. Who's the exercise instructor in *The Main Event*?
45. What's the name of the restaurant which welcomes Dolly back in *Hello, Dolly!*?
46. What songs did Barbra perform as a guest on *The Burt Bacharach Special*?
47. Who took the picture which appears on the cover of the *My Name Is Barbra* album?
48. In which film does Barbra have a black eye?
49. For which two films has Barbra recorded songs to be played over the credits, only to decide afterwards to let the credits roll without the songs?
50. Is Barbra right- or left-handed?

(Right) In *The Way We Were*, Katie was a whiz with a pot roast. But was it served with or without carrots?

Barbra had a very special dedication for *Yentl*, and if you recognize this scene, you can probably recall what it was.

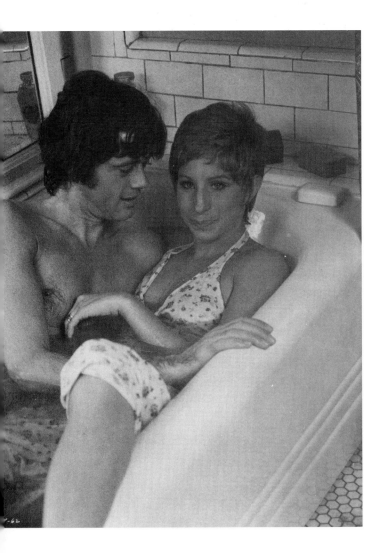

14. They all played either her mother or father
15. Yetta Tessye Marmelstein
16. The Dupler
17. Bernard Baruch
18. Richard Rodgers
19. *For Pete's Sake*
20. *What's Up, Doc?, A Star Is Born, The Main Event, All Night Long,* and *Yentl*
21. True
22. Elizabeth and Peter
23. *The Way We Were*
24. e—all of the above
25. Her French poodle, Sadie
26. *People, ButterFly, Songbird, Wet, Memories, Guilty, Yentl, Emotion,* and *Nuts*
27. Baltimore
28. A newborn baby
29. *What's Up, Doc?, The Owl and the Pussycat, The Main Event, The Way We Were,* and *Up the Sandbox*
30. *Yentl*
31. September 6, 1986
32. *The Owl and the Pussycat, Up the Sandbox, The Way We Were,* and *The Prince of Tides*
33. Streisand's character in *Nuts*

Hint, hint . . . if you recognize the movie and Barbra costar, you'll be able to get one of the films in which Barbra's in a bathtub.

34. Barbra Streisand and Herbert Ross
35. He's wearing a ruffled tuxedo shirt
36. *Funny Lady* and *The Main Event*
37. Marilyn and Alan Bergman
38. Steve Ross
39. *Shivouth!*
40. Billy Joel
41. The International (later changed to the Las Vegas Hilton)
42. *Funny Girl, Up the Sandbox,* and *The Way We Were*
43. *Funny Girl, The Owl and the Pussycat,* *What's Up, Doc?, For Pete's Sake,* and *A Star Is Born*
44. Gilda Marx
45. Harmonia Gardens
46. "One Less Bell to Answer"/"A House Is Not a Home," "Close to You," and "Be Aware"
47. Sheldon Streisand
48. *Funny Lady*
49. *Up the Sandbox* ("If I Close My Eyes") and *The Prince of Tides* ("Places That Belong to You")
50. Right-handed

17

Collecting Streisand

Playbills from *Funny Girl* in London and Philadelphia. The Michel Parenteau Collection

*B*arbra Streisand collectibles are in the form of all kinds of books, posters, programs, records, and bric-a-brac. However, unlike many other stars, Streisand has rarely licensed her image for any kind of merchandising. In fact, many of the items collectors hold dear are things which were probably never meant to be sold to the public at all.

The following items are some of the most interesting, prized, and valuable Streisand collectibles.

Programs/Playbills

- *I Can Get It For You Wholesale* playbill (Shubert Theatre or Broadway Theatre)
- *Funny Girl* playbill (Winter Garden Theatre)
- 1965 World's Fair playbill—Barbra on cover in *Funny Girl*
- *Funny Girl* London theatre program (Prince of Wales Theatre)
- *An Evening With Barbra Streisand*—concert program, 1965–66 (two different covers, one color, the other black and white)
- *Funny Girl* souvenir movie program
- *Hello, Dolly!* souvenir movie program

- *On a Clear Day You Can See Forever* souvenir movie program
- *Funny Lady* souvenir movie program
- *The Prince of Tides* souvenir movie program (embossed cover; full color, glossy photos; forty pages)
- *Back to Broadway* listening party program, May 13, 1993
- Friars Club Roast—Entertainer of the Year program, 1969

Other Movie Collectibles

- *Funny Girl*—unlicensed, unauthorized wristwatch with picture of Barbra from film; her name is misspelled "Striesand"
- *A Star Is Born*—jigsaw puzzle
- *The Main Event*—lavender tank-top style T-shirt
- *The Prince of Tides*—canvas tote bag and T-shirt
- *The Prince of Tides*—invitation to New York premiere, September 18, 1991; the opening was switched to December 25, 1991
- *The Way We Were*—T-shirt and key chain, "Streisand & Redford Together"
- *Yentl*—bootleg plastic puff stickers

This stunning photo was the cover shot for the 1966 Barbra Streisand concert program.

Stand-Ups

- *A Star Is Born*—bigger than one-sheet poster
- *Superman*—life-size cutout of album-cover pose
- *Guilty*—Barbra and Barry in a clinch, miniature version
- *Songbird*—Barbra and Sadie, her French poodle
- *Back to Broadway*—full-size and miniature versions of Streisand with microphone

Picture Discs/Colored Vinyl/Promo/Demo CDs and Albums

- *Superman*—promo album, only five test-pressed
- *Yentl*—"The Way He Makes Me Feel" 12-inch single
- *Emotion*—commerical release, entire album
- *The "Second" Barbra Streisand Album*—promo album in blue vinyl
- *Color Me Barbra*—promo album in red vinyl
- "Second Hand Rose"—promo 45 in red vinyl
- "People"—promo 45 in violet vinyl
- "Why Did I Choose You?"—promo 45 in blue vinyl, both 3:44 and 2:59 cuts

- *Just for the Record . . .* —demo tape/CD featuring excerpts from the boxed set
- "All I Ask of You"—four-song, picture CD
- "We're Not Making Love"—three-song, picture CD
- "The Places That Belong to You"—four-song, picture CD
- "With One Look"—three-song CD
- "With One Look"—promo CD single, with Barbra's name misspelled "Striesand"
- "The Music of the Night"—three-song CD, including duet with Michael Crawford on title cut, and version of "Children Will Listen" different from *Back to Broadway* album
- "Children Will Listen"—promo CD single, featuring album version with spoken intro
- "Speak Low"—promo CD single
- "I've Got a Crush on You"—promo CD single of Streisand's duet with Frank Sinatra, from his album *Duets*
- "Ordinary Miracles"—tour CD, 1994
- "As If We Never Said Goodbye"—3-song CD single, 1993
- "The Event of the Decade"—2-CD promo retrospective (U.K.), 1994
- "The Broadway Collection"—2-CD Australian special edition, *The Broadway Album* and *Back to Broadway*, 1994

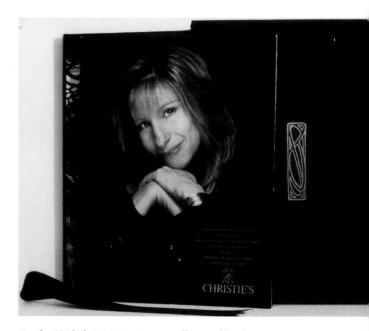

For the 1994 Christie's Auction, two illustrated books were designed with a special cloth sleeve to hold them.

Movie, Video, and Music Posters— U. S. and International

Barbra Streisand has made fifteen motion pictures which have been seen around the world. She has recorded fifty albums and has appeared in many television specials. The posters created to advertise these events make for some of her most interesting collectibles.

• *A Star Is Born*—concert poster from Sun Devil Stadium
• *A Star is Born*—mass market version of one-sheet film poster
• *Up the Sandbox*—original film poster featured Richard Amsel art work. It depicted Streisand strapped to giant baby bottle on the cover of *Time* magazine as "Dustmop of the Year." The Amsel posters was pulled after the picture's release—*Time* objected to their publication being used in the ads—and replaced by a photo-driven poster
• *The Belle of 14th Street*—three art deco mini-posters
• *Playboy* magazine cover—reprint poster
• Blackgama ad—"What Becomes a Legend Most?" reprint poster
• *Live Concert at the Forum*—poster of album-cover art, inserted in first pressing
• *Barbra Joan Streisand*—poster of album-cover photo, inserted in first pressing

(Top) The souvenir program for *Hello, Dolly!* was originally sold in movie theaters.

(Bottom) This was one of three original, art nouveau-inspired posters designed to promote *The Belle of 14th Street* television special.

• *What's Up, Doc?*—photo from film, pop poster, horizontal
• 1968 Ron Galella photo—celebrity poster, Barbra in corkscrew curls, black gown
• 1962 Bon Soir photo—celebrity poster
• *Emotion*—poster depicting Barbra as she looked in the title video from the album; it was a one-sheet poster, similar to motion-picture posters, and was printed to be displayed in theatre lobbies

Other Collectibles

• Barbra's personalized audiocassette invitation to *One Voice* concert
• *Color Me Barbra*—color brochure insert from album's first pressing
• Grenada postage stamps, 1993—her name is misspelled "Barbara"
• St. Vincent & the Grenadines postage stamp—Barbra in Concert, MGM–Grand Garden, 1993
• *Streisand Superman*—sew-on patch

Postcards and Other Paper

• 8" x 10" easel portrait—1966 picture of Streisand, signed in auto-pen
• 1962 Columbia Records bio-card
• Barbra Streisand Paper Doll Set
• Barbra Streisand at the Riviera Hotel, Las Vegas, 1970

- Barbra Streisand at the Hilton Hotel, Las Vegas, 1970
- Menu from International Hotel showroom, Las Vegas, 1969

Buttons

- *Guilty*
- *The Way We Were*
- *A Star Is Born*

Noteworthy Books, Magazines, and Other Publications

- *The First Decade: The Films and Career of Barbra Streisand* by James Spada
- *The Greatest Star* by René Jordan
- *Barbra* by Donald Zec and Anthony Fowles
- *Streisand: The Woman and the Legend* by James Spada
- *Streisand: The Woman, the Myth and the Legend* by Shaun Considine
- *Streisand Through the Lens* by Frank Teti and Karen Moline
- *Barbra, the Second Decade* by Karen Swenson
- *The Barbra File,* a monthly fan newsletter
- *All About Barbra* (twenty-nine fan magazine issues) 1984–present
- *Barbra Quarterly* (ten fan magazine issues) 1977–82
- *Streizettes*—Barbra Streisand International Fan Club newsletter, 1964–71
- *The Barbra Streisand Collection of Twentieth Century Decorative and Fine Arts*—Christie's Auction catalogue

In the past two years, there have been two Barbra Streisand stamps . . . so far. The Michel Parenteau Collection

The hard-to-find one-sheet poster was created to promote the concert staged at Sun Devil Stadium in Tempe, Arizona, to film scenes for *A Star Is Born.*

- *Mad* magazine—*On a Clear Day You Can See a Funny Girl Singing Hello Dolly Forever,* Streisand spoof, June 1971
- *Time*—cover story, "She Couldn't Be Medium," April 5, 1964
- *Newsweek*—cover story, "Streisand: The Superstar Story," January 5, 1970
- *Life*—cover story, "Great New Star, Her Success and Precarious Love Story," May 22, 1964
- *Life*—cover story, "The Fear-Ridden Girl Behind the Star," March 18, 1966
- *Life*—cover story, "The Way She Really Is," December 1983
- *Look*—cover story, "Superbarbra," April 5, 1966
- *Playboy*—cover story, in-depth interview, October 1977
- *People*—cover story, "She Talks for the First Time," April 26, 1976

There have been quite a few fascinating books about Barbra, including these three.

- *People*—cover story, "Barbra," December 12, 1983
- *US*—cover story, "Barbra, the Way She Is," February 10, 1986
- *Harper's Bazaar*—cover story, November 1972
- *Billboard*—special issue, "The Legend of Barbra Streisand," December 10, 1983
- *Entertainment Weekly*—cover story, "Money Girl," April 15, 1994

MGM—The Streisand Supermarket of Collectibles

In 1993, Barbra Streisand agreed to license a wide variety of merchandise in conjunction with her appearances at the MGM–Grand in Las Vegas. It was one of the few instances in her career when she officially sanctioned T-shirts, caps, posters, and more with her name and image on them. The response

Oh, you beautiful doll! *The Barbra Streisand Paper Doll* book. The Michel Parenteau Collection

for these collectibles was enthusiastic. In only two days, Sony Signature reported over $1 million in sales. To accommodate all the interest in the merchandise, Sony set up a toll-free telephone number—1-800-664-8444—so fans could continue purchasing items long after the concert sales booths had closed down. When Streisand went on tour in 1994, more collectibles and merchandise were offered for sale, and the response was overwhelmingly positive. The tour merchandise was later sold on the QVC television network. Here is a list of the Streisand-licensed collectibles from the MGM:

- Concert program—December 31, 1993–January 1, 1994 (twenty-four pages)
- Two specially-created posters—one was 22" x 34" in full color, the other 16" x 24" in black and white

Barbra made the *Time* magazine cover by becoming the hottest thing on Broadway in 1964.

One of the essential magazines for a Streisand fan is the special *Billboard* issue, "The Legend of Barbra Streisand."

The *Newsweek* cover of January 5, 1970, included a fabulous cover by Steve Schapiro.

Noted novelist Chaim Potok did an in-depth *Esquire* interview with Barbra while she was preparing *Yentl*. The killer cover was shot by Scavullo.

One of three "Barbra" booths located at the MGM-Grand. Two days after the concerts were over, the booths were gone.

The coffee mug and jade crystal paperweight from the MGM-Grand concerts in Las Vegas.

● Set of thirteen different postcards (5-1/2" x 8-1/2") in color and black and white, presented in a special envelope with gold seal (all but two photos have never before been published)

● Silk jacket—bomber style, 100 percent silk, in black with logo embroidered across the back

● Black T-shirt—with full color image of Streisand silk-screened on front

● Scoop-neck T-shirt—black with printed burgundy and gold concert logo

● Crew-neck sweatshirt—black with black and gold embroidered concert logo on front

● Jewel-neck sweatshirt—black with gold and black concert logo

● Donna Karan and Barbra Streisand (BSDK) Designed Nightshirt—ivory or black with satin stitching, embroidered with concert logo

● Baseball cap—black with grey, black-and-gold embroidered logo on front

● Crystal paperweight—jade crystal paperweight, hand-etched to resemble concert ticket

● Coffee mug—black ceramic mug with concert logo in white

● Commemorative stamp set—first-day-of-issue collectible Barbra Streisand stamp in vinyl presentation folder; included in folder is a 23-karat gold-foil embossment of the stamp. Limited edition of 3,500. Each piece is hand-numbered.

● Shopping bag—glossy black paper bag with gold concert logo

Acknowledgments

"There are moments you remember all your life. . . . " I had one of those moments in 1968. So, thanks to Shelley Tunis, who took her little sister all the way to Manhattan to see *Funny Girl* at the Criterion Theatre. Who would have ever guessed that that trip would lead to this book. In the years that passed, my interest in Streisand never waned. I read voraciously every article about Barbra, went to her movies, listened to her albums, watched her television specials, and shared everything with my two younger sisters, Ellen Leibovitch and Meryll Katz. Thanks for always being there for me and sharing all those times. You have always been the best of sisters and the best of friends; and Ellen, you've been a powerful ally . . . thanks. To my brother, Mitchell Waldman, thank you for your constant, unconditional love and support. Being the middle child in this family was a blessing, not a boon.

You've got to have friends . . . and I've been fortunate to have many who've helped me with this book. To Michel Parenteau: you have been more than helpful to me, and at the same time, a true, loyal friend. I'm glad you've been a part of my life, and I will always be grateful that you contributed so unselfishly to this book. Karen Swenson is perhaps the best-informed and most resourceful person I know when it comes to Barbra Streisand's career. A special thanks for all your help personally, and a grateful mention to your book, *The Second Decade*. It's a dynamite research source. Chris Nickens has been of immeasurable assistance and provided keen insights and opinions about Barbra. He is also a terrific friend. Both Karen and Chris were integral components in the creation of *Barbra Quarterly*, a fan publication which was of great use in the writing of this book. With that in mind, thanks, too, to Bob Scott and James Spada. Jim also wrote two books about Streisand, *Barbra, The First Decade* and *The Woman and the Legend*, and I have found both to be excellent references. Bob's photography and design were an inspiration.

Barbra Quarterly lasted only ten issues, but since then there's been one, very special fanzine to carry on the legacy: *All About Barbra*. Thanks to Lynne Pounder, Steve Baxter, and everyone involved in the magazine, both in America and England. A special nod to Guy Vespoint, *AAB's* music editor, for those long hours on the phone, talking Barbra.

Over the years, Streisand fans have been very generous to me, like Rain Burns, Anne Zarraonandia, Greg Rice, Steve Sanders, Bruce Mandes, Bob DeLucca, and Bill Moore. Sadly, there are some wonderful Barbra fans who are no longer with us: David Little, John Ramirez, John Graham, Dennis Pallante, and Randy Emerian. I think they would have enjoyed this book; in fact, were they still alive, I know they would have been first in line to lend a hand. I didn't know the late Dennis Ryan personally, but because of his friend Andrea Schafer, his collection helped me in the creation of this book. Thanks to both of them. And for the support, encouragement, and friendship they've given me, I would be remiss if I did not thank Joanna Zulli, Mindi Schulman, Annemarie Allocca, Gretchen Keene, Rosemary Rossi, John Penzotti, and Maryann Cooper. To my agent, Faith Hamlin, your encouragement meant a lot, and hopefully our relationship will flourish in years to come.

Simply the best, that's Mary Keesling and Tom Gilbert, my two closest and dearest friends. If I had another sister and brother, Mary and Tom would fit the bill. They have both been ardent supporters and the truest of friends. A special note about Mary: her contribution to this project has been tremendous, making it far more than it might have been. I appreciate her unfailing interest, infinite patience, all-out enthusiasm, and nit-picking perfectionism, more than I can probably say. Also special thanks to Joe Keesling, for putting up with all the time Mary's spent working with me on the book, and also for the generous help he's given me with the Mac advice. For all the years of friendship and loyalty, the hours and hours of fun and laughter, and everything in between, thanks to my gin buddies, Janelle Morris and Cindy Flora.

To Jerry Ohlinger's Movie Material Shop—I'm grateful for the association and the materials you've shared with me; I'm also thankful to have been able to find a wonderful husband working on the other side of the counter in your store. A nod of thanks as well to Retna, Ltd. and Walter McBride; Steve Ahlgren of Sygma Photo News; Robin Platzer of Twin Images; and Rosemary Rossi of Hollywood Spotlight. I appreciate William Moore of Moore Legends for his magnificent illustrations and his generosity.

My father, Irving M. Waldman, was a great and wonderful man. Everyone who knew him loved him. He died when I was just eight years old, but I remember him very well, especially how he loved me. I remember, too, the confidence he gave me to do my best in everything I endeavor. I hope he knows how much I loved him then, and love him still. My grandmother, Gussie Stark, loved the movies and shared many, many hours watching them with me. She gave me an early appreciation of musicals, and more than that, she shared everything else she had with me. She was a terrific woman: inde-

pendent and strong, funny and warm, loving and protective. Whatever I do, I feel her spirit inside me.

Jean and Hy Corn, my mother and stepfather, are the kind of parents other people wish they had. I love them both and appreciate their love and support. To my ever-growing, always-loving clan—Elliott, Ben, Evan, Amanda, Nancy, Erik, Ian, Mark, Sam, and last, but not least, Jordyn: what a great *mishpocheh* you all are! I'm proud to be one of you.

A special note to my husband, Leslie Solow: thanks for being my partner in every sense of the word. Thanks for hanging in there; for doing everything I have asked of you; and for your many ideas, suggestions, opinions, and reactions to the contents of this book. You have been there in the high times—like Las Vegas—as well as the low points, making the highs soar higher, and the lows seem less dire. If I had to choose again, I would still choose you.

One last word: To Barbra Streisand, this book is possible only because of the many accomplishments you've achieved and the contributions you've made to the world. In my life, you've been a major influence and a great inspiration. Thanks for giving me so much to write about. Let's do lunch sometime? I'll bring the Chinese chicken salad.

—ALLISON J. WALDMAN

Photo Credits

Unless otherwise credited, all the photos and poster reproductions in this book are courtesy of the film producing companies—Columbia Pictures, Twentieth Century-Fox, MGM/UA, Universal, Paramount Pictures, Warner Bros., and National General Pictures. Additionally, the author gratefully acknowledges photographs provided by Columbia Records and CBS Television, as well as any materials from the files of Barwood Films and J. E. G. Productions.

ORDER NOW!
Film, Television and Music Books

If you like this book, you'll love the other award-winning movie, television and music books from Carol Publishing Group.

If you like movies, you'll love Citadel Film Books. From James Stewart to Moe Howard and The Three Stooges, Woody Allen to John Wayne, The Citadel Film Series is America's largest and oldest film book library. With more than 150 titles --and more on the way!--Citadel Film Books make perfect gifts for a loved one, a friend, or best of all, yourself!

A complete listing of the Citadel Film Series appears below. If you know what books you want, why not order now? It's easy! **Just call 1-800-447-BOOK and have your MasterCard or Visa ready. (Tell the operator code #1488)**

FIRST, A LIST OF BARBRA BOOKS:

Her Name is Barbra: An Intimate Portrait of the Real Barbra Streisand (hardcover biography)
Barbra Streisand (Film Book)
The Barbra Streisand Scrapbook

CITADEL FILM BOOKS:
STARS

Alan Ladd
Arnold Schwarzenegger
Bela Lugosi
Bette Davis
The Bowery Boys
Brigitte Bardot
Buster Keaton
Carole Lombard
Cary Grant
Charlie Chaplin
Clark Gable
Clint Eastwood
Curly
Dustin Hoffman
Edward G. Robinson
Elizabeth Taylor
Elvis Presley
The Elvis Scrapbook
Errol Flynn
Frank Sinatra
Gary Cooper
Gene Kelly
Gina Lollobrigida
Gloria Swanson
Gregory Peck
Greta Garbo
Henry Fonda
Humphrey Bogart
Ingrid Bergman
Jack Lemmon
Jack Nicholson
James Cagney
James Dean: Behind the Scene
Jane Fonda
Jeanette MacDonald & Nelson Eddy

Joan Crawford
John Wayne Films
John Wayne Reference Book
John Wayne Scrapbook
Judy Garland
Katharine Hepburn
Kirk Douglas
Laurel & Hardy
Lauren Bacall
Laurence Olivier
Mae West
Marilyn Monroe
Marlene Dietrich
Marlon Brando
Marx Brothers
Moe Howard & the Three Stooges
Norma Shearer
Olivia de Havilland
Orson Welles
Paul Newman
Peter Lorre
Rita Hayworth
Robert De Niro
Robert Redford
Sean Connery
Sexbomb: Jayne Mansfield
Shirley MacLaine
Shirley Temple
The Sinatra Scrapbook
Spencer Tracy
Steve McQueen
Three Stooges Scrapbook
Warren Beatty
W.C. Fields
William Holden
William Powell
A Wonderful Life: James Stewart

DIRECTORS

Alfred Hitchcock
Cecil B. DeMille
Federico Fellini
Frank Capra
John Huston
Steven Spielberg

Woody Allen

GENRE

Black Hollywood, Vol. 1 & 2
Classic Foreign Films: From 1960 to Today
Classic Gangster Films
Classic Science Fiction Films
Classics of the Horror Film
Classic TV Westerns
Cult Horror Films
Divine Images: Jesus on Screen
Early Classics of Foreign Film
Great Baseball Films
Great French Films
Great German Films
Great Italian Films
Great Science Fiction Films
The Great War Films
Harry Warren & the Hollywood Musical
Hispanic Hollywood
Hollywood Bedlam: Screwball Comedies
The Hollywood Western
The Incredible World of 007
The Jewish Image in American Film
The Lavender Screen: The Gay and Lesbian Films
Martial Arts Movies
Merchant Ivory Films
The Modern Horror Film
More Classics of the Horror Film
Movie Psychos & Madmen
Our Huckleberry Friend: Johnny Mercer
Second Feature: "B" Films
They Sang! They Danced! They Romanced!
Thrillers
The West That Never Was
Words and Shadows: Literature on the Screen

DECADE

Classics of the Silent Screen

Films of the Twenties
Films of the Thirties
More Films of the 30's
Films of the Forties
Films of the Fifties
Lost Films of the 50's
Films of the Sixties
Films of the Seventies
Films of the Eighties

SPECIAL INTEREST

America on the Rerun
Bugsy (Illustrated screenplay)
The "Cheers" Trivia Book
The Citadel Treasury of Famous Movie Lines
Comic Support
Cutting Room Floor: Scenes Which Never Made It
Favorite Families of TV
Film Flubs
Film Flubs: The Sequel
Filmmaking on the Fringe
First Films
Frankly, My Dear: Great Movie Lines About Women
Gilligan, Maynard & Me
Hollywood Cheesecake
Howard Hughes in Hollywood
More Character People
The Nightmare Never Ends: Freddy Krueger & A Nightmare on Elm Street
The Northern Exposure Book
The Official Andy Griffith Show Scrapbook
100 Best Films of the Century
The 1001 Toughest TV Trivia Questions of All Time
The Quantum Leap Book
Sex in Films
Sex In the Movies
Sherlock Holmes
Son of Film Flubs
Who Is That?: Familiar Faces and Forgotten Names
"You Ain't Heard Nothin' Yet!"

For a free full-color Entertainment Books brochure including the Citadel Film Series in depth and more, call 1-800-447-BOOK; or send your name and address to Citadel Film Books, Dept. 1488, 120 Enterprise Ave., Secaucus, NJ 07094.